THE IT
IMPERATIVE

THE **IT** IMPERATIVE

KEVIN J. SMITH

The Anima Group

Paperback ISBN: 978-0-578-20197-9
Hardback ISBN: 978-0-578-20198-6

Library of Congress Control Number: 2018938432

Cover Photo © 2018 thinkstockphotos.com. All rights reserved - used with permission.

PRINTED IN THE UNITED STATES OF AMERICA

AUTHOR DEDICATION

To Julie, Christopher, Michaela, Zachary,
Taylor, Isabella, and Gianna. My everything.

For Mom and Dad.

ACKNOWLEDGMENTS

The journey that lies within every book is a daily revelation of ideas and emotions—this mix carries us forward and is ultimately made complete through a collaboration of many wonderful people with each contribution necessary in its own way.

My heartfelt thanks to Steve Daly and Steve Morton for believing in this project and what might yet lie ahead. Your enthusiastic support has meant so much.

Continued gratitude goes to John Ferron for his support of my first book, thereby allowing me to take the first steps on this remarkable journey. I will not forget your leap of faith.

To the talented and passionate people of Ivanti with whom I am blessed to work every day.From the countless spirited discussions with my colleagues to my work alongside hundreds of global market leading organizations of all sizes have sprung the framework presented in this book—the exhilarating transformation and rebirth of IT as shaped by The IT Imperative.

It has been my pleasure to work with the professionals at Outskirts Press throughout the publishing process, and my thanks for holding to an aggressive schedule and making this book the best it can be.

Once again, my talented illustrator Julie Felton brought my rough sketches to life.

im-per-a-tive

Of vital importance; crucial; essential.

PREFACE

The wonderful world of Information Technology (IT) continues to surprise us and refuses to be defined. Just when we begin to believe we know what IT is and is not, we are reminded that we simply don't.

The widely accepted models, processes, frameworks, tactics, and strategies of IT today have evolved with good cause for the past three decades and have served us well. However, a rapidly changing world, a global marketplace, and a number of powerful forces within and surrounding IT are colliding to fundamentally change the course of our future as IT and business professionals.

This book is a look at the exciting and dynamic future of IT.

The beginning of this future is not somewhere yet ahead of us—it is already upon us, and the forces reshaping IT are both unstoppable and accelerating. Embracing this vision is vital and increasingly undeniable and in this spirit the following pages will provide a new framework for the daily operations, priorities, and strategies of IT teams everywhere as well as the surrounding organization.

IT will increasingly be seen as a role model and leader of the business, and the lines we often describe between IT and the business will fade away as a natural part of this evolution.

> *The role of IT as a leader in the business is very different than how IT has been seen in the past. But the world around us has fundamentally changed and for many reasons the business needs this leadership to fill a growing void.*

Although certainly not the only elements that will reshape IT, I have offered seventeen themes in the following pages which together will provide a new and needed foundation for plotting a course of action for how we will reshape IT over the next ten years. To help you in making best use of the book and to understand the building blocks behind each of the seventeen elements, I have structured each chapter as a series of short stories. This should make it easier to read through the chapters and easier to understand the forces that are driving the rebirth of IT. I hope you will find it an easy book to navigate.

I reference a window of ten years because we tend to think change will occur more quickly than it will inevitably occur, and at the same time the forces driving these changes across IT have reached a point that can't and won't be slowed. Big changes do take time—some growing level of force exists in the beginning of any cycle of change and then ultimately leverage emerges to help organize and launch the necessary actions described in the following chapters.

I fully expect us to emerge from this decade of change with a new IT model that will serve us well for the next two to three decades. A reset, if you will, that will create a new baseline with some staying power.

It would be easy to claim all these changes must occur immediately, but that simply won't be possible. Some changes can occur quickly, in the next one to three years, thereby giving us a springboard from which to launch into the following years. Other changes will take longer. And of course, the ability and appetite of organizations to make lasting change varies greatly.

> *Make no mistake, while your organization*
> *will have unique needs, the remaking*
> *of your IT operations and embracing*
> *dramatic change are not an option.*

This is at the heart of the Imperative—a mindset and spirit that we must first accept and then, even with some healthy caution, embrace. Change can first take hold and then accelerate, driven by the passionate and talented people across IT who I believe know at some level that we must change. With the framework of a new IT strategy in place and the people of IT mobilized, anything is possible.

Of course, all of this must be done with the recognition that the fundamental mission of IT has not changed and the Imperative cannot and should not replace this fundamental mission.

> *This mission is timeless—IT must continue to manage and secure the evolving infrastructure of assets and data, while delivering high-quality services.*

While increasingly clear to us today, that has not always been the case, and this association has not always been recognized or appreciated. Meaning, a healthy estate of assets with poor service is a problem for everybody. At the same time, unreliable infrastructure and assets will all but make good service impossible.

This is an important point. What I'm proposing in this book is that the fundamental mission of IT has not changed and will not change, but how IT thinks and acts must change dramatically. The results of these strategic and proactive actions will create a new dimension to IT that complements and even improves the core. The core of what IT must deliver to the business will carry on. If we look far into the future, much in our world will have changed but every business, regardless of size and regardless of market, will leverage technology and information to deliver goods or services to their customers.

> *This brings us back to the enduring model and mission of IT: maximizing the ability of an organization to leverage technology in*

*a way that creates competitive advantage
while winning and retaining thrilled
customers.*

Only this approach will allow us to rise to the challenges the future will inevitably hold and achieve the remarkable potential that IT represents for the broader business. The vision for IT that many of us have passionately embraced for years is now coming to life. We stand at the threshold of what will become the most significant transformation experienced in the rich history of IT.

The Imperative will both improve the daily performance of IT while fundamentally realigning IT within the business as an engine of innovation and a source of customer loyalty and market leadership. Yes, among the many things that will change about the daily operation of this organization is that we will move IT closer to the customer and closer to revenue.

This is another simply stated principle but one with many ramifications. We will explore this more closely in a chapter dedicated to the customer connection (Chapter 2). And this is another element in our broader assertion that IT is not only capable of leading the business, but that IT must lead the business. This is born of what IT is uniquely capable of today, and also a reflection of a fundamental void that must be filled.

*The business needs the leadership of IT
more than ever.*

What this means is that IT must seize the potential that has to a degree lain dormant for many years and set a direction for the broader organization. By virtue of controlling the technology and information every worker relies on every day, IT is uniquely positioned to make this vision a reality and in many ways has a unique means to monitor the pulse of the organization.

You will note a number of themes that appear throughout the book, and this is not repetitive but rather reinforcement of what is core to our rebirth. Notably, our path to the rebirth runs through passionate people and a new culture of IT, and while there are a number of priorities we must balance, the number one priority will be our focus on the customer. With this, we simply can't go far astray.

The journey that lies ahead for all of us will no doubt hold some surprises and challenges, but we who hold so much admiration and affection for IT are fortunate to be part of this remarkable rebirth.

TABLE OF CONTENTS

CHAPTER 1

CADENCE

Cadence carries a great depth of meaning and is the perfect way to begin our discussion on the future of IT.

The perpetual clock we apply to everything we do across IT must change. This begins with setting new expectations and then demanding more of ourselves and every person in the organization.

> *Our mission is to take up a relentless investigation of every task and business process performed each day in IT with an eye to both how we increase the tempo of IT and the speed with which we complete our work.*

This reference to business process is intended to capture the sequences of work that are performed every day in IT. These tasks can be simple single-step activities or more complex workflows consisting of a few to many individual tasks. The key here is—it is all right in front of us and under our control. It helps to make a list of all the things we do in IT every day and include both internal-to-IT responsibilities as well as what IT delivers to the broader business. This becomes a complete inventory of work that is performed across the organization and therein a surprising number of opportunities to increase our tempo and compress our cycle time.

> ***This list should then be prioritized by strategic value to the business and then ordered from the longest elapsed time down to the shortest.***

This naturally gives us our highest impact and largest potential time-saving tasks and workflows at the top of the list.

Now, we can go to work.

We then assign individuals (this can work well for the tasks) or small teams (normally best for more complex business processes) to scrub through every step and every minute of what is required today to identify and then recommend time savings and improvements in efficiency. These recommendations are then reviewed with an executive sponsor and members of the other teams representing the full **IT Cadence Task Force**.

These reviews are a great exercise. It is important to have experts from other teams across IT gain visibility of what work is occurring for every task and business process.

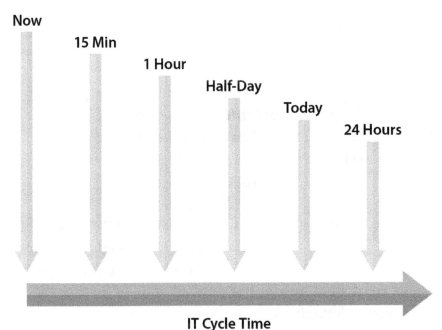

Figure 1.1 The New IT Cycle Time

Figure 1.1 is a simple depiction of what we must be focused on—the new thresholds of cadence for IT. This shows six thresholds that will define the pace of all work that is executed. We must be focused on completing all tasks and workflows within one of these thresholds ranging from now to twenty-four hours. This includes all the work performed by IT, large and small.

What then follows is a relentless pursuit of evaluating, questioning, and optimizing every element of these time windows. And it is important to understand that every second matters. This mindset must be preserved throughout all our work on the Cadence Task Force. Yes, it is great to find time savings of days or weeks, but those big chunks of time alone won't get us to our goals. In some cases, we will get there with the stacking of seconds and minutes. This adds up over time.

> *A great opportunity to save time is the elimination of steps altogether in a multi-step business process. This is often very possible and very productive.*

An increase in the tempo of IT will have countless benefits within IT but will also bring value to the broader business. It is both a very measurable thing, and one of intangibles. An increase in tempo will be noticed and felt by everybody. And this is contagious. Saving some time, we are then driven to save even more.

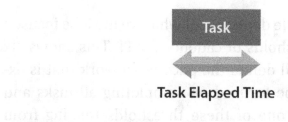

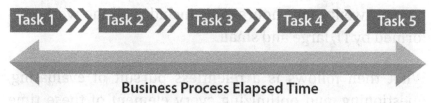

Figure 1.2 Task and Business Process Elapsed Time

Figure 1.2 shows the anatomy of elapsed time for a single task and for a multi-task business process. Each is important and each of these models will be put on the clock when we are looking to complete our work within one of the six thresholds of cadence shown in Figure 1.1. Of course, the multi-task business processes offer a bigger opportunity for time savings, but every second counts, so we need to review every task and every business process in order to maximize our improvement of cadence and speed.

One of our challenges here is that the IT organization has traditionally been seen as somewhat slow and methodical. Yes, it is true, my friends. Having said that, methodical can be good and there is certainly a time and a place for precise and meticulous work.

But it is critical that we know the time and the place, and beyond these special cases we are committed to placing a strategic emphasis on speed, and increasing the daily operations of IT. And with this speed created in IT, we then begin to accelerate all the work that occurs across the organization every day. This is a wonderful source of energy and velocity and coming from a place that many would say is unlikely—from within the depths of IT.

This speed is strategic and fundamental to the transformation that lies ahead of us.

NOW

There is a powerful mindset and set of actions that go hand in hand with the concept of *now*. The key part of making *now* a reality is a readiness to take immediate action. No waiting, no delay, no hesitation at the initialization of the work. Only with eliminating any initial waiting time that might be wired into our standard IT processes can we make *now* possible. This is the first and most important step—finding and extinguishing any initial delay in taking action is the greatest natural barrier to making *now* happen.

> ***When we are able to complete actions
> immediately, in a few minutes, it takes an
> enormous load off the organization and
> makes what was impossible previously,
> possible.***

A key within the deeper key of *now* is the ability to first immediately detect a need and to then take the first actions to complete the necessary process. This detection and action sequence needs to be instant and real-time—but the good news is that this is possible with the systems and automation we have available to us today.

Let's use the common example of a service request coming to the service desk. This occurs many times every day, and we described earlier the greatest enemy of *now* is any waiting that normally occurs prior to executing the first step. If we are able to recognize the creation of a service request and are prepared to take the first steps immediately, then we have won a crucial battle in making *now* possible.

And we will find there is a cascading effect, and in the best possible way.

Every delay we can eliminate then clears the way for the next improvement.

We all carry with us a natural desire to accomplish more in a single day and at the same time understand we can't continue to add more hours to our workday. This is not a sustainable model, as much as we might ignore this fact early in our careers!

While there is no magic here, accomplishing tasks immediately is a highly effective way to create more time in our day. This simple concept is a very powerful one—working in a way that gives us valuable time back in our day to think and to find a better way.

Because *now* is our first threshold, it is important that we make every possible effort to complete work immediately, and every task or business process that can be completed at this threshold offloads this work from flowing into the next set of thresholds.

We need to think in terms of fighting hard to hold the line on the next threshold and not allow tasks or business processes to move to the next time boundary. This can be said for each of the six marks that occur in the first twenty-four hours.

ONE HOUR

It is important to be aggressive in setting the next threshold of time beyond now. When now is not fully possible, the standard for speed should be less than one hour.

An hour is more time than we might think at first. It is remarkable what we can accomplish in the course of an hour with a focused effort.

An hour gives us sixty minutes, a full 3,600 seconds to complete the task at hand. And with the tools we have available today, we can accomplish a lot in a matter of seconds. Improved tools and automation can now accomplish work in a matter of milliseconds—this is beginning to reset our expectations around task durations in everything we do.

A lot can be accomplished in this one hour window, and the approach is the same as the one we take for now. Given that we have made every effort to fit the completion of a task or business process into a few minutes, much of the work has been done to compress the overall elapsed time required, thereby giving us a good head start on meeting the goal of one hour.

It might be the case that the elapsed time can be well within the one hour window although not quite meeting the standard of now, which we expect to be less than fifteen minutes.

As we progress through these time thresholds, it is a good exercise to avoid the natural temptation to dismiss the value of a few minutes. In fact, we should celebrate every second that can be saved. The benefits of this approach really begin to add up over time.

When looking at this threshold of one hour, it is a good time to remind ourselves that every effort should be made to meet the standard of the current threshold before, <u>and only reluctantly</u>, accepting that we must move to the next time standard. In this case, we only accept one hour work completion when the first goal of now is simply not possible. What we will learn is that these efforts to meet the standard of the current time threshold will pay back to us at the next threshold and that we are delivering precious value not just to IT, but to the full organization as we squeeze precious time out of the work performed every day.

This is a remarkable chain of dependencies and linkages that are both virtual and physical across the organization and that knit together everything that must occur to deliver a product or service to a customer.

This fabric is fundamental to every organization, and this chain of action is critical to accelerating the full cadence of IT, which then unlocks the market velocity of the business.

HALF DAY

In the manner of how we work, a natural and meaningful time threshold is a half day. Most workdays consist of two halves, separated by a lunch or midday break. Even with our new obsession with tempo and speed, there is some good in a midday break, although we want to keep it short. As an extension of this evolving mindset, there is value in getting our blocks of work completed before midday in the case of a morning start, or by the end of the day in the case of an afternoon start. Let's think about this for a minute.

> *When we allow a task or business process that is under way to continue into the next day we are taking a risk that additional delays will happen—and often these are beyond our control.*

Priorities can change. A new crisis can occur overnight that requires our attention and pushes out the work that is currently under way. People can be out of the office due to vacation, sickness, or travel. Escalations can hit IT at any time. As much as we might hope this won't happen or that we will have visibility of these schedule issues, stuff happens.

With this in mind, we need to fight against any day-to-day carryover in order to avoid this risk of losing more precious time. Push hard to finish our tasks at the half day and end-of-day marks, and that might require an extension to the first half of the day, or to the end of the day. This is not always easy, but drives down our risk and protects the next day. This brings us some immediate value each day, but brings us a much bigger benefit over time as it becomes a more standard way of working and the savings build.

> *My use of the word "fight" here is not by accident—we need to view this pursuit of time savings every day as a true fight.*

Often not easy, this fight at every threshold is absolutely vital to changing the cadence of IT.

We can view the first threshold of now, and the third threshold of one hour as the best opportunities to avoid the new risks created by the half day threshold, but when we do get to the half day marker, we need to redouble our efforts to hold our tasks or business processes from crossing this fourth threshold. This protects a level of cadence within the workday—allowing us to complete key work before midday or before the end of the day. Let's think of this as a compression of the business day, which changes our productivity and yield. The same-day completion of a task or business process energizes the business and catapults us to a new tempo for the organization.

TODAY

Beyond the numbers and actions we take within this new model of cadence, <u>the mindset we adopt</u> in concert with these elements is critical. It is a new sense of urgency that we carry with us every day as part of the new lifestyle of IT. Embracing this sense of urgency will bring us a focus on preventing incomplete tasks and workflows across IT from moving into the next day. We touched on this in the previous discussion on half day.

> *Why all the fuss? That's simple—because there is just so much that can go wrong or slow us down when the day ends and we are left to wait until the next day to complete our work.*

This is, of course, beyond the growing push to 24X7 operations, which we take up in a dedicated chapter.

Changing priorities, travel, sick leave, planned vacations, holidays, downtime, and planned outages—everything gets more complicated and our risk goes way up when we cross the boundaries of Today. That is why it is so important to complete our work within the first five time thresholds in our new model of cadence.

In the case of our work not being completed on a Friday, we now face the bigger task of completing our work on Monday, three days later. This simple example highlights the importance of completing all the work we have started, today.

In many cases, it will make sense to extend the day in order to complete our work in progress today.

This is not necessarily in line with the traditional model of IT, but with only a short amount of additional work at the end of a day, we can often give big value back to IT. Even thirty minutes can go a long way. This effectively clears the way for a fresh start at the beginning of the next day. This can include team huddles across IT with one or two hours remaining in the day to review what work remains to be completed, and what it will take to get it done. Then, we can rally around these open tasks.

We should also recognize that people across the broader organization are waiting for much of this work to be completed, and when IT completes the task(s) and business process(es), we are having a widespread and important impact on the broader organization. We are eliminating downtime and any waiting for what can potentially be many of our coworkers. The web of waiting can really slow down the organization, and at the same time, eliminating any waiting can bring a much-needed boost.

24 HOURS

This is our sixth and final time threshold for IT cadence. While we have only stepped through twenty-four hours in the course of evaluating the first five thresholds, we have illustrated along the way the vast resource of time available to us in the initial period of twenty-four hours as we launch through the completion of tasks and business processes. This is simply the normal day of IT. Lots of work to be completed with limited time and resources.

The Imperative mindset should be that in virtually every case, we need to focus on completing the work of IT in twenty-four hours or less. Large, complex projects, implementing and going live on a new ERP system for example, can be exceptions, but virtually all of our daily work must be completed in twenty-four hours or less. Of course, now is best, but even in the case of twenty-four hours, we have delivered a key element for the future of IT.

A valuable byproduct of our mindset for speed and fighting at every threshold is that in most cases, our work will be completed well before we get to the twenty-four-hour mark.

This comes along naturally with the push to compress our total elapsed times, and meet the standard of what in many cases will be the first two or three time thresholds.

Expectations and perception are everything, and it must be made clear across the IT organization that the full list of tasks and business processes elapsed times cannot exceed this 24-hour standard. And in some cases organizations will require an explicit approval from the CIO or VP IT in order to go beyond twenty-four hours as we complete the full inventory of IT tasks and business processes and a reset of the IT timeline. This accountability is a good thing and is indicative of the pressure and urgency we will all feel to get faster at everything we do. Not previously on the radar of the CIO or VP IT, the value of raw speed climbs the list of priorities and occupies a top spot in the IT agenda of the future.

We should not be surprised to see a new set of daily reviews and explicit approvals and exceptions created to support the visibility that is increasingly called for.

This is yet another element of the circle of focus and urgency that will then change everything, both from a mindset standpoint and in terms of what the hard numbers will tell us. More on that later.

A PROCESS FOR GAINING SPEED

You might be wondering how exactly we can go about squeezing seconds, minutes, and hours from our IT tasks and business processes. Good question. This is close to the heart of the Imperative and so worth us taking a closer look.

The first step in this process is understanding <u>this is an iterative process,</u> and every time savings is important, be it large or small. It bears saying again that every second is valuable, and it is nothing less than extraordinary how simple seconds grow into minutes, which in turn change into hours saved. We are then on our way to achieving the necessary 90 percent (a description of this is coming shortly) elapsed time savings.

> *In every business process there lies a great opportunity for saving chunks of precious time—the elimination of steps altogether.*

What we learn during the careful inspection of a business process is that some existing rules/steps/approvals/reviews are a legacy that no longer makes sense. In these cases, we should seize the opportunity to simplify the process; this normally brings a nice time savings as an added benefit beyond simplification, which is in itself good for many reasons. Simplification improves the consistency of our performance and improves decision making. This brings added value to the business as it allows us to work smarter and faster. This simple thought brings us again to the core of the Imperative.

As we embark upon this process of gaining speed, <u>we should question everything</u>. That means nothing is off limits, and beyond eliminating full steps in a business process, this approach will allow us to uncover many other sources of time savings. The strategy of iterative improvements is important because there will be cases of a simplification, elimination of a step, making a change to how a task is performed, or other process improvement that then reveals another opportunity that was not visible previously.

These opportunities might not come to light until we make another pass through the inspection of the task or business process. Some of our most impactful time savings will only come through the inspection that comes with the second or third iteration. Don't assume any limits on the number of iterations. For some organizations two or three might be enough. For others it might take four or five or even more passes through the process to get the results we need. It is a healthy exercise, and very productive for many reasons.

AUTOMATION

Automation is a strategic and increasingly capable ally in the urgent push for speed. Not only does automation assist us in saving time, but it also brings with it a number of other clear advantages.

> *Automation enhances consistency, improves decision making, and unshackles people to find smarter ways to work every day. Without the savings of time, this would never be possible and is a timeless trap in business.*

And with these improvements in how we work, we can for the first time shift both the reality and the perception of IT from simply a tactical arm of execution to a strategic leader in the organization. Our dream and, lo, our vision for many years is now within reach.

There is some good news in that automation tools have improved greatly in the past ten years and are now capable of realizing the vision we've held for these tools for many years. The timing is good because we need the help. Both in the form of business rules, which are single automation blocks, to many-step and complex workflows, automation tools can help offload IT in running these elements with little or no human intervention. Automation is important enough to the future of IT that we have dedicated a full chapter in the book to it (Chapter 6).

For now and in the context of cadence, automation holds an important place as it can deliver both incremental and significant time savings when implemented correctly and with the new generation of tools. And, the broader the scope of automation across the elements of IT, the greater the potential value. We explore this important concept in the chapter on the unification of IT (Chapter 7).

As highlighted earlier, the added benefit of consistent decision making and offloading redundant tasks from our people gives automation a clear place in the future of IT.

A KEY METRIC FOR CADENCE

Much of our discussion in this chapter has been in the absence of hard numbers, so let's take a closer look at measures that will help us monitor results and set goals. The previous sections have defined the time thresholds of now, one hour, half day, today, and twenty-four hours. This gives us some guidance on setting expectations and compressing our total elapsed time for all tasks and business processes. With focus comes the natural question of how much faster must we be in order to meet the demands of the Imperative? Is a 20 percent reduction in total elapsed time good enough? What about 50 percent? These are great questions, so let's explore the numbers for a moment and apply the time-yardstick of the future.

While every time savings is important, a 20 percent reduction in elapsed time is simply an incremental improvement and does not bring strategic value. And, while 50 percent is better, this is not fast enough to become strategic. It does not fundamentally change the life of IT or create the opportunity to think and act differently.

Our goal is a 90 percent reduction in the elapsed time of all tasks and business processes performed by IT every day.

This level of speed changes everything. This level of time compression leaps across the threshold of tactical and becomes strategic. This changes the cadence of IT and ultimately of the business. The shock waves of velocity will be felt throughout the full organization and make things possible that were simply not possible before.

A wonderful thing about the good people of IT is that they will invariably take a goal and push to do even better. So, our first thought in looking at the goal of a 90 percent reduction in all the work performed by IT might be: *This is a big number and an aggressive goal.* So it is. But what we should expect, and I'm confident will occur, is that IT will take on this goal, find remarkable ways to meet the goal, and to then take the time savings even further. In the end, we are likely to see a full 90-95 percent time savings in most cases. It is not an exaggeration to claim this will change everything and in ways we simply can't imagine today.

To keep track of our targets, the IT organization should make a complete list of all the tasks and business processes performed on a regular basis. Earlier we called this an "inventory," and I like this concept. I'm a big fan of lists; there is something quasi-magical about checking things off a list.

This inventory is inherent to IT and is in fact critical to the full business because the speed of IT is ultimately the speed of the full organization. We simply can't move the business faster without the engine that is the technology and data of IT moving faster.

In terms of what tasks and business processes make the list, a good measure is the frequency with which they are performed. Monthly is a good test—if activity is performed across IT once or more monthly, it should make the list. A good secondary measure is the total elapsed time of the task or business process. The longer of these presents a bigger opportunity and is likely a source of waiting and risk of delay. Together, these factors bring us our inventory of opportunities, and the 90 percent reduction goal then is applied to every item on this list. As we hit the goal for the first few items on the list, we immediately begin to see the benefits as well as develop a more efficient process for meeting the 90 percent standard for the remaining items.

Remember to celebrate when hitting a small or large goal. Make a big deal out of hitting the first 90 percent milestone. This will encourage our teams and everybody will understand what we can achieve when we follow the process and focus on what we need to extract in the way of time savings. Celebration and recognition are a powerful thing, and everybody wants to be part of a winning team.

Even better, track the percentage improvements for each task and business process and post the results, in a running tally, in a public place that is visible to everybody.

Communicate and market these results and the benefits back to the organization. This builds a real sense of achievement and supports the resources and budgets we will need for future projects. Everybody, including the CIO, CFO, and CEO, will understand what this means to the organization.

KEY TAKEAWAYS: CADENCE

1. Always start with the goal of completing tasks imme-diately. This will increase the speed of everything, even those that ultimately can't be done immediate-ly, and creates a sense of urgency for all the people in IT.

2. A focus on speed is not a technology thing—this is a cultural shift and a mindset. Technology can help, but people ultimately make IT what it needs to be.

3. The technology of automation has improved dra-matically in the past decade—these tools must be leveraged in the pursuit of speed. Smart systems will provide another boost and are enjoying their own curve of improvement.

4. The single best method for improving the speed of performance is the removal of unnecessary or re-dundant steps in performing tasks for business pro-cesses. Be ruthless about lifting this unnecessary work from our shoulders.

5. Communicate the goal of 90 percent time savings of-ten and widely. Then, celebrate the achievement of the goal and recognize the people who made it hap-pen. This will accelerate the cultural shift.

CHAPTER 2

THE CUSTOMER CONNECTION

If there is one element of the Imperative that best embodies the IT organization of the future, it could very well be our relationship with the customer. This connection is vital to everything IT will do every day over the next twenty-five years and beyond.

A new and passionate focus on the customer is uniquely capable of lifting IT to heights never before possible.

> *In many ways this is nothing short of a collision of the unstoppable forces of technology evolved with the business, but this technology needs a guiding light in order to be great.*

Having said that, it is certainly not the case that this connection has failed to exist for the first thirty years of IT. Much work has been done with customers throughout the history of IT. However, due to many factors that have governed and steered the evolution of the IT organization to date, a singular and consistent focus on the customer has been difficult to find and is often missing altogether.

We should not immediately label this an oversight or as a shortcoming of IT. Taking a step back for a moment, this is, in fact, wholly understandable. We can appreciate that IT was born with a focus on technology and safeguarding the assets of the organization. The scope of these assets has grown and technology has evolved dramatically, but this charter has been one that was very much inwardly focused, and as such we tend to think of IT as an internal organization and not charged with the mission to be external facing.

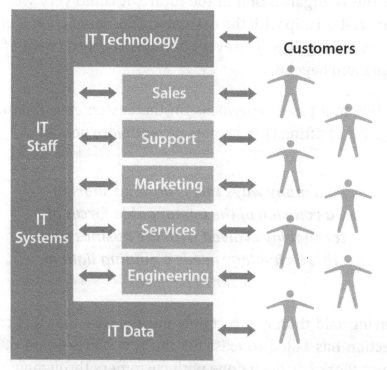

Figure 2.1 The New IT Customer Connection

The customer connection has typically been the business of Sales, Support, Services, and Marketing organizations. Figure 2.1 shows a new model where IT surrounds and complements the traditional customer relationships as owned by other parts of the organization. This direct connection will be owned by IT but highly collaborative with Sales, Marketing, and Customer Support, for example, to ensure all our efforts with the customer are coordinated and transparent. The customer will welcome this new relationship with IT and recognize that IT, as the stewards of technology and data, will bring a unique perspective that complements the partnership between the customer and the business. Every customer has a natural attraction to "the experts" and will enjoy the insights and expertise IT brings to the partnership.

The time is right for this change and the evidence to support it is, in fact, everywhere.

IT is uniquely capable of creating a bridge from the customer to the very core of the organization.

This is a far superior model versus the traditional model of multiple linkages that attempt to loosely connect the customer with IT. Through these multiple and disjointed linkages, we have the risk of interpretations and delays that ultimately result in some dilution and distortion of what is most important to our customers and the description of their most essential needs.

This is a large and potentially serious risk that exists in our business every day. The Imperative calls for us to move beyond this model and build a fundamentally new, direct, and open connection with both internal and external customers that will bring us clarity where we have been lacking it in the past.

> *This changes everything and will infuse*
> *our people with a new level of energy and*
> *conviction that only the customer can*
> *provide.*

The customer has a unique ability to light the path and remove confusion and ambiguity. We only need to listen to tap into this remarkable source of learning.

Taking this a bit further, when we do find ourselves faced with difficult choices, needing to clarify priorities or improve our focus, the single best way to achieve any of this is working with the customer. Think of this as starting with the customer and working our back into the business. This keeps us on track and protects us from going too far astray. A simple model that is good for everybody.

A PASSION FOR CUSTOMERS

The single best wellspring for a successful customer connection is a passion for happy and successful customers. There is no substitute for this commitment and energy, and this will become in every way the very sap of our daily work across IT.

It is easy to say this commitment must come from leadership, but that is simply not the case. This commitment can come from anywhere in the organization, and like many desirable behaviors, it is highly contagious.

Yes, leadership can role model this emphasis and lead the way, but if this does not exist in an organization, all hope is not lost. Every person in IT, regardless of role, can carry with them this passion for customers every day and thereby become an example for all the people around us. Never underestimate the influence you can have on the broader organization, including on leadership and executives.

> *This is a case, a wonderful case, of role modeling from within and from any level of the organization. Role modeling is not just about "down" in an organization; we can role model "up" and "sideways" just as effectively and maybe even more so.*

A passion for customers is something that our people instantly recognize as right and good. This takes no convincing—it is an instinctive ideal that people are naturally drawn to. As a further testament to its power, our frontline teams in IT will yearn for more customer contact if they don't have it today.

This is true from all sides of this relationship, meaning that our people in IT will always have a natural desire for more customer contact and, at the same time, customers will welcome the opportunity to work more directly with the talented people who watch over the technology of the organization. This natural partnership, although strong, has not always been cultivated, but make no mistake—it is there and waiting patiently to come to life. IT has not been seen as customer-facing, but we will shatter this outdated model. All it takes is a small opening and a nudge, and remarkable things will follow.

What we are called to do in the Imperative is create the opportunity that will fan the flame of this remarkable business-borne passion and the connection with customers and one that goes hand in hand with an organizational drive that is uniquely sustained with customers. These two are inextricably linked and will ultimately prove to sustain and propel one another.

With the catalyst of the passion for our customers, we are drawn to move IT closer to both our internal and external clients, and when this occurs, our passion grows stronger. It is a wonderful cycle that can uniquely take our organizations to new levels of performance, levels that are simply not possible without this partnership. When we face tough decisions in the business and when we struggle with strategy or investment priorities, look no further than the customer for clarity. We will repeat this mindset and principle throughout the book.

A DIRECT RELATIONSHIP

All that is fundamentally good about our connections with customers can't be muted, diluted, or translated lest we lose some of the depth of understanding that is so important.

This demands a direct relationship that is available to us as a valuable and necessary vehicle when our programs and projects can benefit most from a direct engagement. This direct connection won't be necessary every day, but when it is necessary we really need it. There is no substitute. As such, it should be established early and then be leveraged when needed without any delay. This connection should <u>never be sought only in response to problems</u> or a lack of communication that has become a challenge for the partnership.

> *Create this model early and it will pay back to us many times over and serve to prevent many problems that arise in the absence of the direct connection.*

It is not uncommon for our people in IT to hesitate in

contacting customers and establishing these critical connections. This is understandable, and very much the traditional model of IT. But, as with much of what we will
do in the rebirth of IT, this, too, must change. When we
make this change, and embrace the customer connection
as a daily and natural part of our work in IT, we will look
back in amazement that we did not build this engagement
sooner.

It is best to work through the existing relationships we
have in order to make the necessary introductions with
our teams in IT. These relationships can be in account management, sales, technical support, customer marketing,
consulting, technical account management, and more. It is
not difficult to identify the people in our organization who
work directly with our external customers. These people
are normally happy to introduce IT project managers, program managers, directors, or VPs to our customers. This
introduction is in the interest of better understanding customer requirements and how we can better meet these requirements now and in the future.

> *This expansion and enrichment of the*
> *customer relationship will be welcomed*
> *by the customer themselves as they will*
> *instantly recognize it is in their best*
> *interest.*

With the introductions made, and the goals of IT outlined,
we can work with the customers directly toward specific
milestones and deliverables. This work then becomes

self-sustaining and we discover there is always something the customer can help with.

Always be respectful of the customer's time and keep the engagement and the connection focused on more strategic projects.

SEEK WITH GREAT PATIENCE

This is a critical sub-element of the customer connection. In every customer, there is an essence of value that must be understood and appreciated. This is fundamental to the customer's organization and therefore fundamental to our partnership. It is always there, and sometimes it will reveal itself quickly, and sometimes it will require some patience in order to first achieve an understanding and then to grow that understanding into appreciation.

This timeline can't be rushed or subject to artificial structures and milestones.

It must be sought with what we can call great patience and only with great patience will we ultimately understand the core of the customer and their associated needs. While it is easy to slip into assessing a client business as being "just like client X," this is rarely the case when we look deeper. Yes, it is common for clients in similar markets to share some characteristics and practices, but there will always be some number of unique traits that make an organization what it is, and give it a unique character. Sometimes this is easy to identify; other times this takes time to understand. We don't know how much time will be required, but we must commit to taking whatever time is needed to discover the organizational fingerprint.

The core of this character is normally simple, whereas the satellite needs can be numerous and quite complex.

We must not confuse the two; this is the very reason why patience is so important. If we find the body of satellite requirements without understanding the core essence of the customer, we will be without direction and without purpose. This insight is everything.

> *But when we do understand the core and fully investigate and define the supporting requirements, then we have something that is very powerful and timeless.*

This fundamental insight can carry a customer relationship forward and to great success, for decades into the future, and is the basis for what will ultimately prove to be our very best partnerships.

In stark contrast, when we lose a customer or when we have a partnership that is struggling and unable to find success, it is very often suffering from the lack of this understanding. We never did find the core essence of the customer or we confused simple needs or business requirements with the essence.

When we take on and truly embrace the mindset from the

very beginning of seeking to understand our customer with the necessary patience, we have made a priceless investment that will pay back to us many times over.

I have been fortunate to be part of this process on many occasions. I've also experienced enough confusion and frustration, along with a few moments of glorious insight, to assure you the understanding can be achieved in a day, or it can take months. In a few cases, it can take years. In the end, it takes what it must take, and we are willing to invest the time because it gives us so much in return.

TRANSPARENCY

An open sharing of information and inherent honesty are important parts of any partnership and this is a fundamental part of the customer connection. If asked to describe the ideal partnership in a few words, most customers would quickly use words like honesty and trust.

> *A wonderful thing once embraced, this healthy and natural cultural change is another contagious behavior that spreads across the organization with great speed.*

We simply need to commit to transparency and get started. Much of the rest will happen naturally. This is another lifestyle element that has not been a normal part of the IT we are leaving in the past. Once again, much has changed and the full organization can benefit from increased transparency from IT, including internal customers and external customers alike. It is a behavior that stimulates sharing—when we work with a partner who is clearly transparent, we feel the pull to do the same.

*This cycle stimulates many working
style adjustments including honesty,
communication, and trust.*

When transparency begins to occur, we also make better decisions. As highlighted in other sections of the book, when we have access to high-quality data in a timely manner, we are able to make better decisions when all other factors are constant.

This discussion on transparency is a natural complement to timely and trustworthy data as it flows from our commitment to transparency. If I were to point to one element that builds a good partnership above all others it would be trust—and trust and transparency go hand in hand. This combination creates a remarkably powerful cultural momentum.

Role modeling is a wonderful thing, and an authentic form of leadership. Where there might not be transparency today, IT should take the first step in making this commitment. This will benefit the organization, and our internal and external customers are likely to follow suit...another example of leadership that can come within, and from IT. Being pragmatic, this makes even more sense; IT is the steward of our data and corporate information, so transparency is close to home.

OPEN DIALOGUE

An open and ongoing dialogue with the customer is a natural extension of the transparency and the direct connection we discussed earlier. The dialogue is good for IT and good for the customer in that it helps all parties involved to stay informed, shares information in a timely manner, and helps prevent misunderstandings. So many challenges and potential problems can be prevented with an honest and open dialogue with the customer.

An open dialogue drives trust, and as our grandparents love to say, trust must be earned. The saying is as true today as it was then, and we earn trust every day through transparency and open dialogue.

> *While the direct connection is important, its value is limited and will wane over time if we aren't committed to keeping this ongoing dialogue.*

Transparency is a mindset, while this open dialogue is how we operate every day. You can see that the power of this communication model is in the combination of having the direct connection with the customer, keeping a commitment to complete transparency, and in running an open dialogue for the frequent and mutual sharing of updates and relevant information. Any one of these elements is helpful, but the real value comes with the combination of these working together. Then, of course, trust is created.

These concepts are not revolutionary when taken in the context of account management or support today. But what *is* new is the application of these customer-focused concepts for IT.

This is part of the shift the Imperative brings to the operations and strategy of IT and will forever change how we think. Every day begins with a focus on what is most important; the customer ascends to the top of the list for IT, and this will remain the case for many years to come. The customer has always been important to all of us in IT, but we were not always able to operate with the level of understanding and direct engagement we will have as we create our new models. This will not be easy, but the customer connection brings a new dimension to how we plan, how we think, and how we act every day.

> ***This brings us a new and strong sense***
> ***of clarity where there might have been***
> ***ambiguity and confusion in the past.***

Those IT organizations that understand this best and take it to heart will be engines of innovation for the market leaders of the future. In many ways this removes one of the few blind spots IT had in the past and is a further catalyst to bring a more strategic dimension to IT.

A final comment about this open dialogue with customers: We will all gain an appreciation for the beauty of this model in that we will receive immediate and clear feedback on what is good and what is bad. Customers are very direct on this point because a lot is at stake. Ultimately this gets us to the right place with our customers faster, which is all that really matters.

CUSTOMER REQUIREMENTS

We simply can't point to a single thing that stands alone as the essence of the customer connection, but a few things do emerge as at the core of this connection. One of these is the understanding of customer needs, today and in the future. These needs are often captured and described as business requirements. The existence of these requirements is not new, but what is new and what we are called to do in the rebirth of IT is to have IT participate actively in the discussion and documentation of these requirements.

Often the IT staff participating in this process is a program manager or project manager who can take the customer requirements and make them available to all the people in IT with a need to have access to this information. These needs will of course vary widely from one organization to another, but there will always be individuals and teams that are designing, developing, and delivering technologies that will ultimately directly touch our internal and external customers.

This is fundamental to the charter of IT and goes back to its beginning—the teams of IT serving as stewards of technology and information on behalf of the broader organization in order to deliver high-quality goods and services to our customers.

With the advent of IT taking a large step forward and joining in, or in some cases driving, the discussion and capturing of customer requirements, we are able to more quickly and more clearly represent these requirements to the full IT organization and as such those that will ultimately build or buy these critical customer-facing technologies. It is not that the previous process, one that often did not include IT directly, was fundamentally flawed, as that process did produce the necessary results the majority of the time.

The distinction we are making here is that by eliminating our dependency on the intermediaries that delivered this information on behalf of IT in the past, we are able to move faster and with less ambiguity than ever before.

This equation is not just about IT *taking*. We are giving a lot in return, in having a deep understanding of technology, data, and client systems and with this being able to connect the resources and assets of IT and the business and put them to work for the customer. In the end, this results in a better solution.

This model empowers IT to deliver a superior result more consistently and with more economy of effort—not re-markable within the context of a single deliverable, but quite impactful over the course of the many projects and deliverables demanded of IT in a typical month, quarter, or year. This is a wonderful case of leverage, and we are searching for precious leverage every day. When we find it, it is a beautiful thing to behold.

CUSTOMER USE CASES

An important element in customer success and a natural complement to the definition of customer requirements is the ability to validate, in a consistent and empirical manner, these same requirements. It's a long and sometimes perilous journey from the definition of a business requirement to the final delivery of the technology intended to address the requirement.

> *We are fond of calling this a solution, and that is a good way to capture the intent— we are solving a business problem for our customer.*

And if we are putting time and resource into this solution, it is important.

Test cases, or customer use cases, are to be represented during the development and testing phases performed by IT and development teams leading up to a customer delivery. This commitment and process will significantly de-risk the larger process and help create a successful delivery milestone. It's a complex process targeted at solving complex business problems, so the risk can't be eliminated completely, but the use of a core set of customer test cases is a big boost.

Beyond the technical merits of these real-world test cases, the use of authentic customer data and use cases permits the customer to have a presence in the development cycle, and this brings us even closer to the customer. We can make this personal—and allow the customer test cases to be identified with the customer name. After all, there are real people and a real organization behind this data, and there is no need to keep this detached and impersonal. This personal element should be encouraged so all IT staff involved in the process understand where our test cases have originated from and we are helping real people.

It is also true that real-world test cases are simply better.

Despite the best efforts of our testing and QA staff, it is very difficult to replicate the authenticity of customer use cases.

This representation of the customer through development and delivery both strengthens the partnership and helps to ensure a successful completion to the project. There is tremendous value here. As a further extension to this principle, if we have customers with unusual complexity, unusual scale, or other requirements that will cause us to test the limits of the solution, these customers should be sought and not excluded due to their demanding needs.

Far better to understand these advanced requirements early and when they can be addressed with less time and expense, than later when the cost of accommodating advanced requirements is much more expensive. This is not always natural, but it's very important we face these robust requirements head-on and early. It's an advanced and ultimately wise, shrewd behavior that saves precious time, money, and resource.

NETWORKING

As our connection with the customer grows and evolves, one element that customers will want to explore is the introduction to and communication with other customers. This is something that IT can facilitate, and as such, we as the facilitators can benefit in the process and learn even more.

The partnership that is borne of the customer connection brings us so much. One great example is our ability to bring customers together, thus bringing more value to our customers and expanding our ability to enhance learning and more effectively deliver the right technology and solutions along the way. This is another good case of leverage—delivering more effective solutions for a given customer while at the same time gaining insights into how we better serve the needs of a larger customer community.

We should begin by embracing this opportunity to bring customers together.

For some, there is a natural aversion to this request. There are concerns this might create more work; it might become complicated; customers might share problems with other customers; it might cause us to take on the responsibility of moderating any discussions that occur; we might be accountable for any problems that follow, to name a few.

As with most things, there are exceptions, but in virtually every case a customer will appreciate the opportunity to meet other customers and will be professional and considerate at every stage. The rare exception should not shape our behavior nor cause us to steer away from doing the right thing, which in this case is to be a willing and enthusiastic channel for bringing customers together.

Customers can learn a great deal from other customers and, in many cases, more than they can learn from our full organization or from IT.

> *Customers have a wonderful and unique*
> *perspective that other customers will*
> *appreciate and value.*

But, that opportunity to learn must begin with the right introduction, and we are uniquely qualified, in having a full view of the customer community, to help a customer take that first step. My experience has been that the pairing of customers is a natural thing, and both customers will appreciate the introduction and recognize the value in this networking. Very little oversight is required; customers are good at taking the appropriate steps following a one-to-one or group introduction.

Over time this networking grows quickly from but a few simple introductions. We just need to be open to starting the process, and well-intentioned customers will take it from there. Be willing and prompt in helping launch this process when the time comes.

TRUSTED ADVISOR

Our connection with the customer will call us to change some of how we work with our internal and external customers day in and day out. One such change will be a shift from simple, short, and tactical interactions to one of a more advisory consultation. In many cases, both the customer and our IT staff are making every effort to keep our interactions short and focused on the matter at hand. Typically, this is answering a very specific question or working on a specific ticket/incident that is blocking our work. These interactions won't go away; they are part of the daily operations of the organization.

What we are called to do is add a new strategic and consultative track to complement this existing tactical track.

The new strategic track will provide the opportunity for senior IT staff to meet with internal and external customers to discuss and brainstorm creative solutions to existing challenges or new opportunities, which could include the offering of new products, the launch of new services, changes in the marketplace, meeting the needs of compliance and governance, opening new geographies, and much more.

This model moves IT into a fundamentally different role with our customers and one that IT is uniquely qualified to fill.

In the past the business has often looked outside for this type of consulting and strategic planning activity. Now, we have begun to understand that likely our best option for this advisement is just down the hall and in our own IT organization.

We need only to create the opportunity to bring the right skills in IT together with the business owners in the organization, and a very powerful model is born from within. Making this a reality requires IT leadership to make time for the right skilled people in IT to serve in these advisory roles and book time with their counterparts in the business. Not easy, of course, because our most skilled and experienced people in IT are always in demand, but this brings tremendous value to our customers and is very much in line with our new focus on the customer connection and the mindset of the Imperative. When we recognize this is a high value and organic opportunity to bolster our customer partnerships, the decision becomes much more clear.

LISTENING

Few things are as simple yet at the same time so hard as listening.

For some, it is simply unnatural and uncomfortable. For others still, it is more of a natural skill that then must be recognized and developed. Too often we just can't wait to quickly communicate the information we believe our customers need to know or should receive, and we forget to slow down and listen. This happens in so many meetings in so many organizations, and really wherever people come together. If anything, it is the norm in our me-first world. Yet, by starting with the willingness to listen, we will often learn the conversation can and should be very different than what we had envisioned.

I include this topic because listening seems to be an endangered skill, but one that is so central to the customer connection.

Of the many skills that our IT staff possess, the skill of listening is not one of our natural strengths. But I'm a big believer in the talents of our IT staff and with an understanding that something is important, our people are remarkably adaptable. And so it should be with listening to customers.

> *It is possible that no trait brings us so much good as does a commitment to listen to our customers.*

This is a great place to start when meeting with a customer—the goal to listen more than we talk. Check that, listen <u>a lot more</u> than we talk. We could call this a Conversation Strategy. It is remarkable what we can learn when we listen, and when this opportunity is lost, we might not have it again. Listening is about more than learning, although this is important. Listening helps to shape a partnership.

> *Our willingness to listen says so much about how much we value the customer and how much we value the partnership. Our sense of value naturally gives rise to this desire to listen.*

The best salespeople, marketing people, account managers, and technical support staff I've worked with share the trait of being good listeners and truly caring about their customers.

Customers can see it in your eyes—that you really care about what they have to say. This creates a very powerful cycle—when we show that we care about our customers and are willing to listen to them, it creates the desire in the customer to treat us in the same way. It is a beautiful thing, and we should be willing to take the first step with our listening strategy in every customer interaction, whether it be a ten-minute meeting, or an all-day workshop. The same rules apply. At the end of our time together with the customer, did we listen more than we talked? What did we hear? What are the key bits of information the customer shared?

I'm confident that if the answer is yes, we listened more than we talked, it was a productive session. And if the answer is no, then we could have done better and learned more.

GOOD NEWS AND BAD NEWS

We all love to share good news. It's easy and fun, and when we have it we just can't wait to spread the good word—without any urging or training or encouragement. But where there is good news, the cycle of business will always bring some level of disappointment, and bad news will inevitably come. Even the very best of organizations and the very best of people will have setbacks. Bad news then creates a very different set of challenges.

> **But how and when we share this information says a great deal about the quality of a partnership. Even more so, it says a great deal about the _quality of a partner_.**

This matter is a fundamental part of the customer connection and, as such, needs to be addressed, because how we manage information that will be disappointing to a customer says a great deal about an organization and our people. Although the fundamentals of this discussion are simple, the actions that must occur are anything but easy.

Bad news should be delivered quickly and directly. Customers don't want to hear bad news, of course; good news is much more fun. But we all understand that the course of business does not always go the way we have planned, and the sooner we have the information, the sooner we can get to work on making things better. At this point, there is another important behavior for the customer connection, and that is our willingness to immediately switch over from bringing bad news to getting to work on solving the problem before us.

When possible it's always best to bring a couple of ideas on possible solutions when we must share bad news with a customer so we can move together directly into brainstorming and problem solving.

In a good partnership, we celebrate success together and we meet challenges head-on together. It is best to keep an even temperament for both good news and bad news, and we can set the tone for this across the culture. Don't get too low with bad news and don't get too high with good news. In the long term, this is best for the performance of the business and avoids too much up-and-down in the daily operations for IT.

THE USER EXPERIENCE

A discussion of the customer connection would not be complete without looking at the user experience. Only a few things stand at the highest level of priority in the future of IT, and the user experience is one of the select few. This stands in contrast with the past, when this was something that mattered, but not something that drove the daily performance of IT.

As with most things that are truly important, answering the question "why" is easy. The user experience now rises to this new status because it is at the heart of what is driving the transformation of IT—a boundless passion for the customer that builds loyalty and a long-lasting partnership, standing the test of time and trial.

> *With this focus on the customer, the experience of the user demands our attention; we can't grow happy customers consistently if we are not investing in the user experience.*

This is a multifaceted issue requiring thoughtful planning and execution. A great user experience means many things, and we can consider the user to be any individual, team, or organization that utilizes the resources or services of IT. We tend to think in terms of internal users and external users, and this is not a bad overview because these groups share many things in common.

The user experience continues to change and evolve, so doing this well is an ongoing commitment and investment. The skills of IT staff must be matched to this activity as not everybody will have the right skillset. The emphasis here is on communications, capturing key user requirements, a knowledge of the business, and some creative design to investigate how we get better.

This is a recommended role for IT going forward, specifically ownership of the user experience across IT and across all our user groups. As outlined previously this can be a new skillset and might require a recruitment plan to bring these skills into IT. It is an important investment, and this mix of skills will be increasingly needed in IT, and far beyond this user experience requirement.

We can't expect to see ongoing focus and improvement in the user experience without the necessary dedicated resources, and this can't be a part-time position.

As a complement to this skillset and the enlistment of dedicated resources, we must recognize the user experience has a

long lifecycle. We can't confuse just one segment of the user experience with the full lifecycle.

It takes time to fully understand the full scope of the lifecycle and only then can we build a plan and implement a solution that delivers a great user experience.

KNOW THE USER

We need to make a distinction between the "customer" and the "user." Sometimes they are the same and sometimes they are very different. A customer is any individual or organization that consumes our products or services. Regardless of the type of organization we are part of, somewhere we are delivering a product or a service to a customer. A user is a subset of the body of internal or external customers and represents the user of a product or system we provide as a business or as an IT organization. The user can be readily identified, and in those cases an opportunity is created.

> *This opportunity is important and it*
> *requires patience and time.*

But it pays back to us many times over when we fully leverage the opportunity in front of us. This is all about knowing the user—really knowing the user. It is easy to collect information about the user indirectly, or at a high level directly. But knowing the user is about much more. This is about both informal and formal communications, working sessions, whiteboard brainstorming, and much more. This is about context and depth. Simply collecting information about the user is not enough. Not nearly enough.

A few questions that can help guide the way:

1. What are the primary goals of the user?
2. How many distinct user groups are we addressing?
3. What are the key business requirements to be supported for each?
4. Do we understand the key use cases of the user?
5. What is the natural working style of the user?
6. How can we make the user more productive?
7. Have we defined the two to three critical things the user must have?
8. How do we add more value to the experience of the user?
9. How do we improve the overall performance of the user?
10. Do we fully understand any current shortcomings of existing systems?
11. How do we accommodate system changes or new requirements over time?
12. Have we established an open line of communication with the user?
13. How will the needs of the user change in the next 12-24 months?
14. What big strategic initiatives can potentially impact the user in the next 36-48 months?

This is just the beginning, but with a good beginning and a commitment to listening, we can learn a great deal. This is a good time for a gentle reminder—patience is key. Listening is key. Honesty is key.

Understanding the user is worth our time and attention, and a good understanding does not come easily or quickly. But the user is a willing partner and happy to invest the time with us, and so this is the basis of a good partnership.

KEY TAKEAWAYS:
THE CUSTOMER CONNECTION

1. Although far from the traditional model, IT must create a direct relationship with customers if that relationship does not exist today. Customers will welcome this expansion of the partnership.

2. Customer requirements must be developed in a rich language that ensures IT has a detailed and full description of what technologies and systems will be delivered.

3. The unique expertise of IT can be leveraged by both internal and external customers in a trusted advisor model that works to the benefit of both the customer and IT as it expands the understanding of all involved with real business problems.

4. All the work we do in the future of IT will be driven by a new and heightened passion for customers that will shape our daily work and daily decisions.

5. Take the time to know the user as a complement to our overall customer relationship. This includes a multilevel understanding of strategy, goals, requirements, and use cases. As always, change is

inevitable, and we must establish a process for on-going communication and how to manage changing requirements.

CHAPTER 3

THE CONSUMERIZATION OF IT

Powerful market forces and the accelerated evolution of consumer models have had a strong and increasing influence on how IT thinks and operates. This is, of course, a good thing, although not always seen as such by those who cling to the traditional models of IT. We are kidding ourselves if we deny the overwhelming influences of consumer models on IT in the past ten years and to the good of both IT and our customers.

Some slowness to embrace this consumerization is both natural and understandable, but make no mistake, these forces will not go away. If anything, they will continue to gain momentum. Looking a bit deeper, we should recognize the consumer influences are not simply influences, but good and necessary influences from which we can learn a great deal. They represent a strong element of customer desires and behaviors—the behaviors of a new market and a new world.

This consumerization of IT intersects with a number of other elements of the Imperative, and this calls attention to the synergies of these influences and new operating models that are remaking the wonderful world of IT.

It is all but impossible to ignore the influences that online commerce, ubiquitous Internet access, mobility, and social media have on everything we do.

Ultimately these influences are to the benefit of our internal and external customers, and this needs to be the focus of those people in IT who take on the heavy lifting in order to make these new models a reality, including bringing the best of consumer experiences to IT.

At the root of this consumerization of IT lies the pursuit of a thrilled customer who gets exactly what they want, every time.

This is about more than just achieving that result; this all needs to happen in a way that is comfortable and natural and fits with our lifestyle. And, of course, through an experience that builds loyalty and much more. We are naturally drawn to return to organizations that provide exceptional service and value our business. An organization that is paying attention, getting better, and making an effort to better serve us. This is the persona that IT will take on, which naturally pulls us closer to the customer and generates a higher level of passion for quality of service.

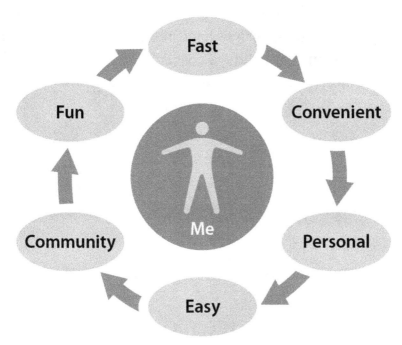

Figure 3.1 Consumer Influences on IT

Figure 3.1 depicts a few of the consumer influences that will help to reshape how we think and how we execute our daily work across IT. We will look at a number of these in the remainder of this chapter, but in scanning this figure we are struck by both the simplicity of the model and how much common sense is here.

Who is not attracted to a fast, fun, and easy experience? Who would argue that convenient is not a good thing? Good common sense, yes, but not always present in the operations of IT. In many ways we will find it natural to adopt these elements in IT because we have all been touched by the influencers we touched on earlier—including social media, mobile devices, the Internet. These elements are now part of our lives, so any barriers or resistance to leveraging these models in IT have likely faded away over the past five to ten years and we are ready to embrace the best of what these influencers offer. So, here we go.

CONVENIENCE

The concept of convenience is another element of the new model for IT that is not often associated with IT but is a natural for the rebirth of IT. It's a natural because it's in our nature. Everybody likes convenience.

Convenience saves time, convenience makes people happy, convenience makes us more productive, convenience keeps customers coming back. There are few absolute truths in business, and one is that when we make a customer happy, lots of good things will follow.

To make convenience a reality, some careful evaluation, communication, and observation is needed. This should not be slow and take a great deal of time, just thoughtful.

Overall, we should pursue this with gusto, knowing it will be a relatively small investment of time that will bring us a big return.

We're looking for a set of opportunities to offer services and complete our IT tasks and business processes in a manner that offers a more convenient experience for our internal customers/employees first, then, if appropriate, our external customers.

Often, but not always, these opportunities are linked, and the improvements we make will benefit both constituents. When it does happen, it's a beautiful thing. A good process to follow is meet with a specific group of business owners to discuss how to offer IT services in a way that is more convenient to users. How can IT save them time? How can IT enable them to complete work more quickly? Are there any limitations in our systems today that slow them down?

To make the session more productive, IT should bring two or three ideas to get the discussion started. A whiteboard session is a good way to conduct this discussion. This will normally bring out good ideas from the business team, and these ideas will complement the ideas the team from IT brought to the meeting. Keep these meetings relatively short, and focus on brainstorming without too much concern on structure. We want lots of rough ideas, and from these ideas we will likely identify a few that can make a difference. Structure can come later. The jewels from this work are the ideas themselves. From this, we can build our improvements.

With these brainstorming sessions comes a need for follow-up. Any follow-up from IT should be quick and informal, just to give the business owners or internal customers feedback on status and any ongoing work that is leveraging the ideas discussed in the whiteboard sessions. This is good team behavior, good transparency on the part of IT, and helps to prevent any frustration that might come when no follow-up happens. Just a small thing that makes a big difference.

EASY

Easy is magnetic in its attraction. We can all use more *easy* in our lives, and IT is no exception. *Hard* is not fun. *Hard* slows us down. *Hard* is discouraging. *Hard* costs us time and money. Even worse, *hard* makes us grumpy.

This brings us back to *easy*, which is a much better discussion to have but has simply not been a big part of the dialogue and strategy of traditional IT.

> ***The great responsibility that comes with easy is to ensure our quality does not suffer and our costs do not rise.***

Put another way, *easy* can be strategic when we deliver it in a way that keeps the quality of our work high and holds costs constant, or in some cases reduces costs. This is an example of leverage—easy in combination with reduced costs. This is a win for the user and a win for the business. We can again look no further than the influences of our consumer markets to find the origins of a new generation of *easy*.

As the Internet began to influence how we access information, learn, and purchase goods, the concept of *easy* became more attainable than ever. *Easy* has flourished in the consumer markets and with good reason. People, both in our personal lives and in business, are drawn back to *easy*. This strategy—making people comfortable and saving people time—has a strong place in the rebirth of IT.

The concept of *easy* is another great example of the shifting strategy of IT. Ideas that have blossomed in our world outside IT but have not been able to penetrate the psyche of IT previously now become a natural fit for our future.

> **This cannot be questioned. The only question can be, why has this taken us so long?**

Easy does take thoughtful design. *Easy* is anything but simplistic. Easy does not happen by accident. The best implementation of *easy* is easy *and* powerful. This result must rely on a strong understanding of use cases and business requirements complemented by careful design and a highly iterative test and validation process.

It is beyond the scope of this summary to give a lot of attention to the development of IT applications, but the concept of user participation in design and testing and an iterative development process is very effective.

One of the valuable byproducts of *easy* is making internal and external customers more productive by saving precious time. This gives us time back in our day, which then allows us time to think—time to think about how we work smarter, time to think about how we better serve customers, time to focus on more strategic activities. This concept of saving time runs throughout the 17 elements. It is fundamental to the future of IT and we discuss this further in the chapters on Cadence (Chapter 1) and Automation (Chapter 6) among others.

There are a few thoughts we should carry with us every day in IT, and one of those is *How can we make this easier?* When we find the answer to this question, we create a powerful engine of value that ultimately grows from happy and loyal customers.

FAST

The speed at which we do everything in IT is changing. It is always best to be driven by desire and to act proactively, but make no mistake, this is not an option. We dedicated Chapter 1 to the element of cadence, which provided a more detailed look at how we will change the tempo at which we perform every task and business process in IT. Here we will take a brief look at *fast* through the lens of the standards we apply to the world of the consumer.

> **We owe a lot to the greedy and impatient consumer. From these high expectations, business has been forced to change and to change quickly.**

This is a matter of survival first. Then the new market leaders understand that beyond survival there is an opportunity for innovation, and from innovation springs leadership and then success is likely to follow. At the heart of the consumer influences on IT is *fast*. This is a significant shift from our preoccupation in IT with efficiency and cost savings measurements throughout the past thirty years.

Now we must view the speed of our
daily performance as a higher priority
than the somewhat parochial efficiency
measurements of the past.

Yes, IT will forever be required to secure the IT estate and deliver great service. Recall this is what we have called the timeless mission of IT. But there is now another dimension to this, and it is raw speed.

Speed done as a quantum leap is strategic. Speed is transformational and fundamentally changes how we live and work. This must be a long-term strategic initiative and not a short-term project. It must drive a shift in mindset that results in a continuing search to remove seconds and minutes from all the work we perform in IT.

It is important to emphasize that while we feel this pull to be faster at everything we do across IT and across the business, these same pressures are at work in the world of our customers. And so we push the envelope of speed so we can then in turn bring speed to our customers.

Our customers need this from us to
better serve their customers. This chain
of dependencies is part of what forms a
strategic partnership; we are only as fast
as the slowest link.

An ongoing commitment to speed and to the customer is vital, as it is often necessary to claw back our time savings one small step at a time and, in some cases, to complete a simple step that brings only seconds in savings before we can then see another opportunity to save time. Meeting our goals here is normally an iterative process, and these improvements in speed clear the way for many other consumer-like behaviors that will bring IT a fundamentally new customer experience. We give this iterative approach some structure in the chapter on Automation (Chapter 6).

ME

There is a fundamental element of *me* in the consumer influences on IT and certainly the remaking of IT through the Imperative. This next point is an important one—a degree of selfishness is a good thing, and can be cultivated into a very good thing.

This focus on the individual, a very demanding individual, has been a key driver in the evolution of the commercial marketplace over the past ten years. This includes elements like social media which begin with a focus on the individual but then as a natural course of evolution grows from benefitting one to benefitting many.

> *So the strategy we take forward here is*
> *that a focus on the needs of the individual*
> *is a major shift in the natural DNA of IT, but*
> *ultimately is our path to a very different*
> *and a very personal IT.*

The talented people of IT must first embrace the concept of *me*, which will take us on a journey to discover many valuable strategies, designs, technologies, and operating models that will build more productive individuals and happy customers.

To begin this journey, it is important to focus on the needs of individuals who serve in key individual contributor roles in the organization, are key revenue enablers, manage strategic systems, or are key leaders in the organization. This investigation must not be biased by budget in the beginning.

We start the dialogue with an exclusively individual focus on a thread that looks something like this:

1. How can IT make you more productive?
2. What systems-related frustrations do you experience every day?
3. What tools can IT provide to increase the speed of your daily work?
4. Today, what work do you perform that seems to be a waste of time?
5. Do you perform regular tasks that can be automated?
6. Rate your user experience for all the systems you utilize regularly.
7. Can we help you to delegate responsibilities/work to others?
8. How can IT assist you in spending more time on strategic tasks?
9. What are the best IT systems you use today?
10. What are the top two or three qualities you value in an internal system?

You will have other questions as well that can be more

targeted at your business/organization. With answers to these questions, we can evaluate where we can have the biggest impact on the individual as well as the cost associated with these improvements.

> *We want to remain focused on improving the performance of the individual, which then brings benefits to teams and the broader organization. This is a case where a bottoms-up model in the organization can be very productive.*

This then becomes a building block that results in leverage when we focus on the right individuals in the organization, and by making these individuals more productive, this spreads quickly. This is not meant to imply that we never move beyond this select group of individuals—we can look at other employees over time after we have reaped the benefits of our original selected individuals.

FUN

The inclusion of *fun* in this discussion might surprise you. But a bigger element of fun in many things we do in IT is a part of our future.

Everybody likes to have a little fun, and we should not accept that fun has no place in IT. We could argue that fun was hard to find in the IT of the past, but the remaking of IT will shatter many standing conventions, and this is one. There is no magic here, as fun is not as elusive as we might believe. A big part of finding fun is committing to creating some fun in our daily work.

> *This is good for everybody. And there is nothing more contagious than a smile.*

A smile is a very powerful thing, and is a catalyst for great service and customer loyalty. Who would argue that we need to smile more in IT?

Fun can come from many places, including:

1. Small contests among teams in IT to drive the right behaviors
2. Brainstorming sessions to create improvement in how we support customers
3. Social events planned at lunch, break time, or after work
4. Designing fun into our interactions with customers
5. Team building with exercises that carry over into the workday
6. Recognition of a team member doing something great
7. Events planned with customers and IT staff—yes, this is a great thing
8. The design of stylish and creative elements into IT applications

A point to take away from this discussion is that IT can be the unlikely origin of fun for the organization. Surprising maybe, but we are trying to do some things that have not been done by IT in the past, and yet things that IT is very capable of providing to the broader business.

Each is somewhat small on their own, but together begin to change the perception of IT and the expectations of IT going forward.

> *An element of fun in our daily work is not without a strategy.*

Yes, we know that fun is fun for fun's sake, but there is

much more to it. Fun will help our teams to be happier, to be healthier, to be more productive, and to provide superior services and products to both internal and external customers. A happy team does a better job. This is simply good for business, and as it is occurring and we begin to see the results, it emerges as a very smart and shrewd investment.

We should be reminded that retention of staff is a challenge of many organizations, and some fun in IT goes hand in hand with a happier and more satisfied organization. It then follows that our people will stay longer in a given role. This makes those individuals and all the people around them better and more productive. These up-and-coming stars then have a chance to be recognized and promoted and then become our IT leaders of the future.

COMMUNITY

As powerful forces borne in consumer ecosystems increasingly influence IT, it will bring a sense of belonging to something bigger, a sense of community. This offers a natural attraction to our people and is a great complement to other elements, including fun.

> *Community is about many things, including sharing, communicating, belonging to something bigger than ourselves, and a sense of giving back.*

What this means to IT and to our Imperative is that we must first create a stronger sense of community within IT, and this will then influence the culture of the broader organization. The change in IT has its own strong set of benefits, and this then grows exponentially as the influence of community spreads across the broader organization.

Community is all about people, and the future of IT as well as the future of business is about people and service. Yes, we love our technology, and no organization appreciates technology more than IT. We know this in our soul.

What better team to be the catalyst for leading our organization to an understanding of the synergies between people and technology? People can leverage technology to be better than we can be with no technology, but technology alone will not save us. Technology alone is not driving the rebirth of IT. A healthy culture with talented and passionate people leveraging technology to perform at their best every day—well, that is really something to behold. And IT can lead the way.

It is important to understand that we have two equally vital sides to this discussion.

These opening thoughts are around the internal encouragement of community that makes an organization closer and stronger. I'm also suggesting there is a twin to this strategy—IT must lead the way to create social and community experiences for external customers. Sometimes, but not always, the business owners will recognize this is an important element of the customer, and that is great, as all that matters is we get to the right place.

However, in the absence of the necessary push from business owners to create social experiences and a community for external customers, IT should be proactive in leading the way. This is good for many reasons, including IT having the resources to make this a reality. It will ultimately create happier and more loyal customers. We make this point repeatedly throughout this book because it is the foundation to everything.

IT can also uniquely open a window to the core of the business—our assets, our infrastructure, our systems, and our data. This core then gets plugged into our community activities and creates a greater depth to everything we do. People are fantastic alone, but we are even better when we think in terms of the powerful pairing of people and our technology assets working in unison. This extends our thinking around community even further and knows no bounds.

KEY TAKEAWAYS: THE CONSUMERIZATION OF IT

1. It is possible your IT organization is doing some of what is outlined in the chapter today. That is excellent, and you are likely off to a good start. But the power of these consumer elements is in the combination of multiple improvements, so be committed to implementing the other improvements.

2. Assign owners and small teams with cross-functional membership to drive progress for specific elements. It takes focus to drive change, and it won't happen by accident. For example, create a team to focus on improving the community experience of internal and external customers.

3. Communicate consistently across IT to reinforce the commitment to a more authentically consumerized IT operation. Good ideas and improvements can come from anywhere. We need to get the dialogue started.

4. "Convenient" and "easy" are a good place to start. This drives optimism and excitement across IT, which will spread quickly to internal and external customers. You will be able to see and hear the excitement that comes with improvements that make our daily work easier and more convenient.

CHAPTER 4

A REAL-TIME VIEW

The systems and data of IT have evolved dramatically in the past decade and today can offer us a unique and valuable view of the business. Good data supports good decisions, and with some thoughtful planning, we can create an accurate and up-to-date view of the business. The power lies in the combination—meaning that good data that is not current, or poor data that is up to the moment are not singly able to drive good decision making.

This is good common sense, but surprisingly sometimes overlooked. What we must demand, and what is now readily available to us in IT, is data that is effectively real-time <u>and</u> highly accurate.

This is a very powerful thing and what a remarkable resource accurate and real-time information can be for the IT organization of today.

This high standard of quality and timeliness is able to bring tremendous value to the business and has earned a place in the Imperative as a result. This is a very exciting opportunity for project teams, mid-level management, and the senior leadership of IT. It should not be assumed that the usefulness of this data is limited as it has a place on both the front lines with project teams and domain experts as well as in the office of the CIO, CFO, and CEO. The implications of this are huge.

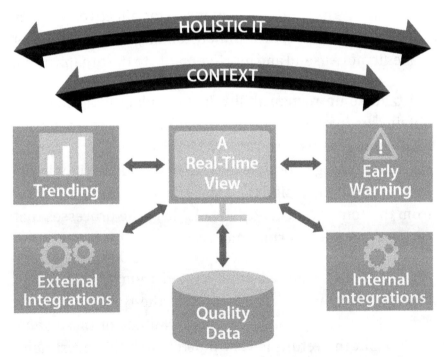

Figure 4.1 A Model to Enable a Real-Time View of IT

Figure 4.1 show examples of the sources and assets we pull together to create this real-time view. These elements today are more available and of a higher quality than ever before. This reminds us of the powerful combination of immediate access, high quality information, and more advanced systems and, in an increasing number of cases, intelligent tools to help us process this information.

Together, this gives us a pulse of IT and of the business that will drive faster action and improved decision making.

Later in this chapter we will address both the vertical fidelity of the data as well as the context. This effectively creates a horizontal and vertical dimensionality to the data that makes it more useful and more versatile to the organization.

We take some responsibility in first identifying how we obtain this information and the systems that can meet the high standards we are required to maintain. This can be seen as a mining effort; we need to first find the right information and then design the most effective way to extract it from the source and make it available to the processes that can leverage the information.

After this first step, we then should thoughtfully design how the information is presented in the right form at the right time and to the right people. Neither of these steps is easy, but the return is very much worth the investment. This real-time view is an engine of effective decision making across all the elements of IT.

QUALITY DATA

When we set out to assemble our real-time view of IT and the enlightenment it brings, we begin with a commitment to trustworthy data. My experience in working with many IT organizations of all sizes is that the careful inspection of data will almost always bring some big surprises. And normally these surprises are along the lines of the general health of data not being what was expected.

This is a critical point—the sooner we can validate the current quality of our data in IT, the sooner we can take steps to elevate the quality of this data through the spectrum from Poor to Average to Good to Great.

Very few organizations would rate their data as Great today. Very few. Most IT organizations will fall in the categories of Poor or Average. This is to be expected, and should only serve to increase our resolve to make it better and identify this data cleansing as a big opportunity for the organization. This idea of it being an opportunity is a healthy way to think about the work that lies ahead.

It is important to understand that the initial investment to improve the quality of our data is not a small investment, but this first step is the hardest. When this first step is completed, we now have a solid foundation on which to build our processes, reports, and dashboards and can now trust the information we are shown.

With this foundation of trustworthy data now in place, the ongoing cost to maintain the quality of the data is much smaller than what it took to uplift the quality of our data baseline.

That initial bit of pain will pay back to us over time and potentially for many years. This reinforces another priority of the rebirth of IT—take the time to build a quality foundation that will scale. This investment will never be one that is regretted or questioned. It is no accident that the quality of data is the first topic we discuss in this chapter on A Real-Time View. This opportunity to make better decisions and to make them more quickly is wasted if we are not operating with quality data. But, with high-quality data available to us in a timely manner, many doors are opened and the talented people of IT can really get to work.

This is a beautiful thing to behold—getting the right information to the right people at the right time.

DASHBOARDS

Dashboards done well bring our data to life and deliver this valuable information to the right people, who can then take action and make better decisions. These dashboards should be simple, easy to understand, and provide actionable information in a useful way. This is effectively our window into the vast world of data and information. As we have reinforced throughout the book, thoughtful design is always time well spent, and this is no exception. Take the time to understand what our internal and external customers need to see and how it can best be assimilated.

The beauty of a dashboard is in its simplicity. A good dashboard in business is much like what we would expect of a good dashboard in an automobile or an aircraft.

The point is to show exactly the information needed in a simple-to-understand form that can be quickly processed and directly support any decisions to be made. With bad data, there really is no point in building a sexy dashboard. However, with great data, we are able to leverage this valuable information in a dashboard that brings our data to another level as actionable. Now, we are really on to something. We now have within our reach the ability to deliver quality data to project teams and leadership, in a real-time manner.

This can fundamentally change how effective we are in managing and operating IT. The dashboard, when properly designed and constructed, can be a helpful reference throughout the day and aid in better decision making. We can learn a lot in just a few seconds with a glance at the right dashboard.

> *This is the key—we need actionable information that enables better decision making.*

Then, when we can add the additional value of faster on top of better decision making, we are entering the realm of truly transformational. It is important to evaluate what information is required for each role, and to match the view with the individual so the dashboard content is purpose built.

One size does not fit all. We must avoid the temptation to deliver the same dashboard to very different groups of users to save development time or cost. If the dashboard does not present the right information, there is no value whatsoever, and no level of cost savings can justify this big disconnect.

HOLISTIC PERSPECTIVE

As part of the natural and accelerated evolution the rebirth of IT brings us, we are placing more emphasis on broader views of IT versus the traditional silo-based, local, and myopic views. These are the traditional models and, as with many of the existing habits of IT, are simply something we need to move beyond. When we begin to look more broadly at IT and beyond the silos that have limited many of our views from the past, it begins to change both how we see and how we think about IT.

We are able to make decisions based on a more complete understanding of IT, we move closer to the key initiatives of the business, we are shaping more business-oriented thinking versus technology-driven thinking, and we are better able to appreciate the current state and future needs of our customers.

This is an important liability of our silo-based view—we are too far removed from the customer, which dilutes our understanding of what the customer really needs and begins to dilute and distract our actions as well.

However, when we look more broadly across any remaining silos in IT, we get the benefit of not only a more holistic view; we get the added benefit of a better understanding of customer needs. This, in turn, feeds our desire to increase our connection with the customer and in virtually every case will bring us the understanding we need. The information is there, and needs only a small desire to be revealed by a willing customer.

Our only question might be—why did we wait so long?

Although we might find the CIO or VP of IT looking at more holistic views in traditional IT, this should no longer be limited to executives and senior management recognizing this information can be leveraged by the complete team. The point being that it might not be necessary to create these views for the first time. If they exist, we should leverage the information across all of IT. When in doubt we should be inclusive, as this information will benefit all teams and reshape how we view the business and how we think. People will gravitate to the right thing and to the customer and only need a little encouragement and help. Curiosity is a wonderful thing—a catalyst to many other good behaviors and outcomes. The holistic view is but a single example of this, but the premise applies that when we give people access to better and more complete information, lots of good things will happen.

EARLY WARNING

Timing is everything. When we have early visibility of developing issues, we can take action. The ability to take action early can make the difference between a serious failure that can impact the business, customers, and potentially revenue versus a potential issue that is addressed and resolved before having any meaningful impact. This is a fine and very important distinction. Inherent in this concept is the difference between being proactive and the traps of continuing to live reactively.

The concept of a real-time view is not limited to informative information and better decision making.

> *There is another important dimension that relates to our ability to prevent potentially damaging events from occurring at all.*

This highlights the power of our access to quality information at the right time.

To make the most of this information, we need to have our

response systems in place and ready to mobilize. The turn-around for these systems to take action must be seconds ideally, and if this is not possible, it should be minutes. This calls out the importance of our ability to take action quickly as a complement to us receiving information quickly. These go hand in hand.

Just as receiving information slowly is of low value and potentially damaging to the organization, delays in our action following the receipt of the information is equally of low value and potentially damaging.

> *We must insist on being close to real-time in gaining access to the right information and equally real-time in taking action on this information when action is required.* **Fast** *with* **fast** *is a very powerful and strategic model.*

Slow with *fast* greatly reduces our potential value, and of course *slow* with *slow* is a model that all but dooms us to failure. Conversely, *fast* coupled with *fast* is the model of future market leaders, and nothing less will do in the rapidly changing world of IT and in our rebirth.

Early warning is another example of our move to proactive in IT. This has been our goal and strategy for thirty years but it is not often realized. However, proactive is now within our reach, and early warning systems are a high-value variation of this strategic shift in IT. Once again speed changes everything and transforms our lifestyle.

TRENDING

Trending information is uniquely important as it helps us to understand if we are getting better, getting worse, or standing still. With this information we can then plan for how we address weaknesses, leverage strengths, and reach long-term goals.

> *Trending information is important to all of us, but management and senior leadership perhaps a bit more so.*

Virtually all CIOs, for example, want to see trends for key initiatives across IT that allow course corrections and avoid the risks associated with surprises. Surprises are particularly bad in the fast pace of our new IT. Increasingly, key metrics are related to how we are serving customers, the reduction of cycle times, the performance of key services, compliance and audit performance, security threats, and a few other core measurements. The bottom line is creating a highly useful view of how we are doing, and with this information we can be proactive in getting better.

Accurate trending information takes some planning but is well within our reach. It is necessary, for example, to determine what metrics we want to track, the horizon on which it will be framed, and the level of granularity.

Some of this information will be readily available; other elements might require us to identify new sources of data or create the need to leverage additional analytics, BI, reporting, or other tools that will help provide exactly what we need. Again, these are very manageable issues, but the earlier we can define exactly what trending information is required, the more cost- and time-effective we can be in sourcing and creating the right trending views.

> *It is worth noting that because trending information is a bit more complex than simple snapshot reports, it is especially important that our data is both accurate and timely.*

Trending often drives key decisions and ensuing investments, so it is vital that we are taking action on information that is correct. The consequences of anything less are serious.

Looking ahead is a simple but a big change for IT. This has so many levels of meaning, including the ability to be proactive in our actions, strategic versus tactical planning, and acting more aggressively to address issues before they can impact the business. All of this mindset and behavior change requires us to have access to quality trending information.

A HIERARCHY OF INFORMATION

Today, we should insist on multidimensional and dynamic information as the new standard. This means many different things, including the ability to show information at different levels of abstraction to match the different roles in the organization. A view of our data that makes sense for the CIO might work for a VP IT, but would be all but unusable for a network administrator or help desk manager.

The quality of information is so much better today, but if we don't get it to the right people we have wasted a tremendous opportunity to drive value. Taking this a step further as this point has been made previously—this valuable information must be for everybody.

The organization simply can't accept the data being right for only a few.

A simple example of a flexible hierarchy would be a detailed view, a mid-level view, and a high-level view; with this level of detail, we can then shape the data to match the different needs of diverse roles in the organization. As we are designing our databases, and report creation and query/search/sort capabilities, it is important to design in the flexibility to operate up and down and across this hierarchy in order to deliver exactly the information required by the members of IT. Up and down and across is a good model to keep in mind for communications, for sharing of information, and for collaboration.

> *Any lack of flexibility in our vertical and*
> *horizontal abstraction of data is very*
> *difficult and very expensive to fix later.*

So, it is important to have a good schema and report design at the beginning of our processes in addition to designing in flexibility at every opportunity. It is a good exercise to explore and define every role in the organization that will require access to reports and what the form and contents of these reports and dashboards will be.

This early understanding of our data consumption, from the standpoint of people, provides important guidance to the design of our physical and logical data management systems. Remember, up and down and fully across. It is also a wonderful empowerment model for our teams and reinforces just how important the work is they will be performing on behalf of the organization.

Limited access to information shackles the organization and dilutes our ability to make good decisions and act quickly. Of course, this takes many forms, and some of which we have addressed earlier in the discussion including data quality. But it extends even further into this notion of data abstraction and is described here to ensure it does not escape our attention.

CONTEXT

Context is the formation of information in such a way that it can be fully understood and assessed. With this we can make the argument that context is everything with regards to data.

This is an important point to explore—information becomes significantly more valuable and ultimately actionable when we have considered the right context.

A good and sensible goal for data is the right information, at the right level of detail, at the right time, to the right people, and fit for the task at hand to drive effective actions and decision making.

The presentation of data must be far more than something that gives us interesting information to look at. It must guide us to take the right actions and make better decisions and to do all this more quickly than we could without the immediate access to this information and in the right context.

Many people and many organizations spend a great deal of time searching for the right information and then confirming it is up to date, and then finally constructing the right context. This is a very time-consuming process, and while we understand it is important enough to spend time in this pursuit, we also have a sense that we are losing precious time, which carries a cost that is difficult to fully comprehend.

The key dimension here is time. You might recall the first discussion in the book looked at the cadence of an organization, and it was no accident that we looked at the speed of IT as our first element of the Imperative. The demands of speed are strategic and appear in many of our seventeen elements and make another appearance here in our look at context.

> *We should take the time in the beginning*
> *of the lifecycle of data to ensure we have*
> *considered the right context for each of the*
> *target users of this same information.*

Think of this as a logical and then a physical flow model for each element of data.

This investment of time up front will save us many times this investment later. In the worst cases, the information won't be usable. Even in the best cases, we leave individuals and teams to design their own context when it is lacking. The later this work occurs in the lifecycle of data, the more expensive it becomes to correct what we neglected up to that point.

Put another way, the full potential of information can't be reached without the right context. This is a design effort that must be planned for from the beginning. Without a thoughtful design, we are leaving the consumers of this information to fend for themselves, which can create significant delays before the information is truly useful. In some cases the information will be discarded altogether when it is found lacking. This is bad for everybody, so the leadership of IT in this case brings great value back to the organization, including what can be a significant time savings.

KEY TAKEAWAYS: A REAL-TIME VIEW

1. Immediacy will dominate much of our thinking in the IT organization of the future. We can only meet this standard with the equally immediate availability of quality data that is in virtual sync with the current state of the organization.

2. One size does not fit all. We need to deliver the right context and the right level of detail to each and every consumer of our data lest the value be greatly diminished. Every member of every team will do their best work with access to current and high-quality data.

3. Identifying early indicators of problems is a powerful tool that allows our IT teams to act quickly and more proactively. Even a few minutes' notice can prevent significant issues and significant impacts for the organization. We should plan to live in the zones of Green and Yellow, and do everything possible to avoid the Red state.

4. Every IT role should have access to quality dashboards that are updated constantly throughout the day, showing the current state of the organization, trending, key escalations, and indicators of risk. This enables every staff member to move quickly and do their best work every day.

5. **Another level of this evolution will be the use of intelligent assistants that process data in a fraction of the time possible with humans, and then present findings to people in order to make the right judgments and take the right actions. This further accelerates our timeline.**

CHAPTER 5

MAKE IT PERSONAL

The evolution of IT and our first thirty years of IT operations were very much focused on efficiency, cost savings, and productivity based metrics. This model made perfect sense and addressed the needs of IT at the birth of the IT organization in the late '70s and early '80s. We became very good at optimizing our performance around these traditional IT measurements. Technology itself and the evolution of technology is a given and the process will never stop.

> *Our calling in IT is to lead the way in how this technology can best be leveraged to deliver a great service or product to our internal and external customers.*

And the steps from average, to good, to great will become increasingly about the quality of the service we deliver and the degree to which we provide a service that is highly and thoughtfully personalized.

The journey ahead of us will have our people rallying around the ideal that personalized service is a key element in the rebirth and reshaping of IT. This means many things and has many implications, but at its essence we are called to maintain our existing performance and cost standards while at the same time transforming the services provided by IT to be personal first, then very personal. We will begin to appreciate the degrees of personal as we get better and better.

> **This amounts to a journey within the journey of personal.**

In the end, this creates a thrilled and productive customer/employee, which is, of course, a great thing for IT and for the broader organization. Much of the inherent value of IT performance that is personal is in recognizing the investment required is often small and the return that comes back to us is large. This is another example of leverage.

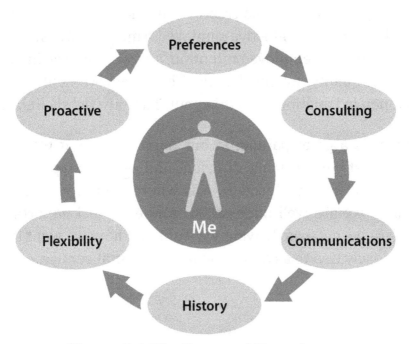

Figure 5.1 The Personal Experience

Figure 5.1 captures a few of the contributors and elements required for a personal experience. Note this model is closely aligned with the consumerization of IT discussion we had in Chapter 3. These building blocks are closely linked and must be when we consider the origin of the new personalization models can be traced back to consumer experiences and expectations. The personalized model includes preferences, good communications, understanding history, and the flexibility to adapt to the changing needs of our constituents.

There are no big surprises among these elements, but the combination is powerful and timeless.

Making IT personal also creates many desirable results, including a more productive employee, a more loyal customer, an increase in employee retention, a strong culture, higher service quality, and much more. These improvements don't happen in isolation—anything but. They are tightly linked.

There is a great parallel in our personal lives if we look closely at how we make decisions and where we spend our time and money. Normally, it is where we are welcomed, where we are well understood, where we feel important, where we get exactly what we want and how we want it—all closely tied to a commitment to **personal** service.

PREFERENCES

We all know what we like and what we don't like. This is personal, and something that helps us to be at our best every day.

For the most part, IT has simply not been able to accommodate preferences in the past, but that, too, is changing. As we make the transition from IT being largely impersonal to a more personal experience, preferences should be part of the plan. Why? Because this is often an investment that is relatively simple to implement but brings big returns with regard to user satisfaction and productivity.

Our internal and external customers will respond to this immediately and improve every interaction provided by IT.

The power here is in the simplicity of knowing the individual and helping them to be at their best and, as a result, happy.

This is very different than how IT both thought and acted in the past.

It would not be a stretch to say that *personal* is one of the last qualities that would come to mind when describing the traditional model of IT. A sobering truth, but one we should take as a challenge. If we can change this, surely we can change anything.

It begins by taking the time to understand what each user or customer wants within a defined set of parameters. This is most productive when it follows a framework of how service can be delivered across the full lifecycle of fulfillment. In this case of preferences, service delivery is the most common example. For example, how does the customer prefer to be notified when actions are taken?

> *Personal information needs to be current*
> *and accurate. A small thing? Not at all.*

This can make a big difference in how we build a relationship with an internal or external customer over time. We should also take the time to update information at every touch and not allow preference information to grow stale, which can happen quickly. It only takes a few minutes and helps to prevent misunderstandings and frustrations later. Little things matter—this is another example of what lies at the heart of the Imperative.

Changing our mindset, changing our culture, changing our attention to detail. Dramatic change is not necessary; it is a commitment to incremental and consistent change over time, and there is no better and meaningful example than the soft touch we use with internal and external customers.

COMMUNICATIONS

Communication is multifaceted and, when improved, brings us so many fantastic benefits. It is also a complex and sometimes funny issue in that the people of IT, the people we are so fond of, are not naturally inclined to focus on communications. Yes, it is true. The inherent ability to be very good at communicating is certainly there, as our people are vastly talented; it is simply not an area that always carries a focus and a priority. This, too, must change.

Good communication is valuable in the present time, but also helps to prevent problems and misunderstandings later.

Good communication takes relatively little effort and has, for all practical purposes, no downside. It is simply all about commitment and consistency.

All internal and external clients appreciate updates, even short and simple updates, on the status of current activities or the progress on a service activity. The traditional model of IT focuses on communications at the beginning and then at the end of the action or business process. This is not enough.

We need to add updates at key milestones during the performance of the business process. This keeps our customer current and also creates a sense of improved customer engagement and more personal service. And, when looking at all the resources available to us in order to create improved customer satisfaction, improved communications is a very effective option.

Our call to action here is to review all the existing communications channels we have in IT today with our internal and external customers. What we must have is both a confirmation for the initiation of action or service and a confirmation of the completion of the same. This is the minimum baseline.

Then, we should add updates at key milestones during the process and take advantage of the existing communication channels to avoid unnecessary expense, and the preferences we have captured from the customer. This can indicate, for example, a desire to be contacted with a phone call, a text, or an email. This creates a more informed customer, a happy customer, and more personal service.

CAPTURING HISTORY

History can teach us a great deal, if only we pay attention. Seems simple, yes, but not easy.

History offers valuable learning that we need not search endlessly for—it is right in front of us. It's often ignored, but never without valuable lessons. In virtually every completed business process or service delivered by IT, we have the opportunity to capture lessons learned and insights. These might be simple or quite extensive.

The key is that the lessons are almost always there, but must be captured immediately as with the passing of time our insights fade and the opportunity is lost. In this context, we want to capture what we learn from each service delivered to and interaction with the internal and external customers we serve. This both improves our future performance and builds a more personal engagement with these individuals and teams.

This process requires an immediate update to our records and the profile for the people we are serving when every task or business process is completed.

As with most things, we need to create a standard for how this update occurs, and something like 48 hours is about right to have the records updated. Anything longer and our clarity of thought begins to fade and other priorities begin to emerge.

It is very difficult to go back and update these records after a week or more has passed. Although a single update won't make a remarkable difference, the accumulation of this information over time will. This brings us back to having the commitment to making the updates to client records when we complete an action for that client. It only takes a few minutes and we simply need to make the time, every time.

It is also important to do a follow-up call with any internal or external client following the completion of every action or service. While a short survey can be a helpful tool and can meet the need in some cases, a phone call or short meeting is better, and I recommend this when possible. The dialogue teaches us a lot. We need to include "what went well" and "what can be improved" into every discussion; this then shapes the content we provide in the update to our records, which in turn enables us to deliver more personal service.

FLEXIBILITY

Flexibility is difficult when it is sought after our services and business processes have been designed and are operating. However, only a modest amount of planning and design effort is necessary to build flexibility into our systems from the jump. This flexibility is important, although it might not be clear from the very start.

> **But what we learn quickly is that the world around us changes, and the needs of our internal and external clients will change.**

We need to anticipate this change and make flexibility a strength in our systems and with the people of IT. We are either flexible or we are not—there is not much in between, so we need to make the commitment to be flexible.

Beyond the benefits to our business, flexibility allows us to deliver a more personal service to internal and external customers. This, of course, is a very good thing. What flexibility does for us beyond today is allow us to better serve our customers over time as needs change.

We won't be successful if we are able to offer a personalized service for a period of time, but then as requirements evolve we are forced to back off and retreat to a one-size-fits-all model. Flexibility should stand the test of time, and this principle should be a design goal from the beginning.

We can capture so much about a customer, including preferences and history, if only our forms and interfaces allow us to define this information. This is an example of flexibility—these forms and interfaces must allow us to add fields and edit fields over time without long lead times and consulting/vendor fees. We know changes of this type will be necessary, so it can't be a surprise and should be accounted for in design.

When this flexibility is designed into our applications, then it all happens seamlessly. If not, these changes are painful and slow and costly and often result in a retreat to generic services.

It is remarkable how much we can be limited to or enabled by user experience behaviors; this is a key place to provide flexibility. Many applications succeed, and therefore their users succeed, through the benefits of flexibility. Our applications should never get in the way of our people doing their best work to serve our customers.

ADVISEMENT

The interactions of IT with employees will evolve dramatically in the Imperative. This model will leverage the expertise of IT and apply this in a manner that is more strategic, more consultative, and more targeted at specific business needs. This model is made possible by the benefits of automation and self-service, among others, to free up some of the capacity in IT to partner with the business.

Although direct interactions with IT staff occur today through phone calls and walk-up support, these interactions are typically on the short side and limited in scope to the here and now of a current issue. This is understandable, and very much in line with the history of IT and the service desk. Beyond the service desk, security and desktop or server teams operate somewhat independently in executing IT initiatives related to these functions.

The reality is that much happens across the organization every day that can benefit from the expertise and insights of our experts in IT.

Why have we not leveraged this valuable knowledge previously? The challenge has included:

1. Meeting the daily needs of escalations, security issues, and operations fully consumes the time and minds of our people in IT.
2. Making the necessary time available with the people in IT who can provide this assistance is a cultural shift and not an easy one.
3. Creating an appointment/scheduling model that allows the right expert in IT to meet with the business owners or project teams.
4. Communicating with the business that IT staff are available and ready to meet to discuss business problems and business requirements.

This model creates a valuable partnership between the teams of IT and the broader organization and shifts the perception of IT to one of the trusted advisor. This model has been discussed in the past, but not often implemented. It's another great example of what lies at the heart of the rebirth of IT—a strategic and proactive partnership with the business.

FOLLOW-UP

When IT performs an action, supports a user, or delivers a service, the internal or external customers will have an experience and form impressions either directly or indirectly. These impressions are clear immediately following the completion of our work and will fade over time.

This creates the opportunity to learn a lot, and a brief follow-up is a valuable source of information that can help us to improve.

Sometimes a lot, sometimes a little,
but every bit helps.

Although this seems like an easy one, follow-up often does not happen. New projects are launched, escalations occur, priorities change, and after just a week or two, it becomes very difficult to perform the follow-up.

This is not a new concept for IT and certainly not for the service desk team. Many service desks regularly perform surveys or other forms of follow-up following the resolution of an incident or the completion of a service request.

What is new here is the need to take the follow-up further, with a view to personal service and how we performed in meeting this standard. Some of the basic questions remain the same, but we take this follow-up a step further to understand how IT performed and how IT can improve in the future with regard to delivering a highly personalized service.

> *Some of our best ideas come from customers, and we simply need to provide the opportunity to receive this valuable feedback.*

It is important to complement automated surveys, which do have a place, with direct live discussions during which more information will come out. These discussions need to be very focused and direct. We are trying to understand if the customer received exactly what was required, and in a way that was most convenient for the customer while meeting all the known customer preferences. We then take this a step further and explore ways in which we can further improve on any element of the customer experience. Sometimes a little prompting is required to bring out the best ways we can improve. This dialogue is important to our ongoing improvement—we can always get better.

PROACTIVE

The all-important shift from reactive to proactive begins with a change of mindset.

This change in mindset is all about moving beyond a response to immediate needs, to anticipating what comes next. With regard to our examples of serving internal and external clients, or performing actions in IT that address security, compliance, or asset management requirements, for example, it is necessary to anticipate and plan.

> *This is a vital duality—acting on the needs of now, while at the same time evaluating and projecting those business requirements that will become the immediate needs of tomorrow, of next week, of next quarter.*

These are the behaviors of high-performing organizations. This is strategic IT. Let's take a brief look at how this happens.

It is necessary to multi-thread our activities to enable the shift to a more proactive engagement. Like most things, this won't happen until we are committed to assigning resources to these multiple responsibilities. In the traditional model where all our people are consumed with reacting to and managing immediate and short-term needs, the shift to a more proactive culture is stymied.

The practical needs of the organization might require that we assign a majority, something like 80 percent, of our resources to the standard response and execution models, but this needs to be complemented by a small task force of a few people who are evaluating trending and performing planning for what challenges are looming for IT in the future.

Our world is changing so quickly, it is difficult to look beyond two or three years, but we do have a reasonable view of what will shape IT in the twelve- to twenty-four-month horizon and only need to give our good people the opportunity to focus on this proactive planning. What new security risks are likely to emerge, what new services will be required in IT, what new compliance requirements will impact IT, and what new technologies will IT steward? These are but a few of the core questions to be considered.

> *When we free a few of our best people in*
> *IT to look at these issues, incredible things*
> *begin to happen.*

It might make sense to treat this task force as something

like a six-month rotation so other people have a chance to participate and our planners stay connected to operations as well.

Our people will appreciate the assignment and the opportunity to think about the future. It sends the signal that we are moving to a more strategic and proactive model, and this then has a ripple effect into the culture. It is hard to overstate the value of this impact.

KEY TAKEAWAYS: MAKE IT PERSONAL

1. Advisement is a critical activity and represents one example of the shift from tactical to strategic IT. We have always been capable of this, but it was difficult to free our people to make this happen. This encourages the trusted advisor role IT can occupy in the organization, and no group is more qualified to deliver this service.

2. Don't underestimate the importance of good communications. This allows us to quickly identify opportunities for improvement as well as confirming what we are doing well. Communications also create the opportunity to be personal. Personalizing communications does not take a lot of effort, just a bit of planning, and it makes everybody happy.

3. Flexibility is a powerful model and recognizes that change is here to stay. The organizations that are flexible and are able to adapt to change quickly will be successful, and those that cannot will inevitably struggle or fail outright.

4. The move from reactive to proactive is not an easy one, but now is the time to make this strategic shift. Not an easy shift, but one we must make now as it sets us on a path to fundamentally changing the

value of IT. It's more about people and culture than about technology, and this understanding is the first step in making the shift.

CHAPTER 6

AUTOMATION

A broad, dynamic, and rapidly evolving topic is automation and one that has a prominent place in the future of IT. Even more so, automation is a key enabler in the rebirth of IT.

This rebirth is not in our future; it has already begun. It is surrounding us today.

Automation is something of a vast puzzle—frequently discussed and often misunderstood. Any look at automation should explore the many aspects of how it can complement the people and strategy of IT and occupy a place that is very powerful, yet does not create expectations that can't be met.

When properly deployed, automation simply makes our people better. It is all about people and not about technology. Automation blindly driving forward without people in the center of it all is folly.

This might be very different than what you believe today, but as we begin to understand automation better, we come to the realization that it is, in fact, <u>all about people</u> and the wonderful ways in which automation can make our people better and more productive.

It is not a bad description to characterize automation as an intelligent partner to IT and our people. Automation and humanity are a powerful combination that is at the core of the rebirth of IT.

> *However, it is important to understand there are limits to how smart we should expect automation to be.*

Expectations should be managed, as there is a gap between the myth of automation today and the reality. Yes, automation tools have improved a lot over the past five years, but there has been so much hype around automation that we need to rein in these lofty expectations a bit. In some ways, automation can't possibly live up to the hype generated around it and AI over the past few years. At least in the next few years, that is, as automation will continue to get better and could potentially exceed our expectations in the future.

Even with some modest lowering of expectations, automation remains powerful and brings us so much value that is achievable today. It goes far beyond the single element of *smart*. Automation is also fast, consistent, and on duty around the clock. This last point is an important one—we are pushing to make IT operate 24X7, and automation can be a great resource in making this happen.

Taking a step back with a look at what is working today, self-service and service catalog are great examples of IT offerings that have proven to be quick to implement, offer strong cost savings, be very productive for users and customers, and operate around the clock. Both these offerings leverage automation and automation that does not require new AI or smart technology to operate.

Yes, AI and smart systems will continue to advance and in ten years will offer capabilities we can't even imagine. But we don't require these new advancements to have a big impact on the business today.

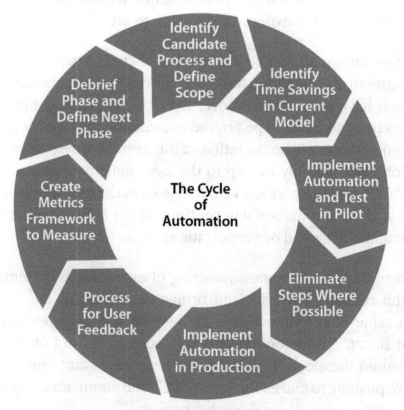

Figure 6.1 The Cycle of Automation

Figure 6.1 shows an approach to automation that captures the tools and technology we can leverage to operationalize automation in order to serve the business. This cycle describes an iterative approach, one that aids us in systematically identifying candidate processes and then moving through the process to bring automation into production and measure the benefits delivered. This incremental and iterative approach should include reviews that help close any gap between expectations and the reality of operating automation as well as preparing us for continued improvement.

The proven automation tools that exist here and now can help IT to make many changes and improvements in how we operate every day, both internal to the business and how we service our customers. Even simple business rules and workflow automation allow us to continue the exciting rebirth of IT and carry us forward.

> *Then when we do see new, smarter, and faster automation tools arrive, we will be ready to push IT and the business to new levels. The processes we need will be in place.*

This is a natural evolution that brings us new technology when we need it. In this increasingly complex and distracted global marketplace, it is important to stay the course and not get ahead of ourselves. It is simply not necessary—we have everything we need to do remarkable things today and fundamentally change how IT lives.

AUTOMATION & PEOPLE

As the technology of automation springs up everywhere in our lives, there is a natural tendency to believe a gap exists between people and automation—that a form of rivalry is developing between the people of IT and automation technology.

Nothing could be further from the truth. In fact, when implemented properly automation and our very human people make each other better and simply can't elevate the performance of IT without working closely together. I like the idea of <u>partnership</u> to capture the right relationship between automation and humanity and believe it best captures the sentiment.

> *Automation is stepping up as a partner*
> *to IT and as a partner to the business and*
> *is both vital and strategic to the rebirth*
> *of IT—but only as a partner with the very*
> *best elements of humanity.*

This idea might very well go against what many people in

IT believe today. We must work together to overcome the thinking that somehow automation is a threat to our people and a technology that somehow has some evil intent for humanity. Everything automation is today and everything automation will become in the future is derived from and has been built to serve humanity.

What automation does very well is capture and consistently execute the decision-making and operating sequence understood by our people experts. By automating some number of our repetitive tasks and routine work, our people are able to spend more time on more complex and strategic work. To spend more time thinking.

This helps our people, helps the business, and helps our customers, and the cycle then <u>allows our best people to find a better way</u>. This discovery would not be possible without automation lending a helping hand and offloading the organization of the normal work that has been blocking us from getting to the more strategic initiatives.

It is very much about creating time to think, and if automation can do only one thing for us, this could be the most important. Time to think, time to design new and creative solutions to the challenges of IT and the challenges of the business has been out of our reach for the past 25 years, and now automation tools can help us make this a reality for the first time.

As automation tools improve and new learning systems can offload even more of our daily work, the opportunity expands and we can offer new services to the business,

including more personalized consulting to business owners and project teams. In many ways, the automation of
simple, repetitive tasks is just the beginning.

Yes, it is important because it then allows us to identify
and then design the next set of activities we can automate.
This second level of automation can become a reality in the
next five to ten years, and the advancement of technology
should be ready just in time to take on this more complex
work. And yes, there is likely to be a third level of activity
automation can offload in the next ten to fifteen years as
our new learning systems become ever more capable.

*Does this create an inevitable collision of
humanity and automation ten to fifteen
years from now? I don't believe so, but this
very point is likely to be a highly discussed
and debated topic in the years ahead.*

PRECIOUS TIME

With IT budgets under pressure being a reality that is not likely to change soon and adding headcount difficult at best, IT continues to wage a war in the search for a few extra minutes in each day. With this time, we have a chance to think about how we can work smarter, how we can work more strategically, how we can be a center of innovation for the business, and how we can better serve our customers.

In this difficult battle, automation might very well give us the best opportunity to find the precious time we need.

Seconds or minutes are enough in the beginning, but this will likely grow to hours or days later. Starting simple is a good model, and every second helps. As with the best of our improvements, advancements in automation bring us much more than time savings. Automation enables us to operate IT differently, in a manner that is highly available and highly reliable as an example. In a manner that is highly consistent and repeatable.

This can mean 24X7 operations, improved access to grow-ing knowledge bases, improved agility, the ability to be truly proactive, and the ability to get ahead of the business and lead for the first time. As automation tools continue to improve, it is difficult to overstate the upside of automation in IT over the next ten years. Expect automation to improve hand in hand with AI, and the barriers we think of today will be removed quickly.

> *This is more than just another change. It is a lifestyle change for IT and the beginning of changing everything we do and how we do it.*

The root of all this change is, of course, driven by exter-nal factors, starting with the customer and extending to a changing market and improving competitive differentia-tion. Real and lasting change always comes from the market and from the customer, and this is no exception. A linkage is then created to the technology of IT and how we get better and faster in the race to save precious time. Automation is real leverage because it shatters the model of IT that stood for the past 30 years.

The old model cast IT as reactive, a little slow to move, lack-ing innovation, and lacking a true customer focus. For the most part true, but IT was not lacking the desire to change, only the means to make it happen.

With automation comes lasting change, and that brings us back to precious time. We can never stop looking for resources that will give us the opportunity to give time back to the people of IT, and the sources of this time will be limited. But automation will be a real source of this time savings, which then completes the cycle by enabling our people to think. With that time to think, and only with that time to think, can we create the ideas that will change IT, change the business, and enable us to better serve our customers.

CONSISTENCY

Not normally our first thought when the subject of automation comes up, consistency deserves some attention because it is, in fact, an important part of what automation offers. When we have defined the constructs and rules of automation and the tools of automation are running, we will immediately notice that our business rules and workflows are executed perfectly every time, over and over again. This means no mistakes and nothing to slow us down. Yes, speed is a big advantage and yes, operating 24X7 is important to our future, but don't overlook the value of consistency when added to this other great stuff.

It is natural that we make mistakes through the course of the day, and these mistakes will have consequences—sometimes small and sometimes large, but the consequences exist nonetheless. The design of automating a process will normally include the help of an expert on that process, somebody in IT who has manually performed the process hundreds of times and under lots of different conditions.

This is a good thing because we are gaining the insights of our best people, and the automation technology will capture this expertise.

Once captured and operational, the automation technology will reflect the business rules and tests provided by our process experts, and this knowledge is then applied every time the automation is executed. Each and every time. This simple model is powerful in the beginning and even more powerful over time because it will scale. Think about this for a minute—the simple business rule or more complex workflow captures this expert insight and then this experience is applied hundreds and potentially thousands of times as the business continues to run.

And the execution is immediate, consistent, and correct every time.

To emphasize a couple of these points, we have the benefit of the execution occurring instantly, when the conditions meet the defined criteria. No delays, no hesitation, no wasted time. So, we have the automation executing instantly, and reflecting the business rules defined by our experts, performed exactly as expected each and every time.

The automation brings with it a natural ability to scale under most conditions. Computing resources today are so capable and so fast, we can execute thousands or even millions of tasks in a fraction of a second. This speed—combined with perfectly consistent execution—is the essence of automation and a great example of how IT redefines itself and brings value to the business.

MENTORS

Every element of automation must have the help of our experienced process experts. Automation is wonderfully powerful once handed the baton from our people, but helpless until that time.

I like the idea of people mentors overseeing the design of our automation models in a form of partnership. This is a good model because it brings us the best of both worlds.

Automation is a fascinating combination of stupid and smart.

In the beginning it is utterly stupid because the technology does not know how to get started or where to go.

Then, with the help of our people experts, we begin to capture experience and expertise. The automation is ready to model and absorb this wisdom, and its own level of intelligence grows. Our people mentors continue to model business rules, decision criteria, exceptions, approvals, dependencies, and much more to fully capture the many considerations that drive our business processes. It is worth our time to get this right, because as the automation begins to execute, we want to ensure the logic is complete and correct as it will be executed many times. These blocks of automation then build on one another, and this expands over time to grow the scope of automation across IT and across the business.

But it is important to remember this process should be done with the oversight and validation of our best people. People mentoring technology is a remarkable model and one we will see much more of.

The result of this expanding scope is the automation of our most redundant and simple tasks first. These workflows are the easiest to automate and then allow us to focus on the more complex tasks. The circles continue to expand, and this does not need to occur quickly because it needs to be done right. Our people mentors should oversee this growing scope because they can both provide the necessary business rules and decision parameters as we design the automation, but equally important is utilizing our people mentors to test, validate, and adjust the automation sequences when they begin to operate. We won't always get the expected and required results, and our process mentors are the best qualified to check the results and make the necessary corrections. Then, when we have verified the automation results are right in every case, we can scale up our operations and turn our attention to expanding the scope of our automation tools.

This work should be done incrementally, in manageable phases.

Remember, begin with the most repetitive and high-volume tasks first. These are low risk, which is desirable on the design side, but bring us some nice value and savings—particularly if these work blocks are high volume. It is great to offload our people in IT from this work, and we should recognize and celebrate our progress and success at every step.

With the success of the partnership between our automation technology and our people experts in the early phases, we then have a proven model and move on to more advanced and more complex business processes in subsequent phases. As automation technology continues to improve, our scope of automation will continue to grow. This work is likely to run for the next ten years and beyond.

INNOVATION

The seeds of innovation have been planted within IT, and we are now able to mobilize in making innovation part of our new lifestyle and an important driver in the expanded leadership of IT across the business. Innovation can be valuable and fun.

> ***What can be more fun that finding new and better ways to run IT and then carry this influence into the broader business?***

We carry with us an understanding that over the next ten years, existing and new market leaders that emerge in the rapidly changing global marketplace are likely to be great innovators. It will be a cultural value and a lifestyle that runs through everything we do every day. Most of us will agree on this point, but I'm taking it a step further and suggesting that IT will become the birthplace of many of these ideas—not a commonly held belief or expectation today.

In this context, innovation related to automation is both

natural and important. So much will happen across the business related to automation.

> *From a technology standpoint, automation will rise into the top tier of a few things that can drive the biggest performance improvements in the business.*

With this focus on automation and how much it can do for the business, it becomes a natural target and launching pad for innovation. It will get lots of attention and lots of good ideas.

A few things will drive innovation related to automation, noting a crossover with smart systems and AI:

1. New and smarter ways to model decision making.
2. Improvements in speed.
3. More complex, advanced reasoning skills.
4. Learning automation that can make process adjustments over time.
5. Intelligent assistants that make suggestions to people in the process.
6. Integrations of communications channels including Voice and Chat.
7. Extensions that will leverage Bot technology.
8. Automation that can recognize risk and take preventive actions.
9. Automation that can provide alerts based on business conditions and trending that requires attention.

And, of course, this is just the beginning.

As a theme, innovation related to automation will focus on smarter and faster.

This combination brings more value and makes automation more versatile and more impactful to the business.

Automation will become more natural for all of us, and we won't think of it as automation or even technology. It will simply be just how we work and how we get things done. The lines between automation and humanity are blurred, and we will work in a seamless combination of tools and teams.

All of this automation will ultimately be to the benefit of our internal and external customers. This is not a short-term trend—we should expect this evolution of automation to continue for the next 25 years and cause us to reconsider and change how we perform most of what we do every day.

CUSTOMER SERVICE

Automation can assist us in providing great customer service. The best of automation is very much in line with where we need to expand the service we provide to internal and external customers. You likely have a good idea what this means—around-the-clock support, self-service, self-help, speedy performance, and personalized service to name a few. These improvements are a natural for automation.

As we are always looking to take our performance in IT to the next level, there is no better galvanizing force and rallying cry than the customer. The pressure to improve with regard to the customer will never go away, but we are fortunate today to stand in the midst of a remarkable acceleration in this evolution.

This service revolution is being driven by a collision of two strong forces—the technology we can leverage to improve our performance in virtually every respect, together with a cultural- and leadership-sponsored focus on the customer and everything therein.

This collision is happening today. It is likely to continue for the next five to ten years and reshape everything we do, from the customer back into IT as the center of the business. And just in time to serve our needs is the advancement of automation tools that are nothing short of outstanding. Ten years ago this was not the case; automation gave us little help in taking care of our internal and external customers.

Our automation tools today are the real deal and include, to name a few:

1. Automated business rules
2. Integrated workflow models
3. Self-service
4. Service catalog
5. Email listeners
6. Smart search tools
7. Chat and chat bots
8. Advanced search tools for self-help
9. Learning systems
10. Intelligent assistants

Each of these items taken individually will make a difference. But, taken as a whole, we begin to understand the remarkable transformation racing through IT and how automation has become a primary driver for this change.

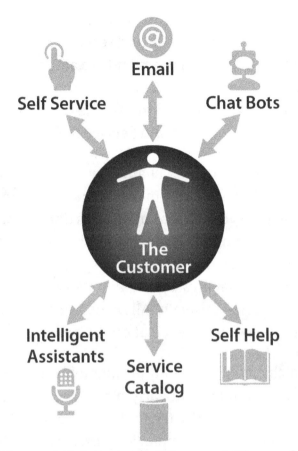

Figure 6.2 Automated Support Channels

Figure 6.2 shows a few examples of automation support channels that can be applied to our internal and external customers equally well. These channels include email, self-service, service catalog, chat bots, and intelligent assistants, and they will continue to evolve and improve in flexibility and sophistication. For example, chat bots and intelligent assistants are new arrivals, appearing in a useful form in the past five years, and they are proving to be very effective when deployed correctly.

Expect these technologies to become both trusted and widely available. Self-service and service catalog have now been in operation for ten years and are among the veterans of our automation models. Yet they continue to be effective in what they were designed to provide—a simple and fast way to submit an Incident or a Service Request.

In another section of this chapter we discussion innovation, and we should expect much of the innovation we see over the next ten years to happen in this domain of automation. It can do so much for us in terms of not just helping customers (enough in itself) but bring us more benefits in the areas of cost savings, speed, and 24X7 operations. Yes, these themes come up again! All roads lead us back to these core principles—the essence of our IT rebirth.

I've had a chance to use both production versions of these automation examples and early prototypes that will be in production soon, and the technology is outstanding—user friendly, powerful, and simple. Very exciting developments for the good people of IT and for the business.

24X7

The global marketplace of business and the insatiable demands of consumers are together driving us toward around-the-clock operations becoming what is simply expected.

This brings us the ultimate level of agility and flexibility in our lifestyle of the next fifty years, and this lifestyle and its many standards and expectations then shape how our business must operate and how we deliver products and services to our customers.

Nowhere is this growing customer appetite more evident than with the expansion of normal business hours up to and including true 24X7 operation. This was something we in IT simply did not see as a priority only five years ago.

Yes, we have expanded normal business hours to expanded business hours, but we underestimated this pull to shatter what for the past fifty years has been "the business day." Soon, very soon, this model will be gone and replaced with what is the simplest and most powerful model of all—anytime, anywhere. This is how we will live, and this is how we will work.

For the first fifty years following the World Wars that changed so much about how we operate in industry, the manufacture of goods, and the new business models that came along with, we have seen structure around the normal business day hours and business take the lead over our personal time in how we live our lives. Now, everything is changing. This is economic and social and very personal.

> *The traditional model has been turned on its head, and now our personal lives are driving our expectations in business. Any structure around the business day is rapidly disappearing.*

Is this just a temporary phenomenon? No way.

This change is here to stay and, if anything, will accelerate. These new expectations are very simple and powerful—every customer expects a product or a service that is exactly what they require, they expect it to be delivered immediately, and they expect personalized service that is most convenient for them. Personal, flexible, and fast. Thinking about the implications of this model, we are drawn back to 24X7 being a key link in the chain of value and service demanded by all customers. What this has done and will do over the next ten years is place a new emphasis on leveraging technology because IT and the broader business simply can't meet these expectations with manual efforts and brute force.

These forces will also cause the business to turn to IT in a desperate search for help. CEOs and CFOs begin to recognize the business is not equipped to make these demanding customers happy and meet the competitive challenges of our global markets. Only IT will have the know-how, tools, and technology to meet the need.

We have a full chapter dedicated to 24X7 because there are so many important points we need to explore more closely around this model. But we could not have this discussion on automation without recognizing the role 24X7 plays and how automation and its technology building blocks first make 24X7 possible and then make 24X7 the new normal.

Perhaps that is the greatest validation of any new technology—it works so well that it becomes just how we do things every day.

SAVINGS

Savings can come in many forms, and normally we realize these savings in combination with other benefits. The broader the combination of benefits, the stronger the value. This is part of our search for leverage. When we find a business improvement that combines multiple forms of value along with savings, well, that is really something to behold—something we should double-down on.

For example, automation of a multi-step and cross-functional business process brings us the following combination of goodness:

1. It saves time in the execution of the business process.
2. It supports the strategic unification of IT.
3. It reduces the number of integration points and handoffs across the organization.
4. Time savings will normally equate to some level of cost savings.
5. Speed in execution creates a competitive advantage.
6. Improved time of response will translate into improved customer satisfaction.

It is easy to see why automation is a powerhouse in the rebirth of IT. We can cite these six positive elements of automation without breaking a sweat, and there are likely many more if we think about it for a few minutes.

Back to savings. Sometimes savings alone are enough, particularly if the savings are large in terms of either cost or time—these are two of our favorites and important in their own right. So we should not discount savings alone, but it is always best when we find savings along with a primary value driver.

Primary value drivers can include:
1. Speed
2. Customer happiness
3. Agility
4. Personalized service
5. Scalability
6. Elimination of waste
7. Unification of IT

Each of these is important and in the top tier of value to the business. But a single value element alone, while important, is not as impactful as multiple value drivers together, or a value driver in combination with one or more savings elements.

And, of course, the best of the best would be multiple value drivers together with multiple elements of savings. This is not common, but it does happen. And when it does, it is remarkable and has the power to fundamentally change the business.

The traditional focus of IT has included cost savings, which are always welcome. But the rebirth of IT brings with it a great focus on velocity—the speed with which we can complete common tasks and business processes. This calls to our attention the importance of time savings, in turn providing a ripple effect of other savings and value for the business.

Another area of savings that will get more attention in the future will be the reduction of integration points or handoffs necessary to complete more complex workflows. This is measurable and not overly difficult to identify in the organization.

These integration points represent cost, time, and risk. This is a significant challenge with many IT organizations that are battling complexity and risk in taking business performance to the next level. Any savings in the form of reduced integrations and handoffs pay back to us many times over in many forms of savings and support our theme of the unification of IT.

BUSINESS RULES & WORKFLOW

Automation of common business processes can include single decision points or tasks, and workflows which are constructed of multiple related tasks. Both are important and both play a part in how we run the business and in the use of automation technology. A workflow model consists of business rules or task building blocks, and with good workflow tools these workflows are virtually unlimited in size and scope.

> *The larger and more complex the workflow, the larger the potential savings.*

However, these savings come with a cost, and that cost is complexity and risk. The creation of these larger workflow models will take time and more thoughtful design, but once designed and operating correctly, they can offload the organization and help IT to realize significant time and cost savings.

It is a good practice to start simple with the automation of business rules and tasks in order to validate a good design and implementation methodology for automation. The single-step objects do offer good time and cost savings, but are by nature much simpler than more extensive workflow models. Then, with some experience around automation and some successful automation of business rules in place, we can scale up to multi-step workflow automation.

The incremental approach is more likely to bring us automation success versus starting with more advanced workflow models prior to the organization having any experience and success with automation. We will learn a lot in the process of automating even the simplest of tasks, and this greatly reduces our risk when taking on the more complex and broader workflow models.

Taking this a step further, it is a good practice to start with well-understood, highly consistent, and highly repeatable business rules.

> *It can be difficult to automate what is not a consistent and well-understood manual process, so these business rules should be deferred to a future phase after we have a strong base of success in automating other business rules and workflows.*

This might seem like good common sense and it is, but it is surprising how many organizations take on what are high-risk and high-complexity processes in the early stages of an automation initiative.

It is time well spent to carefully select business rules for automation that are used in larger and more complex business processes. This effectively gives twice the value in that we can automate the business rule itself, but then we have a proven and working automation unit that can be leveraged when we later create broader multi-unit automated workflows.

This practice of investing in building blocks of automation, if you will, also allows us to accelerate our progress over time. We have an increasingly large inventory of these automated business rules or tasks available to us and can use them to quickly build larger and broader workflows with less risk and less time.

> *Most organizations will have a logical and physical web of related business rules and workflows that are highly related and interconnected.*

This can often be represented graphically, and the diagram can then be a useful reference as we plan and execute our automation efforts over time. This visual representation gives us a map that provides guidance during our efforts to build out the business rules and workflows that will give us the highest level of reuse and the highest level of impact to the organization.

KEY TAKEAWAYS: AUTOMATION

1. We now understand that leverage is critical for the rebirth of IT, and when we find it, leverage is a powerful thing. Automation is a good example of the leverage we need and is a true force multiplier.

2. Automation brings with it a few characteristics that line up well with our core themes for the new IT—speed, 24X7 Ops, consistency, and self-service to name a few. This makes automation a natural for taking a key position in our IT tactics and strategy of the future.

3. Automation is most successful when we leverage people experts who have the most experience and a deep understanding of a candidate business process or business rule to be automated. These people mentors can ensure we get it right and that what we are automating will deliver the right results every time. This is an investment of time well spent, recognizing that some automation elements will execute at a very high volume.

4. Giving our people back part of their day is a powerful thing, and automation can bring IT this tremendous gift, creating time to think, time to find a better way, time to look differently at how we work, and time

to explore innovative problem solving. This creates a strategic engine for the elevation of IT. Only a few things can clear the way to this model, and one of them is automation.

CHAPTER 7

THE UNIFICATION OF IT

Pressed to pick a single element of the seventeen profiled throughout the book that can naturally complement the customer connection, and drive the successful rebirth of IT by bringing a lasting influence over the strategy and operating models of the future IT, it would be difficult to not select the unification of IT.

> *The unification of IT and a focus on the customer are the two wings on which IT will rise to make the rebirth of IT first a reality and then a magnificent success.*

There is so much here that is fundamental to shaping the transformation of and then the next twenty years of IT and the business.

What is remarkable about IT today is the duality of being so much better than we have been before but at the same time living with such fundamental and significant flaws in both the strategy and the operations of IT.

At the root of many of these flaws is a fragmented and disconnected organization that has evolved over the past thirty years and no longer meets the needs of what lies ahead for us.

Common challenges of IT today include:

1. A silo-based organization with limited visibility of other units
2. Highly localized projects with vertically oriented project scopes and teams
3. Specialized skills with very focused deliverables
4. Little or no transparency across the whole of IT
5. Communications are localized and infrequent
6. Highly tactical and delivery oriented culture
7. A program-based work structure and mindset
8. Limited visibility of corporate strategy and objectives
9. Little or no direct interaction with customers
10. A reactive culture
11. A primarily bottoms-up view of the business
12. Localized and segmented automation and business processes
13. Limited focus on career development
14. A lack or limited supply of business skills
15. High number of system integrations and organizational handoffs
16. Top-down decision making and limited team autonomy

With what we can fairly call a fragile and somewhat ungainly organization model,

*the talented people of IT often find a way
to perform at a remarkably high level, and
it is clearly not the case today that IT is
ignorant of these challenges and blindly
plodding into the future.*

In most IT organizations, we have begun to make changes
to address these challenges, and the rebirth of IT is under
way. This does come with a great deal of brute force and we
are by virtually any measure early in the journey with the
majority of our work ahead of us.

We must find smarter and more strategic ways of working
in order to build a more scalable and more elegant model
for the future of IT and the new IT we know lies ahead.

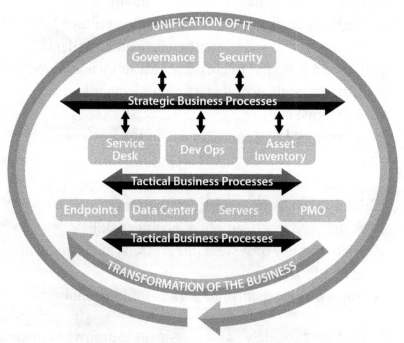

Figure 7.1 An Overview of Unified IT

Figure 7.1 is a rough overview of the anatomy of IT and how we are creating a shift to a unified IT. Although your organization may be a bit different, Figure 7.1 shows a number of typical IT silos and then an example of a somewhat narrow tactical business process as well as a broader, strategic business process.

The paper just can't hold all the dimensions we can show here, but a simple example helps. Also note the sweeping force of a unified IT and the related transformation of the business. These forces are closely related to the extent that one can't occur without the other; they are highly complementary. Also note that while some example IT silos are shown in the figure, they will begin to fade away as we build more cross-functional teams and broader and more holistic business processes and automation. Each of these elements further accelerates our unification. Each of these elements enables the collaboration we need across IT and across the business. With one comes the other.

Increasingly, we will create a planned shift from the current limited model of IT to one that looks very different. It will change much of what we know and assume about IT today and the goals are clear.

The fundamental goals of a unified IT include:

1. Elevated focus on the customer for all IT initiatives.
2. Creating a deep and lasting cultural shift across IT.
3. Remove all unnecessary integrations and handoffs between IT functions.

4. Form empowered cross-functional teams working to the right goals.
5. Use collaboration as a key driver for cultural change.
6. Create holistic work flow and automation models across all of IT and the business.
7. Shift from a vertical to a horizontal work orientation that naturally creates cross-functional teams with cross-functional experts.
8. A new enablement of business problem-based solutions versus localized pain points.
9. Focus on the elimination of all waste.
10. A high level of customer communication and interaction.
11. Drive a new focus on the development of people skills and career paths.
12. Embrace the partnership between humanity and smart systems.
13. Frequent and more informal communications become the norm.
14. New roles are created in IT to drive cross-functional initiatives.
15. Recognize the importance of speed and agility as a corporate competency.
16. The end of project work that is silo-based and with a narrow scope.
17. Empowered teams with high level of decision-making authority.

Note the scope, depth, and value of unification are immense. This is not simply an organizational thing. This is not simply an IT project, not a tactic or a deliverable.

True unification is so much more as we will explore in the coming pages. It is transformational to both IT and to the business.

A NEW WAY

With the rebirth of IT will come cultural change. These concepts are closely linked, and the new IT is simply not possible without changing our culture and values.

This does take time, but a great beginning can be a simple commitment to working in a new way every day.

> *The old way served us well, but now we will create a New IT with a New Way of thinking, and a New Way of performing our work every day.*

The message we are building a new IT will often come from leadership and the CIO. But the daily change we must take on, and the small things we do every day to make the new IT a reality can come from anybody at any time. In some cases, the best ideas and the most impactful changes come from within—anywhere from across the many and diverse teams of IT. Never underestimate the powerful thinking of the talented people of IT. We should always encourage thoughts, ideas, and suggestions regardless of how big or small. These are seeds from which can grow powerful improvements and changes. We are all part of this transformation; only together can we make this New Way and the new IT a success.

> ### *As an individual, never underestimate the influence you can have on your teammates and on your leadership.*

This is an important catalyst for the new culture of IT—lasting and authentic leadership comes from every part of the organization. Role modeling is not simply a top-down phenomenon. Role modeling can occur sideways across the organization, and from the bottom up. This model of leadership coming from within, together with the strong leadership of senior management and our executives, is a powerful and unstoppable force and a joy to watch and to be part of. With it comes the energy, confidence, and passion we need to be successful every day.

Another important leadership concept is to make everything better—one small step at a time. Make every new task just a little bit better; make any new idea just a little bit better.

These small changes add up to big improvements over time. If a new directive comes from IT leadership, embrace it, evaluate it carefully, apply your valuable experience, and find a way to make it just a little bit better.

If each individual and team in IT is committed to making everything we touch in IT just a little bit better, we can accomplish amazing things together.

This makes the New Way a better way. The improvements grow from within, which also increases the likelihood these improvements will stick and be successful over time. This wonderful process also creates a sense of engagement and ownership as these ideas are coming from across IT and not from outside the organization. All of these synergies create a New Way step by step.

ORGANIC LEADERSHIP

As organizations and businesses of every shape and size become more dependent on technology and information, the leadership of IT is needed more than ever. Who better to lead us than the people and teams that know our technology and systems best?

Having said that, it is surely not the case that the business or even IT itself understands this today.

> *Far from it—in many ways IT could be considered the least likely organization to lead us into the future, but as is often the case, I believe history will prove us wrong and lasting leadership can come from the most unlikely of places.*

Clearly, the need for leadership is all around us. Many organizations are struggling today, uncertain of what will happen in the global market and uncertain of the changes that must be made to protect the future of the business and, even more so, to create the competitive advantage needed for lasting success.

It is not necessary for IT to proclaim that we will lead the business into the future, and then expect the organization to fall into line behind us. No, this will be an evolution that occurs over the next ten years. But where do we start? We start at the only place we can start, with the customer.

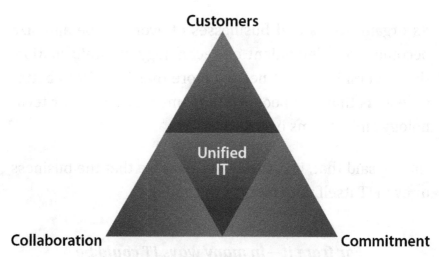

Figure 7.2 The Unified IT Triangle

A simple but very powerful model is shown in Figure 7.2 as the unified IT triangle. At the top of the triangle is the customer; this is where we begin and where we end in everything we do. Alongside the customer are a couple of cultural and people elements in collaboration and commitment. These elements are important because they are required to both rebuild the culture of IT and to ensure customer success. With this simple result, everything else falls into place. A unified IT is only possible with this cultural redesign and a focus on the customer.

A good start is to recognize that we must extend the reach of IT all the way to the customer and create a new relationship, new communication, new engagement, and a new way of working that will give us the guidance needed to make the best possible and targeted investments in the future. This is the best way, the best lifestyle, to ensure we are delivering the best possible systems and business solutions. Only with this strong customer relationship and understanding of customer needs can we build the future of IT. Any attempt to build the future of IT without a focus on the customer is folly.

This new commitment to the customer relationship comes even before we create a unified IT. But the motion to create a unified IT is in play at the same time as our outreach to the customer.

Building this customer relationship is the right place to start our work on unifying IT, and we will come to appreciate that a unified IT in the absence of the right customer relationships is not enough. Not nearly enough. What we will discover is that the building of this new relationship with the customer will serve as a catalyst for many other changes and positive outcomes.

When we think about the profile of a unified IT as shown at the start of this chapter, a good mental checklist if you will, it becomes clear quickly that the items are closely related and bring us a number of synergies.

One great example is the combination of collaboration and commitment. We can't collaborate effectively without improved commitment, and when we focus on an absolute commitment we will see a natural improvement in collaboration. This becomes a very contagious and healthy behavior across the organization. Taking this a step further, the partnership with our customers is the best possible way to start this chain reaction of positive change. Our commitment to the partnership with our customers will come with a new level of collaboration and communication.

With focus and commitment, we will get this right and it then becomes a model for how we work across the IT organization. This will carry over into the business.

> *But we start with the customer as a visible*
> *and critical landmark to rally around.*
> *Think of the customer as our cultural*
> *lighthouse.*

Rallying around the customer then brings us back to the new organic leadership of IT.

With the development of the new relationship with the customer, the engagement of the customer in the development and delivery of successful systems, and the creation of new collaboration and communications models, we have then created a new customer-oriented and results-oriented business model that can be leveraged far beyond IT and across the business.

This customer orientation is a powerful force for the business in that we are improving IT, and we are creating an engine that can and will improve the business.

An increased cultural focus on results can spring from IT due to a number of factors, including our increasing dependence on technology and data and the increased pace and non-stop clock of business. This model of working every day can only become possible by starting with IT, which creates an avalanche that will not stop at the boundaries of IT. The cascade of leadership can't be stopped. What we will come to appreciate is the void that exists in the business today, and that void can be filled with the rebirth and unification of IT.

Crazy? I don't think so. If anything, it makes perfect sense.

CULTURAL CHANGE

A common thread that runs through much of what we discuss throughout the rebirth and the unification of IT is the theme of cultural change. I can't say enough about how fundamental and how important this is. This is where the rebirth of IT begins, and only through this change can the rebirth of IT become a reality. This cultural change touches every person in the organization and should not be assumed to be solely driven by management. In some cases, lasting cultural change comes from within the organization, from our core.

Virtually all of what we must do for the future begins with and is enabled through cultural change. The power of culture is unlimited and regenerative. With an unhealthy culture it is difficult to do the simplest things well. However, with a culture that is empowered and passionate, we can accomplish anything.

There are many characteristics of a unified IT, including the list we outlined at the beginning of the chapter.

To begin, there is only one place for us to look, and that is the customer. This is a unifying force and a source of clarity that can be missing in IT today.

The customer is the beginning and the end.

The beginning in that the customer is our best source of all requirements that drive our daily activity, and *the end* in that the customer is the ultimate validation that we have delivered a successful result. With this cycle in mind, we can't stray far. When in doubt or when we are confused, the customer will bring us clarity.

Extending from the customer is a web of collaboration that also begins with the customer and extends through IT and reaches into the business.

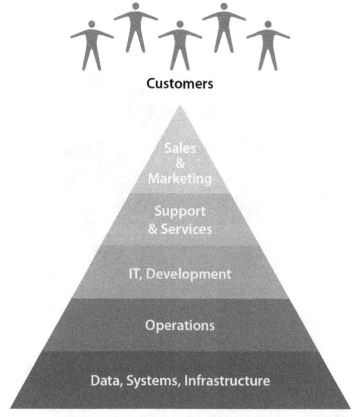

Customers

Sales
&
Marketing

Support
& Services

IT, Development

Operations

Data, Systems, Infrastructure

Figure 7.3 The Old Customer Connection Triangle

Figure 7.3 depicts the traditional customer connection model, with sales and marketing at the top of the pyramid, support and services engaging with the customer sometime later, and IT existing well down the hierarchy with little or no direct contact with the customer. This model is sequential and somewhat cumbersome and so this model must change. In a true collaboration with the customer, we will turn this old triangle on its head, to create a much broader and more direct virtual customer connection, including IT working directly with the customer.

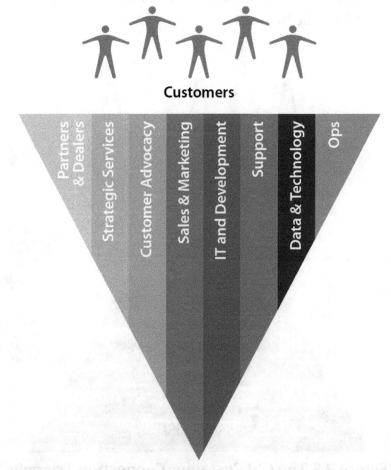

Figure 7.4 The New Customer Connection Triangle

Figure 7.4 is an overview of what this new inverted triangle will become. The key to this model is moving more functions and teams closer to the customer, and adding some functions, including customer success, that help ensure we are living the collaboration model every day and we have people working every day with a sole focus to advocate for the customer and ensure their success. Note that in this model, we have IT, development, and our data and technology touching the customer in a model that puts a priority on transparency and close partnership. There is a lot implied by the model, and it goes much deeper than what the figure suggests at this high level.

We can view true collaboration as the foundation of how we work every day. Open, honest, trusting, and communicative are a few traits that describe collaboration. This applies to small teams of just a few people, to large cross-functional initiatives to how we work with our customers and partners. Collaboration encourages many of the right behaviors and priorities we must have to build the right culture for the future of IT.

> *A good way to describe commitment is the willingness to "do whatever it takes" to achieve the right results with our customers and therefore with our business.*

When we have people, teams, and a culture with this level of commitment, amazing things will follow. Note this commitment is normally accompanied by passion and hope, a powerful and self-propelled mindset. Success is fun, and success creates a strong desire to drive more success.

This model then builds a powerful force that is the energy of our culture.

THE CONSOLIDATION OF TOOLS AND TECHNOLOGY

The unification of IT is a series of actions, some of which happen serially and some of which can occur in parallel. The latter is our preferred path as it accelerates change and reduces our total elapsed time required to achieve the benefits of the reborn IT. Yes, faster is not always better, but it wins most of the time.

One of the actions that can be performed in parallel with most others is the consolidation of tools and technology. This is a natural activity that complements our overall push to create a unified IT. The strategy to unify includes everything—people, technology, processes, our planning processes, and everything in between. Unifying subsets of our world of IT will reduce our value and dilute the opportunity to do this right.

A complex and disparate set of tools including software applications is common for IT. This model was built over time and out of necessity, and was never designed or planned as such. It's more a step-by-step creation based on what was needed at a virtual moment in time. We did not have the ability, or luxury in many cases, of building strategic systems that planned for longer term needs and the evolution of IT.

We always knew this model was less than ideal, but over time this fragmented portfolio creates a number of big challenges, including:

1. High operating costs
2. Large number of complex and costly integrations
3. Multiple vendors are difficult to align with IT goals
4. Too many contracts and renewals to manage effectively
5. Upgrades become problematic and high risk
6. Poor agility
7. Expensive and complex change management
8. Degradation of reliability and availability
9. Difficult to create and manage accountabilities
10. Limited internal control of infrastructure
11. High administration costs
12. Onboarding of new IT staff becomes increasingly difficult
13. Poor alignment across teams
14. Micro-silo model propagates across technology as with organizations
15. Higher training costs
16. Slower purchasing and retirement processes
17. All but ensures localized thinking and localized business processes
18. Creates waste

One good example of a segment of the IT technology

portfolio is software applications. It is not uncommon for an IT organization to have dozens of software applications deployed for managing mobile devices, for security, service management, asset management, compliance, client and service management, identity and access management, event monitoring, and much more.

The growth of our IT technology and tools portfolio must stop, and the unification of IT is perhaps our best opportunity to fundamentally change this model. Stopping the growth is not enough. We need to reduce—better yet, *significantly* reduce—this portfolio, including the software applications, which should be consolidated to less than ten vendors. Difficult in the past, this is now possible with improved software solutions that are broader in scope, more robust in capability, and bring with them a high level of interoperability and integration capabilities built in.

It is easy to get excited about the very real benefits of consolidating the technology and applications of IT:

1. Improved accountability of vendors/partners
2. Shift from large number of vendors to a smaller group of strategic partners
3. Reduced operating costs
4. Reduced risk of problems with upgrades
5. Improved performance of system integrations
6. Improved contracts and business terms
7. Reduced administrator requirements
8. Reduced training costs
9. Encourages the elimination of micro teams and silos

10. Accelerates the creation of trans IT business processes
11. Optimizes and simplifies automation models
12. Improves agility
13. Improved ability to design and implement changes
14. Brings our people together
15. Clears the way to eliminate waste
16. Simplifies the organizational model
17. Significantly enhances the speed of IT

> *Increasingly IT leadership understands, beginning with the CIO, that this consolidation of tools, technology, and applications makes a lot of sense.*

As we evaluate priorities for the rebirth of IT, we should expect this initiative to make its way onto the short list of goals for IT over the next five years. The CIO will understand this is one of the few initiatives that can bring us leverage and save real money at the same time.

OPEN SYSTEMS

Open systems: a simple idea but a very important one with an eye to the future.

The systems of IT, both hardware and software, that we plan to take forward and the new ones we will deploy in the years ahead need to be based on standards and focus on the highest degree of openness possible. This has a big impact on IT and the business over time.

> *Inflexible, proprietary, non-standards-based, outdated and highly customized systems make everything more difficult. This becomes a virtual headwind that saps our energy.*

These systems make integrations more difficult and more expensive, make automation problematic, make upgrades expensive, and slow down the flow of work and information across IT every day. Closed systems block our way forward for both the rebirth of IT and the unification of all things IT.

However, with open systems we encourage transparency, encourage broader business process design, enable collaboration, and reduce the time and cost required to implement the automation we must have over the next ten years. As an added benefit, all of this comes with a lower cost.

Let's think about this for a moment. Open systems allow and encourage us to perform the necessary work for the rebirth of IT, while at the same time reducing our operating costs and reducing our dependency on outside consultants.

This is powerful stuff. It is easy to make the case that open systems should become nothing less than part of the lifestyle for the future of IT. It is simply part of how we live every day.

When we become committed to open systems, again we will look back and be amazed that it took us so long to make this change. Why did we hold onto our older, proprietary, closed, and highly customized systems for so long?

It is helpful to take a complete inventory of all our IT systems; evaluate them in terms of openness and the degree to which we can support current standards; and implement reporting, data sharing, integrations, and workflow. Rate each system on a simple scale, something like one through five, with one being the least open and five being the most. This gives us an understanding of where we are with each system, and although it is unlikely we can correct any challenges we have, or replace weak systems outright, we will understand where we are and begin to put plans in place over time to upgrade these systems with respect to openness.

This is not a technical thing—our work in opening up our systems directly supports our broader work to drive trans IT business processes, collaboration, and to automate many of our repeatable workflows.

It all begins with an awareness of how closed and proprietary systems slow us down and cost us money, while open and standards-based systems give us a boost in many of the key areas we will undertake in the remaking of IT.

THE TECHNOLOGY FULCRUM

Technology surrounds us more than ever. It drives and improves what we do every day in our personal lives and in business.

And, as technology improves and supports our evolving lifestyle, it is increasingly blurring the lines between what we have always considered to be two separate and distinct worlds—our personal lives outside the office and the time we spend working on behalf of our employer.

But for business, technology is not just about the devices themselves and new tools to help us do our jobs a bit better and faster. There will always be new tools and new technology.

For the market leaders of tomorrow, technology creates the opportunity for true leverage and the opportunity to change the business. Technology becomes closely linked with strategy and when properly leveraged can mean the difference between a successful strategy and one that fails.

*But this strategic approach to technology
does not come without specialized
knowledge and the right experience.*

Today this strategy opportunity borne of technology brings together an important need, with what is a unique ability that lives in IT. This is a convergence, perhaps even better described as a collision, that is unique in the thirty-year history of IT. It is, of course, not simple or obvious today but will become more obvious over the next ten years as this destiny of IT plays out before us.

It is quite likely that the business does not yet fully recognize this need and that IT does not yet fully see the opportunity to leverage technology as a strategic enabler. But that day will come and it will come sooner than many expect. When this does occur we will look back, and many will claim it was obvious. But this could not be further from the truth.

The unification of IT creates the opportunity to accelerate this evolution. By unifying IT, we are removing much of the clutter, noise, and waste that is keeping us from driving more strategic activity—including innovation and a strategic approach to the data and systems of IT and how they can better drive and shape the strategy of the business.

Many of the opportunities that exist today to fundamentally change the business live within IT in some shape. We simply need to create the focus and the opportunity to leverage these powerful assets for the greater good of the business.

It is the new charter of IT during our rebirth, to bring new ideas and new models to the attention of the business and the unique skills, expertise, and experience within IT, that makes this possible.

> *We could consider this force to have lain dormant within IT for decades—and only needing the right opportunity to rise and show the business options we did not know existed previously.*

This principle is very much linked to the topic of organic leadership we discuss elsewhere in the chapter. Leadership takes many forms, and there is a great need in business today for strong leadership. Strong leadership driven by technology is a unique capability of the new IT.

HOLISTIC FLOW OF WORK

There is a flow of work in every IT organization that governs how we do our work every day. This flow consists of data, technology, systems, assets, applications, and people. All these elements are working together, sometimes well and sometimes not so well, to accomplish the daily work that is required of us.

Today, and in the traditional model of IT, much of this work is localized and segmented.

Choppy, if you will.

This is driven by many things, including the silos that get a lot of attention throughout the book, domain experts that have a very narrow focus, and systems that are equally narrow. All of this results in the fragmentation of IT business process and workflow. This creates a number of challenges that limit how effective we can be in the performance of our daily work in IT.

In many ways, this model creates a degree of "overhead" that is required to coordinate and synchronize these fragmented and localized workflows.

But we are beginning to understand there is a better way.

We can think of this in terms of stretching and consolidating these localized workflows into broader and more complete business processes.

Our goal is to create a workflow model for IT that spans the full completion of work, from the natural beginning to the natural end. This would eliminate any unnatural and unnecessary integrations or handoffs, each of which is a source of risk and a potential waste of time and resources.

We start with a complete understanding of the end-to-end business process, the natural flow of work, and we then align our people, teams, and organization to align with this natural and complete workflow model.

Transformation and realignment are not easy in the beginning.

We will need to make changes to the organization and systems around the business process model, but this change will make sense and feel natural for our people once we take the first few steps on this journey. Then our momentum will grow, and each subsequent redesigned and broader workflow will come more quickly, and our tempo will increase. In many cases we will ask ourselves how we managed to work the way we did for so long.

The design of this new generation of holistic workflow

models is a natural enabler for our people and for our organization, which leads to the improved visibility and unity of the IT organization. We will now see further across IT, and work in a way that mirrors how we best deliver to our customers.

> ***This is an outside-in model versus the traditional inside-out model. With the outside being the customer, of course.***

This is where we start and where we finish our work.

Good change is highly contagious, and this will be another example of a change that will energize our people and be something that everybody wants to be part of. A natural by-product of this holistic workflow design will be eliminating waste. Every improvement will make the waste easier to identify. There is no blame here, no second-guessing why processes are the way they are. All that matters is getting it right and creating the breadth and alignment that is exactly what the workflow should be, nothing more and nothing less.

No waste, just lean and fast.

THE DEATH OF INTEGRATIONS

Let's begin with the recognition that integrations are fundamentally flawed.

Integrations always bring with them a level of complexity and risk. In no case does an integration improve a system, assuming we can accomplish the same flow of information and same capability without need for an integration.

Although integrations have been a common and accepted part of our IT system and infrastructure for decades, they bring a level of cost, complexity, and risk that is fundamentally a compromise to a higher standard of performance.

One of the remarkable opportunities that comes with the unification of IT is the ability to re-evaluate every integration with the goal to eliminate as many as possible—in most cases this will not be a 100 percent reduction, but it should be significant.

This is the time to question everything,
including long-standing business rules and

assumptions with the goal to exhaust every possible option in the push to eliminate or simplify every integration.

This review of integrations is a healthy and timely process—timely in that some of these integrations will have been operating for five years, ten years, or even longer. What this means is that the systems around them, many technologies, and the business have all changed during this time, and we might discover the integration can be eliminated altogether, and if not then simplified.

Every improvement will make a difference and allow us to move closer to a unified IT, and a stronger and more scalable portfolio of systems.

With each integration that is eliminated, we realize the following benefits:
1. Reduced risk of errors
2. Increased speed of information flow
3. Simplified systems
4. Improved upgrade process
5. Reduced effort and risk associated with making system changes
6. Improved scalability
7. Reduced number of vendors in the IT portfolio
8. Improved speed of diagnosing system issues
9. Improved system availability
10. Reduced cost of system maintenance and enhancements
11. Improved reliability of technology and software applications
12. Reduced cost of system maintenance

And this list is just the beginning. It is likely that the many integrations we live with today are blocking our vision of what can be possible and taking precious bandwidth from our teams—time and thought that can be more valuable when applied elsewhere.

Note the list above contains some very powerful and strategic benefits to IT and the business, including scalability, simplicity, reliability, and speed.

> *And even better, much of this is under our control as it is likely that IT directly, or in working closely with vendors or consultants, created and now operate these integrations.*

It is also very likely these integrations are a source of pain and frustration across IT all the way to the office of the CIO.

Often we build roles and organizations that mirror our systems because it follows a natural pattern. The elimination or simplification of technology and application integrations creates the opportunity to simplify the work our people do every day, which unifies our people and our teams and creates people-related benefits that extend the list of twelve we reviewed earlier in this section. This should not be underestimated.

ENABLING STRATEGY

Another challenge created by the disjointed and plodding work shown by a highly siloed IT organization is the limited ability to drive strategy. The old model of IT tied our hands in many ways and all but forced us to focus on the short term, simply getting to the end of the day, putting out fires that impact us here and now, and literally keeping the lights on.

We felt unable to think about strategy to any degree, and certainly unable to drive strategy. The weight of our tactical work was heavy. However, the best single way to clear the way and shatter the old model is to unify IT. Once again, we are reminded that this changes everything.

The unification of IT will have many benefits, not the least of which will be the ability to create bandwidth in IT, for what might be the first time, to focus on collaborating on and the execution of strategy.

It is vital that IT has a voice in this process because IT brings so much singularly unique value to the discussion.

Recall that the big assets of corporate data, automation, technology, applications, infrastructure, and so much more are managed by and best understood by IT. But too often IT was not at the table when the organization was building strategy due to lack of time, lack of resources, or simply not being invited.

This will now change because we simply can't formulate nor execute the strategy we need for the next decade without the insights and participation of IT. Why? Because the advancement of technology, a mobile workforce, the leverage we gain from automation, the value of smart systems, and so much more is now central to our strategy.

Just a few years ago, this was not the case; the market leaders of tomorrow will be those who best leverage and think strategically about technology. This is new—market leaders of the past were not necessarily great with leveraging technology and were able to make this work.

*But only for a time. The bell now tolls, and
we need to change yet again.*

Ultimately, this is good news for IT and good news for the business. The business and IT need each other to deliver the right strategy to the full organization, which brings us another step closer to the next evolution of the unification of IT—the unification of IT and the business.

IT is the business and the business is IT.

They are inseparable. This is what we will become, and every person in the business and every customer will be the beneficiary of this powerfully unified model.

The role of IT in strategy is not an organizational thing. It is so much more.

IT's collaborating with the business is all about creating a better strategy that enables the business to better serve our customers and to drive more success for the business. This is all that can matter—driving the right results with our customers. Due to the factors shaping our world today, this is only possible with IT in a central role in the strategy process.

Shaping, enabling, and driving the strategy into the future.

ELIMINATION OF WASTE

Waste is a reality today, a force that slows us down and saps our energy—a kind of poison that exists in every IT organization. But we need to see the good in this. See this as what can ultimately be a big opportunity.

Every element of waste we find and eliminate brings us an exciting return on our efforts. This can become an energizing force across IT—a new focus to search for and identify waste, and to then find a new way to work that is leaner, smarter, and faster.

This work will continue for some time, likely for years. But that is okay because waste is likely something that accumulated over time, over many years, and so it will take some time to cleanse IT of what probably took a long time to codify in the organization and in our systems.

Waste can take many forms, including:

1. Anything that is slow
2. Outdated systems that no longer add value
3. Unnecessary or complex organizational approvals

4. Extensive documentation requirements
5. Work product that is highly localized
6. Integrations that create risks or delays
7. Organizational or system handoffs
8. Any task that adds significant time to our business processes
9. Redundant work based on special cases that rarely occur
10. Work product that is solely administrative
11. Single track reviews or approvals that can create large delays
12. Any work product that offers a lack of transparency
13. Processes that are poorly communicated or poorly understood
14. Any complex business process with no good salvage option
15. Complex workflows that do not have a clear and compelling value
16. Single points of system or people failure
17. Consensus decision making that is poorly understood
18. Large teams formed to support a historical business process
19. Systems with a poor history of performance or availability
20. Critical systems with no effective redundancy
21. People unwilling to align with our cultural values
22. Internal-only business processes with no clear connection to customers
23. Systems that impede revenue
24. Work product that is utilized by a small number of constituents

In reading through this list, it is likely you can quickly think of many things to add—a reminder waste can be anywhere and take many forms.

It is important to establish from the beginning this is not about blame.

That sentiment is unproductive and slows us down. It is a complete waste of energy and creates the wrong behaviors in the culture. There will normally be a set of good reasons for why we are where we are today.

All that matters is creating an open and healthy review of all we do, identifying any form of waste, and clearing the way for quickly removing it.

Every case of saving waste, no matter how big or how small, should be recognized and celebrated. In most cases, eliminating waste will save us time and money. Both are precious resources and bring us closer to the new IT—closer to delivering exactly what the customer needs from us. We are removing the distractions that in the end add no value to our customers.

AUTHENTIC TRANSPARENCY

The value of transparency goes far beyond transparency itself. Transparency is a multilayered operational and cultural initiative. When we are committed to the open sharing of information, frequent communication, and inclusive collaboration, we encourage and enable a much larger set of healthy, productive behaviors. This is very much part of a strong culture which enables a strong business.

With very few exceptions, where we find a healthy and thriving culture, we will find a successful business.

The unification of IT directly improves transparency by lifting barricades and expanding the scope of information flow and scope of work.

When this transparency happens, information that was previously hidden or obscured is now visible and becomes available to our teams, which can immediately take action based on a more complete view of the business.

This is to the immediate benefit of everybody, and it is a natural benefit of the holistic business processes and workflow models that span IT. This is very different than the traditional models that broke business processes into pieces and matched silos and created limited and segmented workflow models.

When we realize that our information and data will mirror the work that is done and business processes that are operated every day, it follows that the visibility of this information will be limited, and for many, information will be difficult to access, difficult to find, or hidden completely.

> *In many ways, a unified IT will allow us to lift a fog that has made it difficult to see across IT. With this limited visibility came a limited understanding of IT and our connections to the business.*

The old IT models all but assured that our people would not have access to all the information needed to do their best work. Of course, the good people of IT would be creative and close this gap and in the end do a very solid job.

But this created an overhead, a headwind if you will, that slowed us down and created extra work—work that consumed time in mining data and time that could be better spent on more value-added work.

With transparency across IT, and more open and immediate access to virtually any information, all our people will be better informed and in a position to make more informed decisions.

> ***This is both a technical and cultural improvement, and the improvement can be seen and felt immediately when transparency becomes real.***

Although this transparency is not one of the first benefits we think of when we look at the improvements a unified IT will bring, don't underestimate the impact this will have on the people of IT.

CUSTOMERS AND MARKETS

We close our discussion on the unification of IT with another reminder about what must be our primary unifying force for this transformation—the customer. And because the transformation of IT can only occur with a unified IT, the unification we create is ultimately not about internal objectives or reorganization. No, it is, in fact, all about the customer. Our focus on better serving customers is only possible with a unified IT, and the only valid reason to unify IT is to move closer to and better serve our customers and their markets. These two strategic elements are inextricably linked.

Think of this force of unification as originating from the outside-in and not from the inside-out. There is a big difference here that needs to be recognized and appreciated.

Not the least priority of which is understanding how we trace back to the only authentic source, and that source of truth is not within our own walls. It must be the customer and the markets our customers live in every day. Propagating the idea of operating from the inside-out is a fool's errand.

This is not an easy shift, moving our focus from one that is internal to a focus on markets and customers, but the great value we find is that customers are in virtually every case happy to work with us and will give us the unadulterated truth each and every time.

The customers of today, and our customers of tomorrow, have entrusted us with a partnership that calls us to deliver value that in turn enables our customers to thrive. This is at the heart of our partnership and has everything to do with the unification of IT. It would be fair to say this is the single greatest driver for why we must unify IT. This call to unification is not simply an internal initiative, not an efficiency project, not an IT reorganization. All of this misses the point.

We are unifying IT to more quickly, more creatively, and more effectively meet the needs of our customers today, to retain happy customers for many years, and to win new customers by offering what other businesses cannot. This focus on customers and markets is not natural for some IT organizations, so this change will not be easy.

But when we are thoughtful about what this really means, what it will take to change the DNA of IT, and how it will change our way of thinking and how we work, it will be hard to turn away from this powerful pull.

*I'm confident that many people in IT know
this is right and have begun to think more
about moving closer to the customer, and
in some cases that connection has begun
to grow. In those cases, it is just a matter of
accelerating what we have started and in
synergy with a unified IT.*

When it comes to IT organizations living with a lack of connection to the customers, it is time to start now; one of the surprises we will get is the willingness of customers to work with us. It won't take much convincing—normally we will find the customer to love the idea of working more closely with us and off we go.

In Chapter 2, The Customer Connection, we took a close look at creating this connection and the many good reasons why this should happen. But this concept is so powerful, we will see it come up time and time again throughout the book, along with a few other themes that are central to the Imperative and core to the rebirth of IT.

Once again we touch on this idea of the customer within this chapter on the unification of IT which in its own right is one of the few core themes because it is a natural fit with the customer—and so these should be considered inseparable.

KEY TAKEAWAYS: THE UNIFICATION OF IT

1. The unification of IT is about much more than changing the organization model, titles, or job functions.
   The essence of a unified IT brings everything in IT
   together and changes everything we do. In many
   ways it is working in a manner that is 180 degrees
   opposed to the traditional model of IT. But in that
   change lies a remarkable value, and in many ways is
   at the heart of the rebirth of IT and the journey that
   lies ahead.

2. A unified IT begins with cultural change, a commitment to working every day in a different way. This
   cultural change drives the formation of cross-functional teams, in many cases for the first time, that
   work across IT to drive more holistic initiatives that
   align with the business.

3. A natural byproduct of unifying IT is improved
   transparency and collaboration, which then will
   transition into a new generation of business processes and workflows that reach across IT and eliminate the limitations around silo-based business
   processes requiring integrations and handoffs that
   slow us down and create risk. This then leads into a
   better use of automation tools because we are automating across IT versus locally. These new business

processes will more closely capture how people naturally work every day.

4. The ultimate unity provided by the unification of IT is that with the customer. We will change how we ground everything in IT by starting with the customer and working back into IT from the customer—a model of outside-in versus the traditional inside-out—from IT projects out to the customer. This is fundamentally different and enables the customer to be tightly linked with everything in IT for the first time. This is to the benefit of the customer, IT, and the business.

CHAPTER 8

THE EVOLUTION OF SELF-SERVE

The appeal of self-serve is strong and natural.

The powerful forces that have shaped the consumer markets of the past ten years began to have a growing influence over IT during this same time and have driven the birth, rise, and now evolution of our self-serve models—including but not limited to Incident Self-Service, Service Catalog, Knowledge Access, and Self-Help.

The attraction of self-serve is very simple and yet powerful, including:

1. Immediate gratification
2. Available around the clock
3. No human interaction necessary
4. Independent operation by the user
5. Attractive and easy-to-use interface
6. The user is in control
7. A personal experience
8. No waiting

9. Fast

10. Saves money

The appeal of this model is broad because it appeals to our naturally selfish instincts, which is in no way intended to be a criticism—quite the opposite. Selfishness is an advanced concept in the context of IT and can be a very good thing.

Note the characteristics listed above are very similar to what we see in other elements of the Imperative. This is clearly no accident and we are continually drawn back to fundamentals that will stick with us over the next twenty-five years.

> *It comes down to doing what I want, when I want it, and how I want it in ways that are easy and efficient and likely to save me money as well.*

I have used the first person of "I" because this focus on me is what drives the success of all these models. The behavior of the selfish and demanding consumer has changed all our expectations in the workplace and reshaped the thinking of every business. The proliferation of the consumer web experience has set the tone for what our customers expect and what we as IT must deliver.

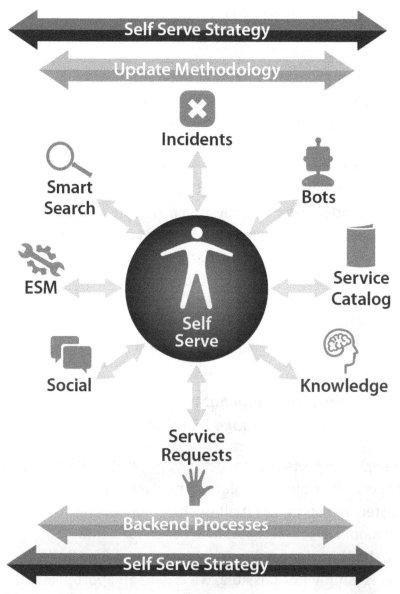

Figure 8.1 An Overview of the Self-Serve Ecosystem

Figure 8.1 is a high-level fly-by of the Self-Serve models, including the hub of this virtual wheel, which is the individual. This model is all about bringing power and happiness to the individual, which then drives the team, drives the culture, and drives the business.

This is an important chain to understand. Moving outward from the individual, we have a number of models available, including Service Catalog, Incident Self-Service, and Social to name a few. We should expect these models to grow in number in the years ahead while at the same time the sophistication, intelligence, and speed will improve. Beyond these models that directly touch the individual, we need the guidance of a Self-Serve Strategy and a robust back-end, including an update methodology and the back-end processes that bring this methodology to life.

Each of these elements is important, and it all comes together to make the whole experience look easy and natural.

> *Easy is anything but easy, but our job is to*
> *make it look so.*

In some respects this model is very intuitive, and in some respects it is quite revolutionary. And we are just getting started, which makes it all the more important to embrace the model of self-serve lest we be left far behind. Our mindset should be to make everything self-serve first; then if this is simply not possible, we create an appropriate they-serve model.

Originally, we saw self-service emerge in IT for somewhat simple incident management use cases. A user could log an incident and then check on the status of the incident over time. This basic use case then grew to include guided knowledge to our knowledge bases to support self-help and self-learning. Our users could be in control, perform the work when convenient, and educate themselves on topics of interest which supported continued professional development. Again, when they wanted and how they wanted.

Recently, the model has spread even further to include service requests and service catalog, and the model will no doubt continue to grow. The benefits are just too strong and the experience too personal to be denied this continued adoption.

The multiple models of self-serve are similar, yet very different in some respects and reflective of the continued evolution of this powerful and flexible model. Staying true to the original concept of self-service, but taking us in new and exciting directions.

Even with the success and widespread adoption of these self-serve models and their derivatives, we should expect to see a continued evolution of this domain and to include some creative surprises. We will likely stay true to the ten fundamentals shown earlier in this section because this profile is timeless. Yes, the details and form of the service might change, but self-service and the generations of its descendants are here to stay.

SELF-SERVE STRATEGY

We should not charge in and blindly slather self-service all around the business, even though it's well understood and has been operating for a number of years.

We need to take some time to create a strategy that will govern where and how we leverage any self-service for the next ten years. The strategy will also govern where self-service will not make sense. Without this strategy these decisions will not be clear and can slow us down or worse, cause us to create models that might need to be undone in the future.

The strategy outline can be simple and should include a number of questions, including:

1. What are the scope and role for each Self-Serve model to be leveraged?
2. What services will be offered through Service Catalog?
3. Where will cost tracking be used and where will it not?

4. What approvals are required for self-serve interactions with a cost associated with them?
5. What user groups will be targeted with our self-serve offerings?
6. What metrics will be used to evaluate self-serve performance?
7. What interfaces and integrations are required to operate each self-serve model?
8. What is the assigned ownership and oversight for each self-serve model?
9. What is the change and update process for each self-serve model?

The creation of this strategy overview should be a cross-functional exercise and include participation from the organizations to be served with the self-serve models and the organizations responsible for developing and operating the models themselves. This is a very good time for communication and transparency. As the self-serve offerings begin to operate, there should be no surprises, with all the details around timing, scope, and offerings of each model being well understood.

> *Many delays and misunderstandings in the daily work of IT can be diminished or prevented entirely with a small amount of planning and coordination.*

This applies to virtually every new project, upgrade, or initiative that IT will take on over the next ten years. We need to take an organization that does not naturally communicate often and well, and shift it to an organization that is not necessarily world-class at communications, but understands the value of communications and so makes it a priority to communicate better, and more consistently.

> *We just need to get a little better each quarter or year, and over time we will be pretty good at communicating.*

This strategy is a good example. Our self-serve models have an important place in the future of IT and bring us the leverage that we discuss throughout the book. As such, these models are a great place to bring some focus. This strategy exercise will get our teams aligned, create some basic agreements to operate with, and establish a process and cadence for communications going forward throughout what is likely to be a ten-year cycle of creating, operating, and improving our self-serve models across IT and the business.

INCIDENT SELF-SERVICE

One of the earliest models to offer the unique ability for a user to operate independently and serve themselves in a productive manner was Incident Self-Service. This provided a very simple user experience focused on allowing users to quickly log an incident and to then check on the status of the incident throughout its lifecycle until the incident was closed.

Following the creation of the incident, self-service included a simple communication and update model to include helpful and related information delivered to the user through the course of the incident process. This model has been a big operational success and is now used as part of most current help desk and service desk operations. It is likely that teams did not know what to expect when first offering this model, but it was an immediate success for both the user and the help desk or service desk.

The Incident Self-Service experience is all about easy, convenient, and fast. It is hard not to like this way of working.

It's easy to log an incident and fast to check on the status when it is convenient for the user. Because *easy* is so important, we design the user experience to be simple. Normally, the user will utilize a simple web interface that requires just a few pieces of information, including:

1. User authentication
2. Brief description of issue
3. Incident priority
4. User contact information
5. User location if applicable
6. Time and date created can be stamped from the system
7. Any helpful comments
8. Confirmation provided to the user, normally including incident ID

This creation process should take five minutes or less.

It is easy to see why this Self-Service model has been so popular, and for these very same reasons, we should expect Self-Service to have a place in the IT Incident Management model for the foreseeable future and certainly throughout the rebirth of IT over the next ten years.

It is in many respects a timeless model, and since incidents will not disappear from IT completely in the next ten to fifteen years, self-service is a very effective process to support the user and to offload the service desk.

In looking at this model, it is important to understand there are two sides to it—the user/employee perspective and the service desk perspective. Incident self-service has a unique appeal to both groups.

As we have discussed, the user is able to quickly create an incident in a convenient way, using a simple interface. We should recognize that each self-service creation of an incident is eliminating an email, phone call, chat session, or walk-up with the service desk. The savings in this are significant in terms of time and money. Incident self-service was one of our earlier examples of an automation model that truly began to offload the service desk and create some time to both think and act differently for our service delivery teams.

While this is simple, it is also remarkable in that we have a happy and productive user and at the same time are eliminating expensive, time-consuming, and often slow manual Incident Management work performed by the service desk.

We will see this powerful duality of value throughout the discussion in this chapter, which is the essence of why Self-Serve is rising.

SERVICE REQUESTS

Service requests reflect the evolution of modern IT and the current state and direction of IT Service Management and service desk. A service request is versatile, and can include user questions, a standard change, the use of a new service, or a need related to the business.

The creation of this request then launches a series of coordinated actions to fulfill the request in an optimal way and to result in a happy and productive user. With what should be a flexible response model, the role of the service desk has grown and will continue to evolve as the needs of the business change over time.

The birth and evolution of the service request have taken the help desk and service desk far beyond the traditional break/fix model driven by tickets or incidents.

The service request model has grown in popularity and in value because it essentially extends the message of "How can I help you today" to IT and to the business. The service request model:

1. Increases user productivity and satisfaction through answering questions and providing access to important information quickly and easily.
2. Improves effectiveness of the broader business by providing access to the right information and to the right service at the right time.
3. Improves control of the costs associated with delivering common services by providing defined and proven processes and quicker approvals where needed.
4. Increases visibility and understanding of services by providing a simple interface for all IT and business users to make a request at any time.
5. Provides a flexible model for the many needs of IT and the business that can't be captured by the traditional processes of IT.
6. Broadens access to IT services to other organizations across the business.

Submitting a service request should be easy and convenient. This is an extension of the incident self-service model described earlier in this chapter, with the primary difference being that <u>a service request is not an incident</u>. Service requests should also represent a great deal of flexibility, by design, in order to accommodate the rapidly changing business and the demands placed on IT. Flexibility should be thoughtfully designed into our systems and not be left to chance. This flexibility becomes a competitive advantage as the rate of change in global markets and in the business is likely to continue and very likely to increase in the next ten years, our horizon for the rebirth of IT.

> *An important element that should be incorporated into the service request process is cost.*

As most service requests have some level of cost associated with them, the service request process is a good opportunity to create increased cost visibility, structured cost approvals, and cost accountability where there may have been none previously. Even with simple cost visibility, behaviors start to change.

The cost dimension of service requests supports our need to create more accountability across IT and to support more sophisticated P&L models as well. This is very much in line with both aligning IT with the business and taking a more business-oriented approach to everything we do across IT every day.

SERVICE CATALOG

Service catalog is a big topic, and as it evolves a complete look at the catalog could become a book unto itself. But it has had such a strong influence over the models of self-serve, this chapter would not be complete without, at a minimum, a high-level summary of where we are with service catalog today and what to expect in the future.

Service catalog has had an undeniably strong influence over the past ten years on how IT delivers services and how we design and operate self-serve models. In many ways, it has reshaped how we think about offering IT services across IT and to the business. Nowhere are the influences of consumer models on IT more evident today than in service catalog. This is a good thing after all, and more and more we are taking a consumer-like and commercially style-driven approach to all we do in IT.

A few examples of why service catalog is a key element in the rebirth of IT and in the evolving self-serve model:

1. Service catalog is a single view of the services currently offered by IT.

2. The service catalog experience is typically easy to use, easy to navigate, and stylistically non-IT in nature.
3. The service catalog is often the vehicle IT uses to offer services beyond IT and to the broader business, including finance, facilities, HR, customer support, and marketing.
4. Service catalog fulfillment is highly automated and delivers fast service at an optimized cost.
5. A current service catalog reduces wasted time due to outdated service definitions, and results in happy customers receiving fast and high-quality services.
6. Service catalog is a unifying force across IT and the broader business. The catalog calls to our attention key integrations and dependencies across the organization and the services we can all rally around.
7. Service catalog is moving closer to the customer—this is not just an internal model for employees and users. We should expect service catalog to be a vehicle to service our clients directly.
8. Service catalog has been a key catalyst is the growth of enterprise service management in the past decade.

The service catalog model is a good reminder of the basic formula for successful self-serve models:

1. Easy to use, with an attractive interface
2. Available around the clock
3. Fast results and fast service
4. Saves time and money
5. Easy to access on mobile devices
6. Puts the user in control

7. Offers quick and easy access to related information and resources
8. Remembers user preferences and history

Regardless of the model or the technology, if we are able to tick all these boxes, we are likely to have a popular and successful result.

Today, we have a minority of our service experiences completed through self-serve models with estimates running in the 15 to 25 percent range. But we expect these numbers to change quickly with self-serve models growing quickly over the next ten years.

Most of us would agree these models will manage the majority of service requests in the years ahead, and by the end of the next decade, I expect the percentage to grow to be in the range of 80 percent. This says a lot about how the fabric of IT and our systems will change.

ENTERPRISE SERVICE MANAGEMENT

The processes, data models, applications, and automation of IT Service Management have extended far beyond IT over the past five years. As the business identified a growing need for more effectively managing services, a careful look across the business found the IT and ITSM teams and tools with the goods and knowledge to help.

Organizations, including HR, facilities, marketing, finance, and customer support, came running to IT for assistance. What we have discovered is that the pressures of audit, governance, compliance, best practices, and the rapid evolution of technology have battle-hardened IT where other organizations have lagged behind.

Although there are many definitions circulating for Enterprise Service Management (ESM), for the purposes of this discussion, we will consider this to be leveraging applications and processes originally developed for IT Service Management specifically for IT, and now for the delivery and management of services outside of IT.

We have confirmed over the past five years that these ITSM solutions are, in fact, a very good fit for the business, and we can leverage the investment made to develop and mature these tools for the broader good.

In many cases, ESM solutions take the form of a self-serve model. This allows the user experience to be scrubbed of any IT content and tailored to fit the targeted organization. When done correctly, there is no evidence the application is derived from anything IT.

Service catalog is a great example of an adaptable ESM solution. The catalog, populated with service requests specific to a non-IT organization, can be quickly configured and mobilized to look like a natural fit for the part. Whether this is finance, HR, facilities, or marketing, the offerings, content, and look of the catalog can be adapted for the business.

Note that beyond the user experience being notably non-IT, the fulfillment of the request would normally not require IT resources to manage the process.

A good way to think of ESM is a business service, delivered by business people to business people.

This is only one example but a good one and very illustrative of how service catalog has been a big hit for the business, and how self-serve models will continue to be adapted for many non-IT business needs. This is just the beginning and a reminder of the broader influence IT people and solutions will have on the business.

This rapid and widespread adoption is no accident and yet another reminder that the formula of easy, fast, 24X7, and personal is a powerful combination that people are naturally attracted to.

KNOWLEDGE

Access to knowledge is a good use of corporate information, and the model we will operate in is increasingly one of complete transparency. There is a limited set of personal employee information and confidential client information that should be protected, but this information is only a small subset of the valuable information we should provide to our teams across IT. Increasingly this will extend to our customers as well.

As with so many elements of the rebirth of IT, this trend has a thread of common sense and a thread of strategy running through it.

Armed with the right knowledge, we are all better.

There is a sense of fulfillment that goes hand in hand with knowledge—a sense of control and a sense of direction. This applies to employees, clients, partners, and the complete ecosystem of the business. The scope is boundless. All people want to learn and to be better equipped to perform a job; we simply need to provide easy access to the right information. From this information springs knowledge, and then many good things start to happen.

For this discussion on self-serve models, access to knowledge is an increasingly important consideration.

This look at knowledge is timely for a few good reasons:

1. Knowledge bases have developed in scope and improved in function significantly over the past five years.
2. Search tools are excellent and help users quickly find exactly what they are looking for.
3. The desire of users to access knowledge is stronger, reflecting a growing desire on the part of internal and external customers to take on self-guided learning.
4. Good use of knowledge goes beyond general learning and includes the ability to self-diagnose and self-resolve questions and problems.
5. The good use of knowledge elevates the ability of the user to achieve complete control and self-reliance, which are at the core of the self-serve model.
6. In the spirit of partnership and openness, users and customers appreciate the sharing of knowledge on the part of an organization or enterprise. This builds trust and loyalty.

This is a good reminder that no self-serve strategy and operating model is complete without a plan for offering access to knowledge.

This commitment to open knowledge access is the right place to start.

Then, with commitment we have other questions that need to be answered, including the shape of the access model and scope of information to be provided. This second element would contain any consideration of confidentiality and other potentially sensitive information.

But these questions will get resolved in due course, and we will then be on the right path to a more complete and more valuable self-serve solution set.

SOCIAL

Social media and the broader social experience and mindset have a place in any discussion on self-serve models. These topics are closely linked because the rise of self-serve in business was influenced greatly by the growth and cultural impact of social media in the past decade. Not long ago, social media had no real place in a discussion on IT services.

Today, that same discussion would not be complete without some consideration of how social media can complement what we offer across the self-serve portfolio.

Once thought to only be part of the personal communications of our youth, social media is now reshaping virtually everything.

In fact, the short list of why social is growing so quickly looks something like this:

1. Highly personal
2. Quick and easy
3. Designed to be great on mobile devices
4. Fun

5. Immediate feedback and gratification
6. Always on

It is easy to see the striking resemblance between this list and the appeal of self-serve itself.

We are drawn to these models for the same reasons. It is no coincidence, as the shape of self-serve has been highly influenced by social media, which has rewritten many of the rules around how we design and operate business applications. Expect this influence and the reshaping to continue for the next decade, on the same timeline as our rebirth of IT.

Coincidence? No way.

If we take the time to study the social media model, we see it has a simple elegance and power. This is a design principle we can take on for much of the work we do throughout the rebirth of IT—and not just the design of our self-serve models as we just touched on, but also in how we work, how we interact with customers, how the employees of IT want to work and live, and how we communicate across the broader organization.

In many ways this highlights a striking contrast between traditional communication models and the new model created by social.

The traditional business communication model was infrequent, formal, and

> *highly structured. The new social media-influenced communication model is constant, informal, and highly fluid.*

The implications in these contrasts are enormous.

BACK-END PROCESSES

To be successful with any self-serve model, we are required to have a complete and repeatable design for the back-end processes. This is the work that is required to fulfill whatever might be requested through the self-serve front end.

These processes must be designed and validated, and often using automation to ensure a fast and accurate fulfillment of the self-serve request. This could be a proper Incident Management workflow in the case of incident self-service, a fulfillment process for each offering in the service catalog, or a business process to support each service request in the case of the general IT service request models.

The approach we use in designing and operating these back-end processes should be very consistent and should include:

1. The use of people experts as process mentors throughout.
2. A validation of the back-end process design with a cross-functional team.
3. Testing of each back-end process using a few

examples of real self-serve use cases in a non-production environment.

4. Use case results should be validated with the process mentors and cross-checked with real production results.

5. Process results must be highly consistent and accurate before promoting the test system into production.

6. The design process should include scalability. Assume the self-serve model will be successful and demand will increase.

7. The majority of the back-end process should be automated using modern automation technology.

8. Discuss and agree to metrics for success to be applied when the self-serve model goes into production.

9. Allocate the back-end processes into multiple phases, with a complete debrief at the end of each phase. Publish the results of the debrief to business owners, process mentors, and IT leadership.

It is important to understand that even the most attractive front end will ultimately fail if the back-end processes are not carefully designed and operating in a way that produces the right results consistently. Likewise, a robust and consistent back-end process will ultimately fail with an ugly and difficult to use front end.

We need to get both the front end and the back end of the self-serve model right in order to be successful.

When we do get both sides of this model right, it is a beautiful thing indeed and a model that will bring tremendous value to the business. A strong self-serve model is likely to grow in usage and remain in place for many years, so the time we have taken to get it right—and this *is* an investment—is resource well invested.

UPDATE METHODOLOGY

Every self-serve model is a vibrant, living, and evolving entity. It requires constant attention and an update cycle that will keep the model fresh and up to date. This update methodology must be designed and confirmed before any self-serve model makes it to the production environment.

Without it, even the very best self-serve experience will grow stale and irrelevant.

The good news is this update methodology can be simple and inexpensive to operate over time.

The key is designing this methodology early, and communicating it to the necessary owners who will ensure the methodology is operated as planned. This design work should not be delayed to late in the testing process or, worse, after the production model is in place and running. This puts us behind and can have a big impact on the value of self-serve over time.

When developed, even in a draft form, this update methodology should be documented and shared with the IT organization so we have an informed team that touches or participates in the update process. In some cases, it can make sense to publish the methodology overview to users as well in the interest of transparency.

The update methodology must consider changes in the market, changes in the business, and feedback from users. All this information should be collected on a regular basis—it is not necessary for this to be done daily or even weekly. Something like quarterly is about right, but yearly is not often enough.

Think of this as a healthy triangulation of the world around us and then making the necessary adjustments, some large and some small, as we navigate an ever-changing landscape.

The process of making these adjustments is important to the overall health of the self-serve experience and the content it provides. These adjustments can take many forms, as in offering a new service in the service catalog, or improving the search engine for our knowledge bases to improve user productivity when working with corporate knowledge. This is all about adding value, improving the user experience, compressing the time required to complete our work, and putting our organization in a position to better serve our customers.

More so, this is a thread of agility that runs through the organization and touches many of our people. Agility is not one big thing; it is a lot of little things that are mighty together.

Given the pace of business is growing ever faster, it is vital that we build systems that can adapt equally fast. And, my friends, this pace will only quicken over time. What we consider to be fast today will be viewed as painfully slow in just five years. A key to keeping up with this pace is the powerful combination of self-serve models underscored by automation.

KEY TAKEAWAYS:
THE EVOLUTION OF SELF-SERVE

1. With so many great options today regarding how we can leverage self-serve models, we need to begin with a simple strategy for self-serve in IT and across the business lest we lose our way. This is about so much more than incident self-service or service catalog. Although these are important models and valuable in their own right, it is now about so much more in how we enable employees and customers to serve themselves.

2. This is another great example of a micro-model that lines up well with our overall goals and characteristics of the Imperative and the rebirth of IT. Speed, convenience, around-the-clock access, and personalized service to name a few. These benefits become compelling due to the degree we can push these advantages forward, and this is a natural fit for the self-serve experience. Better still, this is just the beginning. Always keep these fundamental goals in mind.

3. While our thinking and appetite around self-serve may have been ahead of our tools for a while, these tools and broader automation technology have

improved dramatically in the past five years and now allow us to implement powerful new models. This self-serve automation is now going far beyond IT to the benefit of the business. And while we think of Enterprise Service Management as a big thing in itself, it is just the beginning of what we can do beyond IT, because the needs of self-serve are everywhere. This needs to be an important part of the strategy in item #1 above—how can IT best bring self-service to the full business?

CHAPTER 9

SMART SYSTEMS

The accelerated evolution of smart systems, also commonly referred to as AI, has matured greatly over the past five years. For many reasons this is a good and strategic development for IT and for the business. Only a handful of things have the potential to change how we work every day, and this makes that very short list.

These capabilities have evolved based on both the improvement of technology but also a growing base of experience, which points us in the right direction of adding value in day-to-day operations and in performing real work. In many respects these systems have now crossed a threshold—from being an interesting curiosity with limited real practical usefulness, to providing leverage and real value when applied correctly in IT.

The terminology can be overwhelming and has expanded dramatically during this five-year period of accelerated growth.

A small sample of smart systems and their subsystems include:

1. Autonomous systems
2. Machine learning
3. Intelligent assistants
4. Chat bots
5. Deep learning
6. Neural networks
7. Universal translation
8. Autonomous robotics
9. Cognitive security
10. Text to speech
11. Fuzzy logic systems
12. Thought-controlled gaming
13. Emotion analytics
14. Expert systems
15. Natural language processing
16. Advanced pattern recognition
17. Cloud robotics
18. Predictive analytics
19. Robotic personal assistants
20. Thoughtful simulations
21. Virtual companions
22. Intelligent process control
23. Speech recognition
24. Data mining
25. Gene evaluation
26. Driverless transportation
27. Intelligent risk management

An exciting list for sure, but this is just the beginning—
truly, just the tip of the AI iceberg today.

As much fun as it would be, it is far beyond the scope of this book to consider these examples in any detail—perhaps another example of a subject that could carry another book. Instead we look at smart systems and AI in terms of their place in IT and in the rebirth ahead.

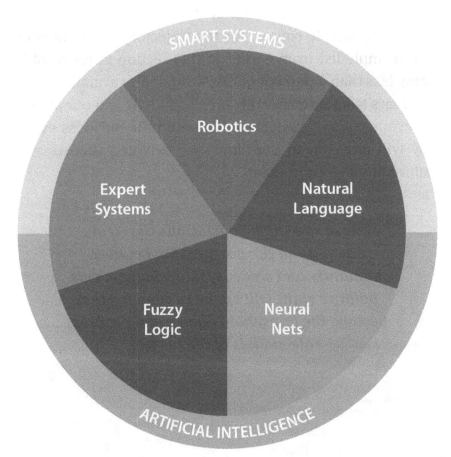

Figure 9.1 The Orbit & Core of Smart Systems

The rapidly growing list of smart systems and AI technologies is hard to track, but certainly bears watching. Figure 9.1 shows a few of the core elements, including Robotics,

Expert Systems, Natural Language, Neural Nets, and Fuzzy Logic. We can debate the categories as they are very much in flux, but this is pretty close. No doubt our terminology and categorization will change, but let's not miss the point of how smart systems and AI are a growing and exciting source of leverage for IT.

To provide a little context for the trajectory of AI, think of our example list from earlier in this section in terms of it being less than 1 percent of the AI capability available to us ten years from now. The advancement of AI and our ability to leverage smart systems in IT and in the business every day will often mean the difference between success and failure in the decade ahead.

> *Those special organizations that truly understand the partnership between humanity and smart systems and get this balance right will be the companies that become the household names and business role models of the future.*

A UNIQUE PARTNERSHIP

With the surge of sophistication and adoption of smart systems in the past decade, a popular point of debate has become the relationship between people and smart systems. Will smart systems replace our people? Does artificial intelligence threaten the future of our IT workers? Will these smart systems expose how limited people really are at performing their jobs? Will people become relegated to simple and repetitive tasks while smart systems take over the more demanding and advanced tasks?

This debate is likely to continue for years to come, but my view is that the answer to all these questions is an emphatic "No."

What I expect to occur over the next decade is something very different and very much opposed to conflict or displacement.

Humanity and smart systems will form
a unique and strong partnership—a
partnership that emphasizes that each

needs the other and together we make our
solutions stronger.

When we look closely and consider this topic thoughtfully, we begin to see the characteristics of smart systems and of people that are lacking in the other and how each can ultimately complement the other.

Our people are uniquely capable of emotion, advanced reasoning, complex problem solving for first-case problems, and creative thinking. Our people have a sense of humor and empathy, both very important and advanced traits. Each of these capabilities and feelings is absent from or a far reach for smart systems today.

Smart systems are incredibly fast, able to evaluate large quantities of data, and able to automate and perform routine and some medium complexity tasks very efficiently and quite effectively. Some would argue that smart systems are able to perform advanced reasoning tasks today, but the reality is that these cases are quite constrained, and this dimension of the technology is not ready to play a prominent role in business today.

In considering the strengths and
limitations of both humanity and smart
systems, we can see how a partnership can
be forged.

By leveraging smart systems to do what they do best and likewise for humanity, we get the best of both worlds and a much stronger solution and model for our business.

As a further benefit, we are able to offload some to much of the work performed by people in IT, thereby enabling our people to be more focused, energized, and better. All the while, our smart systems will be filling their role very well, and better every day, so the limitations we know today fade away. Smart systems, for example, are outstanding at analyzing large volumes of data, evaluating trends, and crafting metrics that provide valuable insights. Smart systems are infallibly consistent and extremely fast.

Intelligent assistants are capable of taking and managing a customer inquiry and answering many of the standard questions that would otherwise go to the call center or service desk. These experiences have improved significantly in the past five years.

A foreign concept to many people just a few years ago, once again our experience in our personal and consumer lives have changed our perception of what is possible in business.

> *For example, think for a moment about your experiences with iPhone's Siri, Google Home, or Amazon Alexa in the past few years.*

It is likely each of us has had some experience with these intelligent assistants of late, and they have become popular stars in the media and TV commercials. In many respects these technologies today are quite crude and will bring far more advanced capabilities to us in the decade ahead. With that in mind, it is much easier to envision how an AI assistant will be helpful to us in the daily operations of IT.

Intelligent assistants in combination with chat bots, which are equally capable, push the value envelope even further—we can offload call volumes from our people analysts or agents by 20 to 40 percent. These numbers are very attainable, and for each interaction saved we are able to reassign our people to other tasks that support our innovation and proactive agenda. We discuss those points much more throughout the book.

Increasingly we will all think about how we can better leverage smart systems and how we can better apply the wonderful and unique skills of humanity.

This is a remarkable and rich tapestry—
and one that is just now coming to life
within IT.

STRATEGY FIRST

It is easy to get excited about smart systems, but these systems should only be deployed across IT and the business in the context of an IT strategy and technology road map.

This strategy will map out how we make the most of humanity and how humanity can be complemented by the rapid evolution of smart systems and AI. We can't simply throw these systems into the business and expect to get the best results.

The strategy will put smart systems and people into the right roles, each making the other better. Putting people and smart systems into the wrong roles would create a collision that would waste lots of time and resource.

These decisions can't be made in flight.
There is just too much at stake, which
brings us back to the strategy.

We need to look carefully at each smart system, as they are each very different with different capabilities, and determine where they can be leveraged to take advantage of these unique capabilities.

And, as AI continues to get better and smarter, it is even more important to have this strategy in place: We need to be thoughtful about the right roles as it becomes more difficult to make these selections and the complexity of our environment grows.

For example, how do we use AI in customer-facing roles? Will customers consider an interaction with an AI technology to be appropriate? Some customers and users are not comfortable with AI technology and some naturally are.

What role can AI play in security and in protecting the business and our infrastructure from threats? How can AI help us to understand the massive amounts of data and information that can tell us so much about our customers? These questions will continue to multiply as smart systems advance and continue to multiply in their own right.

We will need special skills in IT to help us navigate the technology evolution and balance our smart systems with humanity. Strategy development will involve these skilled staff members, likely among our new priority hires, working alongside the CIO, the CISO, and new leadership roles yet to be created.

This is not just about role selection for our AI technologies— as with these smart systems, we have people with unique skills and experience. Don't underestimate the value of emotion, creativity, and specialized experience in our people.

It is just as important to be thoughtful in assigning the right roles to our people as it is to deploy smart systems into the right roles. This, too, becomes a bit more complicated.

Perhaps the selection of roles becomes even more important with our people as we want them in roles of leverage. Leverage is precious and remarkably powerful, but we need to engineer it into our solutions.

HUMANITY & IT

Even the suggestion that the rebirth of IT must consider the role of humanity in IT will be difficult for some to grasp. But this is very much the case and a testament to the remarkable ascension of smart systems over the past five years. We should consider this to be good news: If managed properly, both humanity and IT will be better than ever.

The need to reflect on humanity and our place in IT has not been necessary, and we could make the argument that AI underachieved for much of the past twenty years, either a victim of unrealistic expectations or the slow development of new high-impact capabilities.

IT today is an increasingly complex
tapestry of humanity and technology.

While technology has always been part of IT, its role is becoming more complex and more impactful. This has never been more true than today, as smart systems are demanding our attention and demonstrating capabilities we thought would never arrive in a useful form.

This raises the question of the role of humanity in IT, with good cause, for the first time. This can be viewed as a negative thing or a positive development to be embraced. Why? Because when we best leverage the rapidly improving capabilities of smart systems, it creates the opportunity to better serve our customers and to create a competitive advantage.

Some organizations will get this and some won't. We will attempt to oversimply the issue or ignore it altogether.

Those who appreciate this issue and manage it aggressively and creatively will then build the market leaders of tomorrow. And some market leaders of today, unable or unwilling to embrace and leverage humanity, will fade away, making room for new emerging leaders.

In virtually every case the market leaders of the next twenty years will have carefully considered this very question of humanity in balance with smart systems and found the right answer for their business.

In the thoughtful consideration of how AI technology can best serve IT and the business, we will be pulled back to the question of humanity and how our people evolve in the organization. This has everything to do with focus and being able to look at how we strategically apply humanity to maximize the leverage of our talented, diverse, and very human people. And this is the question we should start with: How do we best leverage humanity versus starting with a focus on smart systems?

We use humanity here with the greatest of respect for the remarkable emotion, sense of humor, creativity, and intuition living in our people.

For the past thirty years we thought of the IT organization as simply composed of people and created to put structure to these same people assets. But now we are finding that any IT organization must call out not just the role of humanity but the role of smart systems. This is a remarkable opportunity and needs to be seen as exactly this—an opportunity to improve everything we do and at the same time to find new ways to innovate. Ultimately, it is all about the creation of thrilled customers.

KEY TAKEAWAYS: SMART SYSTEMS

1. The capabilities and value of smart systems today are real and must take a place in the strategy of IT for the future. However, this is not just about technology, and it creates as many challenges and opportunities around humanity as around technology. Any role of AI must be defined thoughtfully, and equal thought must be given to how the role of smart systems will be balanced with and by the role of humanity. This balance is everything, and IT using smart systems as nothing more than a blunt object will result in a very expensive failure.

2. From the beginning, it helps to think of AI and our people as a new kind of partnership—a powerful and dynamic partnership unlike anything we have seen in IT for the past thirty years. When crafted correctly, this partnership will leverage the jaw-dropping capabilities of AI to the fullest, while at the same time leverage the miracle of humanity and uniquely human traits to their fullest. These partners don't threaten one another, and we should never entertain that idea. This is simply a waste of time and energy.

3. As we are at the beginning of the AI evolution by most measures, our strategy can't merely consider

the snapshot of today. We need to consider the continued improvement and sophistication of smart systems and be ready to leverage these improvements when they become available, without requiring us to rewrite our IT strategy and mission every few years. Take smart systems as a given in IT and design in the trajectory of humanity as well as AI and where we expect the partnership to be in five years and in ten years. This is an exciting exercise that will take us to levels of performance not possible before the dawn of this partnership.

CHAPTER 10

THE POWER OF MOBILITY

Our world has fundamentally changed in the past ten years through the rapid growth—no, we could accurately call this an explosion—of mobile devices. These devices take many forms, but for the sake of this discussion we will reference smart phones and tablets: the coveted and increasingly capable mobile devices of today. These devices are just too easy, too fast, and too convenient to not create a love-at-first-sight reaction from consumers and professionals everywhere.

What we have seen is a "leakage" from our personal lives into the workplace. As the popularity of smart phones and tablets grew in our personal lives, we just naturally brought them to the office with us, on our business trips, and everywhere in between. In the beginning IT was reluctant to embrace these devices, and at some level we hoped they might just go away.

Alas, that is not going to happen. These
devices are here to stay, so we need to
buckle up.

Even more than here to stay, they will continue to grow in use and are likely, very likely, to become the primary device in IT. This is a likelihood we need to think about in IT— what does it mean to all of our systems and processes if the mobile device becomes the primary use case for everything we do in IT?

The user side is an easy fit for mobility, but we should not assume it will stop there. Even the administrator use case could prove to be a good fit for mobility. This might take some time, as there are a few challenges today, but those are very likely to be overcome just as the consumer and user problems have been solved.

As with a few of the elements we discuss in the outline of the Imperative, this issue has many facets that need to be considered. Mobile alone is not enough. Mobile only works when it carries a strong set of characteristics that bring value and broader appeal.

We have started this chapter with a
reference to devices, but The Power of
Mobility has two equally important sides—
the devices themselves, but also the ability
to implement a mobile workforce and
culture.

A mobile workforce enables us to do many things, but there

is no value in a workforce being mobile alone. It is all about what mobility enables us to accomplish that is so important. For starters, a mobile workforce allows us to be closer to our customers. This fact is likely sole justification for mobility.

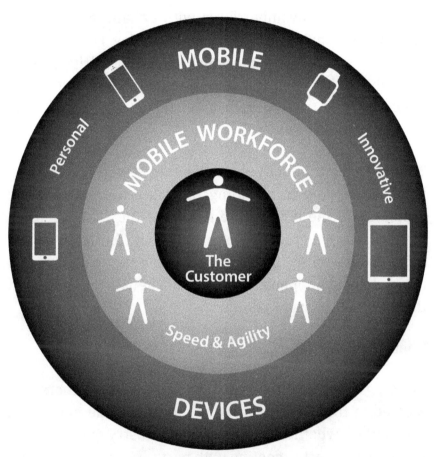

Figure 10.1 Mobility and IT

Figure 10.1 shows the layering of the mobility experience and lifestyle, starting with the customer at the middle. This is really the core value of mobility—our ability to move closer to the customer and spend more time in the market-place with no artificial tethers to the business or IT assets. The customer is then better served by the mobile workforce that is able to focus on the customer, and this workforce in turn benefits from great devices that are increasingly personal and innovative. This cycle of innovation has become a real-time improvement force with enhancements available to individuals and businesses every day. This cycle will not slow. There is just too much commerce driven today by mobility. The winners, of course, are consumers, and now alongside the consumer is the business and a mobile workforce.

We cannot be productive and effective in working in a mobile manner and in spending time face-to-face with our customers if the devices are not up to the challenge. The devices must be great so we can be great. Too often we are seduced by cool technology itself, when the real story and the real value happen only when this new technology is in the hands of the right people.

Then, amazing things happen.

Closely related to spending time with our customers, immersed in their world, is spending time in the market. In the market, whether it is attending industry events, meeting with prospects, meeting with partners, or building relationships with market influencers, we learn more when we experience, hear, and see information firsthand.

*These inputs are best when they are raw,
immediate, and unfiltered. This, after all,
is the reality of the market we serve, and
everything we need to know is here.*

This input then, these valuable feeds of information, are best experienced in person and immediately, which is only possible when we can go where needed and when needed as a mobile workforce armed with mobile devices that enable us to have access to the business information we need, quickly and easily.

CONVENIENT

The rapid rise of mobile devices in our lives and in the workplace has been driven by a single factor more so than all others—the convenience of using a device that we carry with us everywhere we go. This is very much in line with the blending of our personal and professional lives and the blurring of the traditional lines between "at work" and "at home" or "off duty" if you will. This is both a very good thing, and at the same time raises new questions and creates new challenges.

> *With the power of mobility and easy access*
> *to the resources of our business, when*
> *should we and when should we not?*

Again, not a simple issue and in many ways this question is inevitable as the world of business continues to evolve. The issue is multi-faceted in that it is not only about mobile devices that give us access to the resources of our employer, but this is extended further by a workforce that is increasingly mobile itself, and more workers who work in small offices or in home offices. We are accelerating toward a "work anywhere and anytime" model.

This model and the choices it brings is only possible when we are able to be productive while working in a mobile manner. If we cannot perform our jobs well when mobile, then many of these choices go away. We can't compromise the quality of work across the business. It fundamentally violates the principles of our business where we are called to do our best as individuals, which allows our teams and the business to do their best and which then enables us to better service our clients.

> *When the convenience of a mobile device offered and supported by IT allows our employees to be more responsive and productive, it enables our business to better serve our clients in a manner that is more transparent and more agile. This model is good for everybody.*

The model improves the quality of life for our people while growing loyal customers; our employees tend to stay with the business longer and grow valuable knowledge and experience, which further enhances customer satisfaction and customer loyalty. This is a powerful cycle that is directly supported by the convenience of mobile devices.

This brings us full circle back to the power of convenience.

FAST

In many ways the persona of mobility, taken as a single element, mirrors that of the future model for IT and its corresponding rebirth.

Another great example of this is the wonderful quality of speed. Reflecting on speed for a moment, we are reminded again of just how powerful *fast* can be. *Fast* always wants to get faster, and there is no limit to how fast we can become when this is a committed strategy and operating model. In the beginning, speed improvements can be relatively easy and bring us large leaps forward. Later, and as our models for speed become increasingly complete and sophisticated, progress might slow and our steps forward become a bit smaller. No matter, every improvement in speed is important, and the improvements we can make will never stop.

When we view IT as a single unified entity—which will increasingly become our mindset—the opportunities for speed are both compelling and virtually boundless.

Everywhere we look, we can find ways to move faster and complete our work in less time. It is important to remember throughout this journey-within-the-journey of speed amidst the rebirth of IT that <u>the ultimate winner in this wonderful power of speed is the customer</u>.

In this ongoing pursuit of speed, we need to be smart and ruthless about leveraging every tool, technology, process, and means at our disposal in order to achieve our continued steps forward in getting faster. One such valuable resource is mobility. In identifying all the good mobility can do for us, it is also important to realize it is simply an aid in arriving at the ultimate destination—a remarkably fast IT organization serving a thrilled and loyal customer.

Mobility is a natural and powerful complement to *fast*.

> **And remember, we are referencing both sides of the mobility model—the mobile worker amidst a mobile workforce and a powerful mobile device in the bag or pocket of the mobile worker.**

This is an increasingly powerful combination that directly enables the Imperative and the rebirth of IT. And there is even more good news. We should expect to see a continued and rapid improvement in the capabilities provided to us by the mobility model. In many ways we are just getting started; the next ten years will bring us quantum leaps in the power provided by mobility and deliver improvements we can't imagine today.

Taking this a step further, mobility will reveal to us many of the best elements of technology and IT in the future ahead of what we will experience elsewhere. The mobile platform enjoys a large level of investment and innovation because it now crosses over from a personal use and lifestyle model to professional use and, as such, receives a lot of attention from device, application, and communication vendors.

Regardless of what surprises mobility holds for us, we can be confident that speed will be central to the value we can realize in the rebirth of IT.

ROBUST & INNOVATIVE

For many, the thought of a mobile experience comes along with an expectation that this experience and therein its capabilities are limited. This is understandable given how mobility has evolved. With the birth of and then rise of mobility over the past fifteen years, the emphasis was on being mobile itself and the simple convenience this freedom creates.

> *These old biases will quickly fade away as we begin to experience just the opposite— the experience of mobility will begin to exhibit a more robust experience and more robust capability than any other model.*

This fundamentally goes against what many believe is a given for the mobility model. Once again, we shatter conventional wisdom, implement the Imperative, and make the rebirth of IT a reality.

This rise of power within the mobility experience further supports our fundamental mission—to win and retain thrilled and loyal customers. Yes, mobility plays a vital role in this primary mission. The rapid improvement of mobile capabilities simply helps us to accelerate the progress in our mission. The more robust the devices and the experience they provide, the better. This is a case of good combined with good.

Mobility itself is compelling and has been from the beginning. But now, with mobility providing our most robust experience and set of capabilities, we can accomplish what was not possible before. This combination gives us leverage and allows us to communicate, respond, and work in ways not possible before. Immediate access to all our tools and the ability to be proactive in how we work while we focus on results directly with our customers is an unbeatable model.

One example of the power of the mobile device is within applications that cross over from personal use to business use. These applications, which include browsers, calendars, and email, receive much attention from application providers as they have a large target market. We use these applications frequently in business and in our personal lives, and as such they represent a great place to start in accelerating the innovation curve for applications on a mobile device. This trend will continue, with the emphasis shifting to more business-oriented applications that will further break down the barriers to broader use of mobile devices to accomplish our daily work in business. The applications will include ERP, CRM, forecasting, order processing, and expense reporting as a set of use cases that are common for the mobile workforce and much more.

Innovation acceleration will continue for mobility for the next five to ten years, and we should expect to see this platform receive the majority of R&D focus; the return is simply so much larger, with the biggest and fastest-growing addressable market.

We are all winners. This will support everything we do every day, as the lines between our work and our personal time become further blurred.

Ultimately, they become one and we simply focus on the overarching needs of quality of life that brings work and play into the right balance.

PERSONAL

At the heart of the mobility experience is the ability to make it very much our own, a theme that will run through much of what we do in the rebirth of IT and reflective of how we are remaking our designs for how technology assists us every day.

This is turning the traditional model of technology upside down.

For some time the evolution of technology assumed a usage paradigm of a technology offering a compelling set of capabilities, and we as users then found ways to adapt to the technology in such a way that we could make the best possible use of what it offered. Not personal, but that was okay at the time because it was an improvement over the tools we had used previously.

Today, we are ushering in a new era characterized by technology that is more flexible, intelligent, and adaptable. This will forever change the usage paradigm—technology will adapt to what we need and how we want to use it to best fit our personal and professional use cases, which is very different from what we experienced before. It allows us to save precious time and be more efficient and more productive every minute of every day. It's not revolutionary when viewed through the lens of an hour or a day, but very much so when we look at the cumulative value of this model over the course of days, weeks, months, and years.

A wonderful example of this personal usage paradigm is mobility. It's not a stretch to call this one of the best, if not the best, examples of more personal technology, which then in turn enables us to deliver a product or service to a client in a manner that is more personal. If we can't be more personal in IT, it is very difficult to be more personal with our clients.

> *But when IT creates personal models for internal users, and takes a creative approach to making personal service a reality, this creates a powerful cycle that reaches from the core of our organization through the organization and all the way to our customers.*

Another great example of IT leading and innovating from within, changing how the business both thinks and acts in serving customers in new ways.

It is worth pressing harder on this point because it is so important. The business can be stalled, without our knowledge most of the time, in taking new and more creative approaches in how we deliver products or services to our clients because we are limited by the technology, systems, and data deployed internally.

These systems create a model for what we can and cannot do for our customers, which works both for us and against us. We can make this a good news story by committing to more personal models in IT and finding new, innovative ways to deliver personal service internally, changing our view of what is possible with our customers.

IT leads and the business follows where it can matter most—in better serving our customers.

AGILE

Mobility brings with it a natural agility, and an agile IT organization will begin to both influence and then change the business. In many respects, we can view agility as a difficult state to attain in IT given the complexity of our technology and many systems.

But an agile IT organization is now within our reach, and mobility is a powerful catalyst for this change. Due to perceptions of IT being many things but not agile, we have some work to do in overcoming this longstanding view. This, too, is okay. Let's view this as an opportunity to exceed expectations and to over deliver.

It is easy to get excited about agility because it spawns so much flexibility and value across IT. Let's look a little closer at how we can define agility within the context of IT.

An agile IT organization will exhibit the following:
1. Ability to rapidly deliver to new requirements from the business
2. Ability to quickly address changes in market conditions

3. Capacity to reassign resources and technology to address competitive threats
4. Design that aligns with new requirements from customers
5. Ability to maintain low cost associated with reconfiguring internal systems and technologies
6. Ability to mobilize easily in support of new initiatives
7. Design that is equally proactive and reactive as dictated by market conditions and business needs
8. Possessing a minimal set of hard assumptions that limit flexibility in supporting significant changes in the business or market
9. A fundamental commitment to lean and fast performance
10. A strategy to add new skills over time, therefore creating expanded creative and problem-solving capabilities

Note the central themes of fast, easy, and flexible.

And we must do all of this in a manner that is smart and does not take on unnecessary costs.

> *It is not enough to be agile at a high cost, or to dismiss agility in fear of taking on additional cost. This is not leadership.*

What the business needs from IT is lean and cost-effective agility. Agility that is innovative and proactive. This is the authentic leadership of IT.

As we charge forward in making the rebirth of IT a reality,

we look for opportunities to achieve multiple desirable outcomes with a single investment. A focus on mobility is one such opportunity. It naturally brings us speed, agility, and personalized service.

We should also note <u>the trajectory of mobility</u>. It is strong, evolving, and improving quickly, and as such we should expect much more value to come in the next ten years. With a little thoughtful planning, we can leverage this rapid ascent to support our strategies across IT—very much in support of the Imperative and very much a source of leverage.

COST EFFECTIVE

When we are able to take a big step forward with one of our dynamic improvements, including speed or personal service, and at the same time reduce costs, well, that is really something. This is the case with mobility.

We get strong secondary and tertiary benefits while we are enjoying the immediate benefits of working and playing in a mobile manner, which brings us back to the remarkable and powerful value of this model.

> *Mobility allows us to reduce costs by creating a simple and lean model for gaining— anytime and anywhere—access to company resources and at the same time reducing our dependency on physical facilities and tethered resources.*

Recall that we are discussing two sides of the mobility model—the device itself and the workforce, with both being mobile in nature. One enables the other. With this we have something transformative for IT and a model that changes perceptions and assumptions and removes limitations. As IT brings this model to the business, our business teams can think differently about how we work every day, and how we win new customers and better nurture existing customers. The scope of influence for mobility is remarkable.

By bringing the costs savings that come with *easy, anytime,* and *anywhere* access to our corporate systems and the freedom of a mobile workforce, we can then invest in additional areas that can bring us further returns. In today's IT, high-leverage investments include improved customer-facing systems, automation, and AI systems. While it would be fun to discuss these systems further, let's get back to mobility and cost effectiveness.

> *The savings are everywhere because what we have in mobility is the ultimate and naturally lean model.*

Lean in that we can do exactly what needs to be done, when it needs to be done, and how it needs to be done, with no overhead and no waiting. This brings with it an optimal cost model. And highlighting an awesome quality of this model is that we are able to take the benefits of this lean model in terms of time-savings for our people and then take that time and utilize it on other high-value projects.

This could be investing in the customer connection, automation, trans-IT business process design, or being available for advisory appointments with the business. All of this is strategic work and made possible by the time and cost savings of mobility.

As with many of the issues we discuss throughout the Imperative, this matter of savings has more to it than what meets the eye. Savings can occur at many levels, and it is important to be thoughtful when looking at how we best leverage these savings.

Money savings are nice. But time savings are precious and much harder to come by.

When we can create time savings, we effectively have generated an opportunity to change IT and the business; we have given our people the gift of time to think, which is nothing less than magnificent in what it represents.

KEY TAKEAWAYS: THE POWER OF MOBILITY

1. Don't be seduced by cool devices—the power of mobility is all about our ability to better serve our customers. The power in mobility is about people. Enabling the mobile workforce allows us to be more active in the market and to be better aligned with our customers and with prospects.

2. The evolution of mobile devices will never stop, so we need to build workforce models that can take advantage of any improvement in technology and devices that come our way over the next ten years. Mobility is two-sided—the devices themselves and the workforce that utilizes these devices.

3. Once offering limited capability, mobile devices are now getting lots of R&D attention from apps developers and are beginning to match or surpass the capabilities of other platforms. This creates the double benefit of offering both the freedom of mobility and the power of an innovative user experience, further accelerating the appeal of mobility.

4. Never underestimate the value of speed. There is a natural appeal in the speed of a mobile workforce and our ability to compress the cycles of elapsed

time necessary to get work done. This creates new and creative ways to deliver great service and great products to our customers. It also allows us to react more quickly to changes in the market. This is a powerful cycle.

CHAPTER 11

24X7

Increasingly, the clock of business does not stop. Demanding customers, a global marketplace, a virtual and mobile workforce, online commerce, the widespread adoption of Cloud, social media, and the accelerated evolution of devices have changed how we live, how we work, and our perception of the workday.

Boundaries have become blurred, and we expect to be always connected and always working, albeit not within the walls of an office. The future model of business will be "always on."

Because IT is the steward of our technology and data, we simply can't achieve our goal of operating the organization around the clock without IT leading the way. It is true that some IT services are available around the clock, and some IT infrastructure is always available.

> ### *Our mission is about making <u>everything IT</u> available 24X7.*

This has many implications, beginning with a change of mindset and both an acceptance and a commitment to make everything managed by IT operate **24X7**—unshackling the organization and removing limitations that exist today across the business.

It is an important example of how IT can act proactively, leading the business. If IT waits, the business is slowed, and it is only a matter of time before the business comes to IT with a request, or even more likely a mandate, to offer more services around the clock.

> ### *This is a failure on the part of IT—at this point it is too late, and opportunities have been lost.*

With the changing global market landscape, the continued growth of online commerce, and an increasingly greedy and demanding consumer, the need for 24X7 is inevitable. It is not an option. As most of you will agree, we can't wait. IT must lead the way.

This aggressive move to around-the-clock operations then frees our people to think differently about how we can perform our roles differently and better. Taking this further, this cycle encourages innovation and creative thinking without the traditional limitations of a nine-to-five business day. IT holds the key for this remarkable transformation from traditional business hours to around the clock.

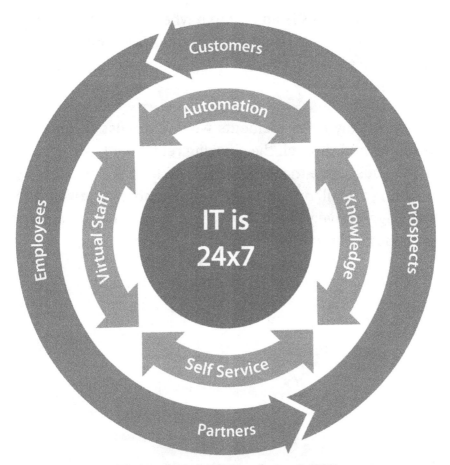

Figure 11.1 IT Leads to 24X7

Figure 11.1 reminds us that IT must be the 24X7 enabler of our workforce and culture so the business can be in a position to serve customers, partners, and the market around the clock. It is not just about our employees. This is only the beginning, where the customer is the end.

Because technology, systems, data, and devices are linked in making 24X7 a reality, the shift created by the around-the-clock model in our culture must be led by IT. There is no other way. This is an example where IT must be proactive in order to be ready when the business understands this is more than desired; it is mandatory to be successful in the market today.

As with many other elements we will discuss throughout the book and through the amazing rebirth of IT—the business needs, more than it knows, IT to lead the business by enabling the full organization to think more creatively and more aggressively about how we can service our customers without any limitations created by the schedule of IT.

IT will then be ready when the business is ready.

TAKING INVENTORY

When thinking about a transition from today to all of IT being available around the clock, we begin by taking stock of all services and asset availability. This includes everything—service delivery, asset availability, service requests, datacenter, security services... You get the idea. Everything.

We then place everything in one of three categories:

1. **Standard hours**

2. **Extended hours**

3. **24X7**

This gives us a baseline for what we have in the way of operating hours across IT today. The goal is to first understand and then to plan how we migrate each element on the list from the standard hours or extended hours of today to full **24X7** operation.

A few will be easy, some will be possible with careful planning and changing old assumptions, and a few will be quite difficult. This is to be expected.

A good place to begin is with the highest-volume tasks or business processes, or those that are the most strategic. In either case, start with elements that are well understood and not overly complex.

> *It is vital that we have early success to generate some momentum and nice recognition for the team.*

This will also allow us to validate a process to be used as we continue working through the list and develop our plans for the future. Be sure to communicate the **24X7 initiative** to the organization to get everybody involved and aware. Good ideas can come from anywhere and should be welcomed. This will also help foster recognition as we make progress and the results are noticed by the business—a chain reaction of synergies that will energize IT staff and business owners.

SIMPLIFY FIRST

The fastest and most productive path to successfully move an element from standard hours or extended hours to full **24X7** operation is the simplification of the task or business process. Simplification has many benefits, beyond bringing us closer to offering the element around the clock.

The benefits of *simple* include:

1. Faster
2. More consistent
3. Fewer mistakes
4. Fewer delays
5. Reduced risk
6. Better organizational understanding
7. Shorter learning curve for staff
8. Improved scalability
9. Reduced cost of upgrades
10. Reduced training costs
11. Lower cost of operations
12. Ease of engagement

The pursuit of simplifying tasks and business processes will also serve us well when looking at candidates for automation, our next step.

When looking to simplify, refuse to accept all the current standing assumptions. It is likely some number of these are flawed. Question everything.

Demand that every step, every approval, every check, anything that requires time or resource must be explained and justified in a clear manner. Set the bar high because any elimination of a step or a simplification pays back to us with the benefits highlighted earlier and much more. This is in fact a great micro-model for how we want to operate the IT of the future. Lean, fast, efficient, no waste, and consistent. This test should be applied here and to everything we do.

Let's not forget that this simplification also brings us closer to moving the element to full 24X7 operation. We get benefits immediately, and ultimately we meet our goal of operating around the clock.

AUTOMATE

A key contributor to the journey of our Imperative is automation. This is a recurring theme, as automation saves precious time and money, frees our people to work smarter, and creates leverage—leverage being one of those things that we pursue in recognition of the remarkable value it can deliver.

After we have done an exhaustive review of all tasks and business processes from our full IT inventory, and the simplification process is complete, we turn our attention to what elements on the list can be automated.

> *The simplification review has scrubbed the tasks and business processes of waste and should leave us with a unit of work that is better equipped to be automated.*

With the improved tools of today, and the dawning of AI and learning systems, we have vastly improved assets at our disposal to make automation a reality. It is a good practice to start simple and automate common tasks that are not complex and occur often. These tasks can be common steps in a business process or a business rule. Automation can take many forms, and our improved tools make automation more flexible.

A good example is an email listener. The listener can be a simple piece of automation that watches an IT email inbox and either automatically creates an alert or takes some other form of action when an email is received. This is good for many reasons. But you get the idea. We want to identify every task or business process that can be automated, as each one that we complete brings us closer to 24X7 operation. It is normally necessary to do this incrementally over a period of months or years, and this is very much acceptable. We can accomplish big things with small and measured steps. The key here is to start the journey to 24X7 now for all of IT, and it will soon become a reality. The first step is the hardest. With this step we begin to build momentum. Then, with every bit of progress, we begin to believe that 24X7 is possible for all of IT, which changes the mindset of our people and the culture.

SELF-SERVICE

Self-service merits a place in this discussion because it has proven to be a very effective tool for IT and as such is a natural for the 24X7 model. Not often seen a decade ago, self-service tools are now developing a strong track record in IT organizations of all sizes.

To keep things simple, we will include service catalog, a rising star in IT today, in this discussion because it shares many qualities with self-service.

While self-service is often focused on managing incidents, and service catalog is best focused on service requests, they share a number of important qualities:

1. Relatively short implementation times
2. Reasonable costs to deploy
3. A great fit for 24X7 operation
4. Lends itself to a simple and friendly user experience
5. Supports cost tracking and accountability
6. Provides a timely response to users
7. Low cost of operations

8. Flexible user/customer access model
9. Often operates in a fully automated manner
10. Easy access by way of mobile devices

These qualities are very real and not a big stretch for IT in most cases.

Put another way, it would be hard to find another tool/process that offers more bang for the buck than the pair of self-service and service catalog in IT today.

Scanning the qualities listed above, it is also easy to see why self-service is a good fit for our push to achieve around-the-clock operations. In most cases we are able to fully automate this process and at the same time create a very happy user. Just when you think there could not possibly be more good news about self-service, it also provides a very cost-effective operating model while achieving the benefits of *fast* and *convenient.* This is a great example of leverage and goes back to the heart of the Imperative.

If your organization has successfully implemented self-service and/or service catalog, and many IT organizations have, it is likely you created and utilized some process for designing the user experience and the automation that makes these models possible. Take advantage of the work that has been done and leverage the success that has been enjoyed. There is no need to recreate the processes we described earlier.

STAFFING

In the spirit of our rebirth of IT, we are required to rethink our assumptions about staffing. We simply can't take for granted that the 24X7 model requires around-the-clock staffing as we know it today. In some cases, we can operate IT 24X7 at current or possibly reduced levels of staffing.

We get a big assist from automation, self-service, and mobile devices, to name a few, and this affords us the opportunity to completely rethink staffing. Where is staffing of the highest impact? How can we deploy staffing to make IT more strategic?

It is also possible, with this fresh look at staffing, to accomplish the goals of 24X7 operations while at the same time providing the necessary staff for the key functions of IT.

Remember, this does not require us to operate in the traditional model of staff members sitting behind a desk in a corporate office.

We can take advantage of call forwarding to mobile phones, chat tools, remote control, and email. These tools allow us to maintain a standard of responsiveness while making the 24X7 staffing model more achievable. In some cases, our people will prefer working in these modes over keeping traditional office hours. For example, an IT analyst might prefer to take a shift on a live chat forum from home in the evening, versus being physically in the office during normal day hours.

Often, it is as simple as meeting with IT staff and determining the preferences and flexibility of the individual members of the team and how we can accomplish the goals of 24X7 operation while maintaining and perhaps improving the staff's quality of life. This might not get us to a 100 percent solution, but it's a good start. We can also take advantage of staff distributed geographically to cover the necessary hours. Staff in the UK and Europe can take calls or support live chat in the off-hours in the US, and the US can return the favor in the off-hours of the UK and Europe, for example. This can support 24X7 operations more readily than we might at first think.

In the case of a single-country operation, we can apply a similar mini-model, especially if the country spans multiple time zones, like the US, with four time zones to utilize. We can take full advantage of this by having staff on Pacific Time provide coverage of late hours on Eastern Time, and Eastern Time staff cover early hours on Pacific Time. You get the idea.

Another creative solution is implementing a four-workday

week, with ten hours per workday with staggered staff hours. This brings the benefit of a four-day workweek, which is attractive to many staff members, while at the same time expanding our coverage of hours in each day and the days of each week. With some thoughtful and creative planning, we can get the coverage we need with our staffing for the 24X7 operations model.

ALERTS

The smart use of automated alerts can be a valuable asset in our push to operate IT around the clock. When conditions arise that require action, alerts can get the attention of a staff member immediately, and the necessary actions can be taken without delay where otherwise the business could be waiting. This is the best of automation and people working together.

In most cases, we can operate automated processes outside traditional hours, but when the expertise of a human staff member is required, an alert can drive the necessary action at a very small cost—a time- and cost-effective model. Alerts must be designed such that the right level of information and context is included. It should be fast and easy for the staff member to access the right information and then take action. If information is lacking and difficult to access, we have introduced further delays, which is bad for all parties.

A smart alert both provides the alert itself but also accompanying information that enables decision making and immediate action.

This is very much possible with the automation tools available in the market today. Taking it a step further, we can leverage technology to set the right thresholds or business rules that constitute conditions that would merit an alert and to distinguish between these conditions and when an alert would not be necessary.

A good model is to have an initial level of warning that indicates a growing risk but that conditions have not yet reached the threshold of an alert. This pre-alert can often prevent the need for an alert, just as an alert can prevent the underlying issue, which then prevents any impact or downtime for the business.

This multi-layer alert and response model enables our teams to take some proactive actions to prevent the occurrence of an alert. In many cases the prevention work effort is but a fraction of what will be required to fully cure the issues associated with an alert.

When implementing IT tools—be it Security, Asset Management, Service Management, or others—it is important to ensure the tools you will leverage have the automation required to support this three-level warning and alert model. In some cases, it could make sense to have a four-level model with single or double cases of early warning added prior to an alert.

MOBILE ACCESS

The quality and flexibility of mobile applications and mobile devices have improved dramatically in the past five years. To a large degree, business has been the beneficiary of advancements driven by the consumer marketplace, where innovation pressures are tremendous. The ability of the IT workforce to utilize applications on a mobile device gives us further support for around-the-clock operations.

Many security, service desk, and asset management functions can now be performed at any time and from anywhere on a mobile device. This was not possible only a few years ago.

The flexibility of mobile access then allows us to perform necessary work while at home, traveling, or simply outside the office. This can be planned work or a response to an incident, a security threat, or an alert.

*This model further blurs the line
between business and personal, which is
increasingly becoming the norm.*

And it is okay with most staff, as it comes with more flexibility around our lifestyle and family time. This flexibility on hours and location benefits both employee and business in that the company saves money when an employee is not required to keep normal business hours in the office, and the employee enjoys the benefits of working from home, when done in a productive manner.

The advances we have seen with the function, power, and convenience of mobile devices have made this model productive.

This is all a matter of timing. The performance of the mobile device, the desire of IT staff to have more flexible schedules, and the desire of the company to transition to around-the-clock operations—all of these goals are aligned and will help make 24X7 a reality.

Of course, from a staffing standpoint our people have different needs and preferences, but that can be managed between employee and employer and is increasingly well understood.

This is an opportunity to improve the quality of life for our employees while accomplishing the goals of IT for staffing. We should not assume that the business or the employee will suffer.

That is simply not the case with the improved tools and resources we have available today. Much of this was not possible just a few years ago, but the timing of our push to 24X7 operations is good.

CHAT AND MORE

Chat tools are another good option to help us move closer to 24X7 operations—*good* today and moving to *great* in the next few years. A chat session with an expert can be quick, helpful, and cost-effective. These sessions can be conducted from anywhere and at any time, which provides flexibility for the IT staff and for the employee or customer on the other side of the dialogue.

In many cases it is not necessary to speak live with an agent; chat is able to answer any questions an employee or customer might have. As an added bonus, these sessions are typically short—just a few minutes. Customer satisfaction is high with chat when done well, and we get a lot of bang for our money in this model.

Another natural benefit of chat is the reduced language issues (versus speaking live with a person) and the ability to utilize staff in other locations, including globally.

***This makes chat a natural for a virtual
team and for virtual hours.***

We can make rolling staff assignments to cover a chat option for users that partially or fully closes the gap in our push to move services to 24X7 coverage.

These preceding comments are assuming our model of today with a human on the other end of a chat session, but this is changing now. New, exciting models are emerging that will automate the chat session with an intelligent and automated assistant that leverages the knowledge base and AI capabilities to provide a great experience and an even more cost-effective model that further frees our people to be applied to more strategic projects.

> *These automated and intelligent chat agents, now often referred to as chat bots, will become the norm over the next five years and help accelerate us toward around-the-clock operations.*

We should view this advancement as a valuable extension to the overall chat experience, but it should not imply the human element will be removed entirely. Where the majority of chat sessions at this writing are with a human agent, this will become the minority in the future, but will not be driven entirely to 0 percent. This should not be expected nor is it desired for a number of reasons.

> *Some types of chat sessions and subject matter will require a human agent, but this is a good thing.*

Let the automation carry the standard interactions and allow our human experts to focus on the more strategic, value-added, or complex interactions. This is a good model that will be repeated throughout the book—automation and AI are best when offloading our people and allowing them to focus on more unique interactions with customers and in finding better and smarter ways to work.

We can also leverage humanity where we need sympathy, emotion, specialized knowledge, a sense of humor, or advanced reasoning skills. There will also be cases where automation and smart systems help us to move much faster, which is another desirable behavior and directly supports the model of 24X7. This gives us leverage.

EXPERTS ON CALL

Experts will always be valuable and will always have a place in our staffing plans. This is a timeless requirement for IT. The key in the rebirth of IT is to use our experts at the right time and in the right way.

The majority of our actions and escalations do not require assistance from an expert. This is increasingly true given our improved knowledge and search tools. But as we look to expand the operations of IT to 24X7, there will be times when the specific knowledge of an expert is required. This need does not go away with 24X7; we simply need to manage it a little differently.

Traditionally, experts have been available during normal business hours, so it was simple. But in the 24X7 model we can require access to our experts at any time.

This requires a level of planning and, in many cases, a rotation of experts on call.

We need to understand the domain expertise of our experts,

and plan for coverage such that we don't have unnecessary overlap of our experts on call, and at the same time we don't have gaps in coverage.

As knowledge, automation, and AI tools improve, our dependency on human experts will be reduced, but it is equally important to understand it will never go away completely. People experts remain a path of escalation and for specialized expertise. People experts will be leveraged for strategic customers and partners. People experts are uniquely qualified to help with high-impact customer issues.

This is what we are planning for—to ensure an expert is available at all times for those special cases when they are singly qualified to address an issue, diagnose a risk or problem, or answer a question. But we must see this as a virtual resource requirement and not simply the expert in question sitting in the office as we have assumed for so many years.

This is another case where we can better leverage virtual teams across multiple locations.

The expert skill is simply another dimension laid across this model.

The most fundamental dimension is staffing of the core skills for standard IT operations, and we extend that model to include the specialized skills in order to support specific activities. This is a general concept that is important to the Imperative—recognize, value, and leverage knowledge and expertise.

We then extend this concept to address our needs for 24X7 operations, recognizing that our push to operate around the clock does not excuse us from making the right expertise available, albeit in a more efficient and leaner model.

VIRTUAL TEAMS

Virtual teams are a powerful and simple concept that have become a reality and will have a place in the operation of most IT organizations. This has been made possible by many factors, including the prevalence of mobile devices, the widespread availability of information via the Internet, advancements in automation tools, the reality of global businesses and global markets, and more. Virtual teams are both a necessity and a great asset when managed well.

A good benchmark for virtual teams performing well is an improved customer experience (both internal and external customers) at a constant or reduced cost. And in many cases we can do this in less time. The implications of this model are huge.

This is an embodiment of **better, faster, cheaper.**

Beyond a useful strategy for the normal operations of the business, these virtual teams are in direct support of our push to 24X7 operations. Virtual teams will normally take advantage of multiple staff members in multiple locations working closely together to provide staffing coverage for IT operations. This is not rocket science—simply a reasonable level of planning and coordination.

These locations and team members can be local, within the same city. They can be regional or global—the model is the same. Only the details and scale change to fit the need and the staff.

The governing concept is leveraging these team members who together provide the necessary coverage for a desired schedule. In this discussion we are focused on 24X7 operations, and we would utilize the team to take this step from the normal hours or extended hours that are kept today.

A simple example would be an IT organization with staff in Los Angeles and London, each operating on standard or extended hours locally. In the push to move to 24X7 operations, we can take advantage of these two teams, evaluate the skills required, plan for the eight-hour time difference, and finally create and implement a plan to provide 24X7 IT staffing at both locations. Some of this then becomes virtual work, but this is okay—the model has been proven to be very effective.

KEY TAKEAWAYS: 24X7

1. Self-service is a natural part of the around-the-clock capability of IT. The model of self-service is at its best when kept simple, allowing users to accomplish what is necessary in an easy and economical manner. This pays back to us by saving time and money and growing happy users.

2. Automation is a powerful glue that holds together and drives an increasingly large part of IT operations. An exciting benefit of automation is that once in place, it can operate with no breaks, no days off, and no distractions. There are many other benefits of automation, but at the heart of what it does best is in line with our need to always be ready.

3. Powerful mobile devices and the growth of the mobile workforce both demand and directly support 24X7 operations. Internal and external customers demand 24X7, while at the same time, the people of IT have vastly improved resources with which to make 24X7 a reality. This is the circle of business and the cycle of renewal.

4. We need to think about our people differently. Our staff becomes a strategic resource and complements the improved automation and smart systems

that can fulfill many of the standard needs of our customers and of IT. This offloads our people to address more advanced and more valuable needs. These needs will occur around the clock, and we must employ creative schedules and staffing models to make our experts available at the right time to keep the business moving.

CHAPTER 12

CULTURE AND PEOPLE

So much of what comes to life in the rebirth of IT is driven by our people, by the wonderful humanity of IT.

Repeatedly I make the point that is at the core of the book— technology is powerful and continues to improve, and today technology can do things that we could not have imagined just a few years ago.

Remarkably this cycle will never stop. But what will ultimately drive the rebirth of IT is our people and our culture. The technology gives us a valuable helping hand, but our people make it happen at the end of the day.

Figure 12.1 The Amazing Storm of IT Culture

Figure 12.1 shows the swirl of forces that are within and surrounding the remaking of our culture in IT. This is the internal-only view, of course. As you will see throughout the book, in most figures we show the customer at the middle or driving the process, but in this case we want to focus on an internal model.

We build the culture by empowering each individual, which then propels our teams and energizes and shapes our culture through a number of important forces that include the ever-present customer and a spirit of passion, collaboration, business mindset, and creative experimentation, to name a few. Each force is critical in its own right and brings balance to all others.

As the wonderful rebirth of IT unfolds before us, there will be necessary changes in our culture that will first start us on this new journey and then accelerate these remarkable changes. The culture of IT will work fundamentally differently and will include new roles, new compensation, new priorities, a new organization, and much more.

> *One simple example of this is turning IT from an orientation that is vertical in nature to one that is horizontal in nature.*

This shift moves us from the myopic nature of the past to the holistic view of the future. With a broader view of IT and of the business, we can make more balanced decisions that consider the needs of the business and the cross-functional implications of everything we do.

> *The new cultural model will offer a powerful attraction for new people with new skills.*

The domain experts of IT today will remain an important part of the future but will increasingly work on cross-functional teams with priorities, deliverables, and schedules more closely aligned with the key initiatives of the business which then take on a life within IT. This will bring to life something that we have discussed for the past ten years but have not often achieved—a true alignment between IT and the business and IT delivering key elements of corporate initiatives.

As we create this alignment, we further drive a cultural shift in IT by creating a business approach to how we run the organization versus the traditional technology and project focus. These IT projects were often formed and directed by IT leadership, but the project teams themselves had very little if any broader visibility into the strategy behind, and any connection to the business.

This lack of context and connection creates many challenges for the team and for all of IT as we are lacking the understanding that is so important for good decision making and awareness, as opposed to simply working heads-down and mouth-shut toward the next milestone.

> *With understanding comes awareness, and with awareness comes enlightenment, and with enlightenment comes conviction, and then everything changes.*

PASSION & HOPE

Passion is a powerful force, possibly the most powerful force of all for the successful transformation of a culture, and a good place to start our discussion on culture and people. Technology alone won't make our future; it is about people and how we work every day.

Hope fuels passion by giving us a sense of optimism, the strong belief that we can be better and the future holds promise.

Although there are certainly IT cultures that have a high degree of passion, this is not a widely accepted standard nor something at the top of the priority list for the IT organization of the past.

This must change.

Passion is remarkable in its ability to transform lives and overcome obstacles.

I would make the case that passion and hope are the only things that can overcome some of the most difficult obstacles that lie ahead. Hand in hand with passion is joy, and it deserves mention because passion in the absence of joy is not enough. Passion and hope together create joy, and these three powerful emotions are all but unstoppable.

Passion, hope, and joy regulate one another. Joy regulates passion and keeps some fun in the mix of what passion can bring us. Passion regulates hope, keeps us focused, and drives us relentlessly forward with action, moving us beyond a feeling. Traveling the journey that lies ahead and finding success along the way will leave us lacking—we need to have some fun and not just *make* the journey but *enjoy* the journey as well.

As we enjoy this remarkable transformation of IT through the years that lie ahead of us, we will push ourselves and our teammates to work in a way that is more focused and calls us to accomplish more in the day. This push requires resolve and requires a level of intensity that elevates our standard of performance.

As we make the transition to a new culture, and that transition must begin now, each of us should do some soul-searching and ask of ourselves some fundamental questions:

1. Am I excited about being part of IT?
2. Am I ready to commit to the transformation of IT?
3. Am I prepared to change much of what we do today and how we work?
4. Am I ready to leave behind some of the old ways of running IT and embrace a new model for our daily operations?

5. Can I bring the necessary passion and joy to our work every day?
6. Can I embrace a new focus on our customers?
7. When challenges come, and they will come, am I prepared to do whatever it takes to overcome them?
8. Am I prepared to be an ambassador for IT to the remainder of the organization and to our customers?
9. Can I commit to be a good teammate within IT and across the business?
10. Am I open to new ideas and willing to bring new ideas to the team?

Just a few questions from what is a much longer list, of course, but it is a good exercise. We need to be honest with ourselves.

Life is short. We should accept nothing less than working in a business we can believe in and being part of something special.

If we are not in a place that we can commit to and be excited about embracing this big change and journey, we owe it to ourselves, our teammates, and our families to find a company and an organization we can commit to and be excited about.

If we can answer these questions with an enthusiastic "Yes," that is an important leap forward. So let's get to work. This is our time.

CUSTOMER FOCUS

As powerful as passion and joy and hope are, they must be connected to something—a higher calling that brings clarity and solidarity to our passion. And this something can only be the customer.

Passion and joy and hope cannot be sustained when pointed inwardly—they must be focused and propelled by a cause, and there is no more powerful cause than the customer.

No remake of IT and therefore a remake of the culture of IT can be complete without a new commitment to the customer.

The closer we look at this connection, the more clear it becomes that the customer is both the beginning and the end.

The customer is the best source of requirements for the products and services we deliver, and the customer completes the cycle of our business by defining success that is the completion of our business processes and all the work performed by the organization.

When in doubt, talk to a customer and everything becomes clear. We have too often lost this connection and clarity in business today and in IT organizations that suffer from the same diluted understanding of what the customer really needs.

In many cases the IT organization has functioned one, two, or even three levels removed from the customer. This must now be seen by IT as unacceptable, and we will create a direct connection to the customer that removes any interpretation and translation of customer requirements before they reach the eyes and ears of IT.

This translation both slows the flow of information and creates a risk that key facts and context are lost in the translation. This is not to suggest that existing customer relationships in sales, marketing, services, and support will go away. That is certainly not the case. The direct customer connection with IT will complement and in some cases enhance these existing connections.

The partnership with IT will only serve to strengthen the customer partnership and will be something the customer welcomes.

Both IT and the customer will understand this enhanced partnership, and additional communications with IT will ultimately improve and accelerate the solutions our business will deliver to its customers.

And there is another benefit to this direct connection: the fueling of the customer-directed passion and joy that are so important to building the new culture of IT. It makes the passion more personal and more directed—at the customer, of course. This is a great enhancement to our culture, and with this new focus, so many good things will follow across every individual and every team in IT.

THE DEATH OF THE SILO

Virtually every IT organization has evolved in a way that created some number of silos, and those silos remain today. The silos were built out of necessity and over time, built around our people experts and the tools these experts used to complete their work every day. These people and these tools were very much focused on fixing immediate problems, of removing pain points if you will. This was tactical, yes, but very much necessary and understandable. With a few small variations, this has been the operating model of IT for thirty years—localized knowledge fixing localized problems with localized technology. A bottoms-up and brute-force lifestyle, and made successful, even remarkably successful given the circumstances, by the talented and hardworking people of IT.

We will look at these silos again in Chapter 7, The Unification of IT, but the context here is cultural, and we simply can't remake the culture of IT without eliminating the silos that slow us down and cloud our vision.

Let me explain. A silo is built around a particular function of the IT organization—for example, security, service desk, servers, the PMO, desktops, or the datacenter.. These can vary from organization to organization, but these are common examples. This function is then supported by technology, software applications, people, and the organization itself that is focused on this single function.

This singularity created and has sustained the silo as we know it today.

The day-to-day operations of this organization are in kind driven by and defined by this single same function. The co-ordination and visibility across silos vary, but are normally limited simply because the silo teams are busy with their function and because there is no real opportunity to think or act more broadly. Their plate is full with the deliverables and priorities of the day, all of which are built around the silo.

It all makes perfect sense. But there is a problem.

While the structure and evolution of the silo are logical, they were born of the world as we knew it in the '80s and '90s during the birth and growth of IT. The world we live in today is very different, and the rate of change is growing faster. The simple fact is that the silo now stands in our way of transforming IT.

The silo slows us down, limits automation, limits visibility, hinders communication, and makes proactive action much more difficult. These are just a few examples, but the closer we look, the more clear it becomes that the silo is a natural enemy of the Imperative, and as such it must go.

But this is okay. What we will find is that the elimination of silos will follow a natural course, and with each step we will begin to see big benefits.

With the completion of each step toward our goal of removing the silos of IT, our task becomes a little easier. It is then easier to take the next step, and with this quickening we are building some real cultural momentum. Our people will notice this and will feel it and know it is right; this will build the confidence of our teams, and confidence is a very powerful thing indeed.

CLARITY & RUTHLESSNESS

Clarity and ruthlessness go hand in hand. We naturally assume ruthlessness is a negative thing, but it has a meaningful, positive side. Clarity brings us a strong understanding of exactly what we must do and what we must not do. Clarity helps us to make the right choices and to create the right priorities. Clarity unites our people and our teams, bringing us a common purpose. In the absence of clarity, confusion takes over and slows us down and creates waste. A wonderful quality of clarity is simplicity, and we can say that clarity done well is always simple but not to be confused with *easy*.

Ruthlessness then gives us the resolve to execute in line with clarity and to not waver. Ruthlessness pushes us to make the tough choices that must be made. Ruthlessness bolsters us when distractions threaten to take us off course.

A high-performing organization of any type will virtually always be clear on what they are working to achieve, normally driven by a common understanding of a vision and goals that support the vision. This is the body of clarity that will bring IT together.

A mission statement for IT brings a sense
of unity and common purpose to our
people and removes any doubt, confusion,
or tentativeness that might exist.

This should speak to the IT organization while being in alignment with the business. The mission statement, done well, answers many questions in itself and brings us back to what is truly important and what is not.

The "what is not" part is very important, because we can't do everything, and this clause needs to remind us of which goals we should be focused on. Normally, two to three goals should earn our full focus. Anything more than this and we are diluting our efforts.

Each goal should pass a simple test: Is it something that is truly critical at this time? Do we have full control over our ability to pursue the goal? Do we have the necessary time and resources to be successful? If we can answer yes to all three questions, then this goal should make our short list of two or three. If needed, a tiebreaker can be the *degree* to which we meet each of the three qualifiers and our likelihood of being successful.

We should, after all, demand and expect
success of ourselves.

This structure of mission and goals is much more common in business than in IT today. But as we look to drive more of a business mindset and encourage more business-like behaviors in IT, the time has come for us to create and reinforce the mission and the goals that will allow us to organize and mobilize our resources.

As an example of a clear mission statement, we can likely relate to the following, which comes from a company most of us have had some experience with:

"To be earth's most customer-centric company; to build a place where people can come to find and discover anything they might want to buy online."

The company is Amazon, and they continue to live by this simple purpose today.

With a simple and compelling mission statement in place and a core set of a few goals in support of the mission, we can go to work. What we need now is a ruthless approach to monitoring and evaluating our focus.

This focus must be narrow and will require us to say no far more often than yes.

This is good, not bad, and if anything, it's an indication we have the required clarity of purpose.

It is easy to say yes, but this is a lifestyle that can lead to us losing our way. Saying yes to the wrong projects and initiatives can undermine our focus and all but ensure we are not successful.

Highly successful organizations stay true to the mission while achieving the critical goals and are able to maintain a high level of focus for an extended period of time. We use the term *ruthless* here as a very good quality for IT—being consistent, clear, and aggressive in continuously qualifying and communicating how and where we invest our time and resources. The *clear* and *consistent* part of this formula relates to the connection to our mission and goals.

For the rebirth of IT, we need more clarity and ruthlessness—qualities that will help us to pass the many tests we encounter every day.

INITIATIVES VERSUS PROJECTS

The deliverables and schedules of IT are normally constructed around projects today, and these projects are in turn aligned around our functional silos. This creates a limited scope, a limited degree of visibility, and further and most concerning, a natural misalignment with the business. Again, this all makes sense as these projects are born within IT and normally constructed by IT management.

One key concept is the creation of these projects from within IT. Born in IT, aligned with IT, staffed with IT.

> *To fundamentally change this model, we look first to customers and then to the business. In both, we will have a willing partner.*

As our silos are systematically removed, we begin to stretch, in a very good way, the visibility of our people and our culture. With this improved visibility comes improved understanding and a greater awareness for all IT. Then, through this natural evolution that brings us a broader and more complete understanding of IT, we can begin to better understand the needs of the business and how IT can align itself with the initiatives of the business.

Taking this one step further, given we are creating direct connections with our customers as described in Chapter 2, we are able to now triangulate the needs of the business with those of the customer.

When this is done, we will have a very good understanding of how we can construct the IT initiatives of the future. Note this triangulation (IT/Customer/Business) is important because while it is vital that we have a direct view of customer requirements, when done to the exclusion of internal business needs, it is too one-dimensional and will create problems. Likewise, a focus on business requirements with limited understanding of the customer creates an even bigger set of challenges.

Perhaps the single biggest risk for IT today and into the future is a lack of understanding how we make the lives of our customers better.

But with this focus on both the business and the customer (and a direct line of communication with both), we can now construct our IT priorities, deliverables, and timelines in a way that has the biggest impact and creates the most leverage.

This initiative structure is very different than the IT project of the past, which was in many cases one-dimensional; these projects were largely constructed around the needs of IT with little or no visibility of the business and the customer.

An additional benefit of this initiative orientation is the new opportunity this creates for the people of IT who will be staffing and leading these initiatives. As part of the team, they will naturally gain new insights and a new understanding of the business and customer requirements that bring life to our triangulation model. This is a very powerful enablement model that begins to fundamentally change the culture of IT—driving how our people think and act every day and shaped by our customers and our business owners.

P&L VERSUS COST CENTER

IT has most often been seen as a cost center, and in most cases sees itself in the same way. The external view of the organization reinforces this perception and has unfortunately put IT into this tactical cost model. This might at first glance seem like a small thing, but there is much more than meets the eye to this issue.

Part of what we need to accomplish with the transformation of IT is to bring a business orientation to IT. One integral part of this shift is the manner in which we manage the financial models that govern IT.

When viewing IT through the lens of a cost center, we focus on expenses and expense line items to the exclusion of all else. This limits our view, our understanding, and our actions. It is effectively a simplistic view of what is a robust and complex model.

The transformation of IT calls us to raise the level of

awareness for all the people in IT as it relates to the operations of IT as well as the alignment with the business. A more complete understanding of IT budgets is an important part of the awareness, and transparency in this case is a very good thing. The future will see us operating IT as a business—this is not possible without a financial view that evolves to a P&L orientation.

This would be viewed as unorthodox by the IT leadership of the past but makes a lot of sense and is a catalyst for changing IT culture. The more our people know, the more effective we can be in aligning across IT and then with the business. Transparency and access to information enable us to create empowered IT staff and accountability. The teams across IT can't be expected to run their respective teams and IT like a business if we don't arm them with the right information.

Although revenue and margin/profit information won't be readily available in some cases, we should start to ask the question which then creates a demand for the right information, and with this, it will come.

The closer we get to a true P&L, the better we can fulfill our goal of creating the needed business orientation. It is a beautiful thing to witness—when our good people naturally gravitate to doing the right thing for the business, driving the organization to success.

This is a significant shift from the traditional model where visibility of financial data was so limited in scope and depth, our team managers, senior managers, and directors—really the valuable mid-level management of the company—were largely blind to the workings of the business and therefore limited in their decision making and ability to support business strategy.

This is under our control and must change.

A NEW SKILLSET

With the understanding that we must operate IT in a different way, we will come to the further understanding that new skills will be required to drive and then operate in this new model.

> *It would be easy to jump to the conclusion that these new skills will replace the existing skills in IT, but that is not the case. The existing expertise around disciplines— including security, applications, servers, endpoints, and service desk, to name a few—will remain important.*

What we will see is an extension of these existing skills with the new skillset, which might require training of existing staff and in some cases the addition of new staff. Knowing we don't have the luxury of adding lots of new headcount, we need to be smart and thrifty about how these new skills are added to the organization. We will defer the *how* discussion for the moment and look at the *what*.

The necessary new skills are a complement to our increased business focus. Our priority is to manage IT more holistically every day and in a way that increases the visibility of the corporate business strategy.

Put another way, we can only create the leverage we need in IT through the unified efforts of all IT teams working toward a common goal. This seems like common sense, but yet remarkable in that much if not most of the work performed in the traditional IT model has been localized, with a localized view and toward silo-based goals.

Some would make the point that the best IT organizations have moved closer to the unified model, but those cases would be the exception and not the rule. When the typical IT organization is working in the high-leverage model across all of IT, then we know a corner has been turned. But we are simply not there today.

While we don't have a name for it today, for the purposes of this discussion we will call one of the new roles the IT business manager.

This role has two key functions—working directly with customers to define and validate key business and systems requirements and then working across the full IT organization to coordinate and communicate all actions necessary to deliver a successful solution.

The business manager will possess a combination of business and technology skills and be able to translate customer business requirements into technology specifications that will fulfill the customer needs. It would be fair to draw a parallel with the role of product manager—a strong combination of communication skills, business acumen, and technical expertise.

Think of the IT business manager as a rising star in the IT organization, with a well-rounded and widely talented skillset. Yes, a few of these exist today in IT organizations around the world, but they are not common. When we do begin to mobilize this new role in the future, these talented individuals will have an immediate impact. It will be a high-profile role on staff to the CIO, or reporting directly to a VP IT.

This is but one example of new roles and new skills that will emerge across the IT organization as we embark on this exciting transformation reflected by the elements of the Imperative. There will certainly be other roles that will be driven by our strategic themes of the unification of IT, the new cadence of IT, automation, and of course the customer connection.

New roles without this sense of purpose simply don't make sense.

EXPERIMENTATION

Two powerful cultural characteristics are the willingness to try new things, and the acceptance of failure as a good thing—as a valuable means to learn and to ultimately get better.

> **The fear of failure can be paralyzing for individuals, for teams, and for a large organization.**

This is very much cultural and something every person in the organization understands—is it okay to make mistakes or is it not? Is it okay to try a new approach with the understanding we might not get the desired results immediately? Does our culture encourage some level of risk taking and new creative approaches as a means to learn and improve our daily performance?

This is a discussion that is relevant to IT because the traditional IT model has been conservative, averse to change, averse to risk, and generally against errors or mistakes. This has been the case for many reasons, and many of these reasons were valid in the past. But today is fundamentally different and calls for fundamental changes in our culture.

For example, with our new emphasis on speed as a strategic measure of the performance of IT, it is very difficult to get the speed improvements we must have if we don't create a culture that encourages some level of experimentation and some level of risk taking. Of course, we can't be reckless. But we need to appreciate that with experimentation comes learning, and from learning comes discovery, and from discovery we find fundamentally better and smarter ways to work every day. This is a journey that can profoundly change IT and the business.

> *This journey begins with the understanding that these valuable improvements would simply never be discovered without some level of trial and error.*

There is another important element of risk taking that needs to be recognized—experimentation brings with it a sense of energy and fun. We all have a desire to do something new, to explore, and we love the excitement that comes along with a degree of the unknown, not knowing what might lie ahead on a new path.

This excitement and energy can only be tapped if our people have the full support and encouragement of the organization and leadership. Excitement spreads quickly and is contagious. It is empowering to our people and ultimately can lead to a few breakthroughs that can raise the performance of IT to the next level. Much of this is closely related to the goals we have around innovation, and this experimentation is not just a technology thing. With experimentation it is true that we can build better systems, but we can also find better ways to work every day. This can include simple improvements or efficiencies that can together add up to big value and big time savings. We should never grow tired of asking questions like *Why? What if? Could we?* and more.

Fail fast, try again, and stay curious. This mindset and the cultural value it brings has been at the heart of innovative breakthroughs for hundreds of years. From Leonardo da Vinci to Thomas Edison to the successful innovators of today, this should have a place in the makeup of our IT culture and for the rebirth over the next ten years.

A BUSINESS APPROACH

As we implement the Imperative and undertake this wonderful transformation of IT, a governing mindset will be to run IT like a business from top to bottom, from left to right, and everywhere in between. Seems like a simple thing, but the fact is that this approach does not drive many of our actions in IT today. It is easy to see the influences of this business mentality across the chapters of this book, but it bears mentioning again as we look at the cultural shift and people influences of the future IT organization.

What we will learn is that culture and people are not just another thing, not just an important thing, but THE thing to the high-performance IT organization of the future.

> *From our people will ultimately spring everything that is good, but they need our help to get started.*

The teams in IT today will need a model from management that helps to establish this improved focus on the business elements of IT. This will include improved visibility of business strategy, customer requirements, communication with owners across the business, budget numbers, and much more.

> *Visibility is a powerful thing. Visibility reinforces trust, visibility is enlightening, visibility is empowering, visibility stimulates thought, visibility makes proactive action possible, and visibility encourages the business thinking we must have.*

This is a natural process, and just a gentle nudge can create a tremendous amount of momentum. Good people inherently want to do the right thing. Armed with a small amount of the right information, they begin to ask questions, formulate plans, fall into line with the right strategy, and work toward the right goals.

Another benefit of this momentum is the role modeling that will occur. Initially, this business orientation will be new, but once it is taken up by a single team, other individuals and teams will take note and fall into line quickly. We also want to recognize the right behavior and highlight the early successes of our business-driven actions. This could be a happy customer, a strategic outcome beyond IT, or a business owner thanking IT for partnering with another organization to achieve some good outcome. And with this the momentum builds, the pace quickens. Winning and positive outcomes are highly contagious, and we use this to the advantage of IT and the advantage of the organization.

There is a hunger in IT that is waiting for this increased focus on the business and on strategy. Once enabled, IT will show a remarkable capacity to take up this business-oriented thinking in everything we do every day.

Encouraging this view will be welcomed by virtually every person in IT and will be a natural improvement to any role in the organization and every career path. We all do our best work when we have a better understanding of the business and more context for the work we perform every day.

We feel more trusted and empowered when we have access to the right information about the business.

COMPENSATION

As our skillsets improve and evolve and we attract new people to IT, there will be a growing need to look at compensation. We should expect IT to be an increasingly attractive organization to join. As such, it won't only be a matter of attracting new talented staff, but also keeping the people of IT in IT and in our organization overall—which is a very good thing for all. Hand in hand with this evolution of the organization and deeper pool of talent is the responsibility to recognize contribution and value through compensation—and don't assume a simple pay raise is the answer. Yes, an increase in the base of some IT staff can make sense, but it is about much more.

Incentives can be effective tools, or bonus plans that are tied to key milestones and deliverables under the control of the IT staff.

Bonus plans have not been common in the IT organization of the past but make more sense going forward.

This investment will pay back to us in creating a highly motivated team that will best leverage the talents we are developing in the IT staff of the future. For example, in the skillset discussion from earlier in this chapter, we took a look at a new IT business analyst role that will work directly with clients and develop solution requirements—an advanced skillset that will make an important contribution to IT and to the broader organization.

> *These are talented individuals who are the impact players of the future in IT and should be embraced and nurtured.*

A business manager position will be a good candidate for a more aggressive and creative compensation plan, which should include a variable/bonus component so our people can share in the success of IT. Other positions will include IT program managers and IT development managers to manage the increasingly complex schedules and integrations that will be demanded of IT.

The need for domain experts—including security, endpoint, service management, and compliance—will never go away. These are high-value skills as well and should be included in our variable and IT bonus plans. The CIO can create a quarterly bonus pool that is distributed by the VPs in IT to staff that make the greatest impact as individual contributors or to the teams that deliver to significant milestones. For the organizations in which equity is available, IT will earn a larger share of the equity pool.

An overall compensation profile will look more like what we have done for key marketing, consulting, or product development personnel of the past. IT will rise to match the plans for the product managers, product marketing managers, and development managers.

This is the standard we should expect and set: The key staff of IT are now on par with the other stars of the full organization, which sends the right message to both IT and the organization and continues to build the momentum in our culture and across IT.

With highly skilled workers charged with changing IT and with the proper compensation and career opportunities, it gets a little easier to attract and retain the talented people who will drive and lead IT into the future. This is an important cycle for IT. Then, with a few more talented people working in IT, it becomes a more attractive option for the organizational stars of tomorrow, which then brings even more skilled workers, innovative thinkers, and leaders to IT. The cycle then repeats, and so we remake our people and culture one step at a time.

NEW CAREER PATHS

The combination of a more strategic focus in IT, increased business awareness, new skillsets, and a faster cadence of IT will result in many changes large and small with regard to the roles our people fill and the path of growth these roles will follow.

One such change is the extension of existing career paths and the birth of new ones. This enrichment of career paths is important to the individual and to the organization in that it represents another means by which we develop, retain, recognize, and motivate an increasingly diverse and talented IT workforce.

Existing career paths will run longer due to the improved standing of IT in the business and the corresponding improved promotability of our people. At the same time, new career paths will open as we create new roles driven by new skillsets and a higher profile of the roles across IT in the business.

*With the trust of the business turning to IT,
we feel a greater sense of responsibility to
deliver more value to the organization.*

The creation of new career paths can take many forms, including those associated with working more closely with the customer and those that help drive accelerated innovation. These paths can then have a positive impact on the business itself and our competitive position in the market, regardless of what markets we might play in. These things are closely linked.

The need for highly skilled people driving deliverables and innovating is a fundamental need for health care, education, retail, manufacturing, food services, legal services, consulting, utilities, transportation, government, technology, consumer goods, communications, and much more. With this common and critical need to enrich the career paths of our good people in IT, it becomes a call for the leadership of IT to be proactive in creating a cultural focus in IT on career development.

We are then called to devote time to career path planning in the existing cycle of management planning, annual retreats, and quarterly business reviews that are currently in place for IT organizations everywhere. If it's not on the IT agenda today for these planning forums, it needs to be added now.

*Yes, we love our technology in IT, but
increasingly we understand that the
difference between good IT and great IT is
all about our people.*

This is a simple truth that you will come to understand and appreciate if you do not today.

With this we recognize yet another new behavior and focus that further changes the face of IT and the place we will hold in the business for the future. Career path planning and enrichment are not limited to our front-line, entry-level management and mid-level management staff.

This strategy extends all the way to the CIO—we fully expect his or her place in the business to be elevated as the star of IT is rising and the impact of IT becomes more compelling.

This can mean many things, including the CIO joining the senior executive staff if that is not already the case, and the promotion of talented and strategic CIOs to be the CEOs of the future. The business will increasingly see the CIO differently, as a strategic and innovative employee who is uniquely able to better leverage technology and data to make the business stronger.

This has not often been the case in the past, but that will change, as the successful CIO of the past was commonly a technologist first, with some business skills—productive for IT, but not necessarily equipping the CIO to be a driver to the overall business and bring value to the executive staff.

With the rebirth of IT, the CIO of the future will be a talented and well-rounded business strategist with a mix of skills, including a good understanding of technology and how technology can be leveraged to create happy customers and drive business growth.

The CIO becomes a must-have at the senior executive table and a strong candidate for the COO and CEO office.

The rise of the CIO further supports and enhances the promotability and compensation of all staff across the IT organization. The upwardly mobile CIO will bring along with them an appreciation and understanding of the talented people of IT, which then supports and protects the further investment we will make in the career development and compensation of the many talented people working across IT. The promoted CIO will be an advocate of the IT staff and willing to make investments that might have been reduced or cut altogether in the past.

This contributes to a realigning of how IT is viewed in the business—from a tactical cost center to a strategic driver of the business and home to some of our most talented and valuable people.

The CIO will remember from whence they came, and from this much good will arise.

REFUSE TO TOLERATE APATHY

Apathy is a dangerous thing that extinguishes passion before it can take flight. Apathy is a poison to much of what is good in a healthy and growing culture and is clearly counter to what we must create for the future of IT.

Not always part of the discussion when we look at the culture of IT, *apathy* becomes more important as we tune and nurture the culture of IT for the future. It is simple— apathy can't be tolerated in any form. It must become completely unacceptable to all of us. It goes against so much that is fundamental to the future of IT. In many ways, we should see apathy as the natural enemy of a short list of what we must have in our culture to remake IT, including joy, passion, energy, empowerment, and commitment.

None of this is possible with apathy.

The good news is that a culture that emphasizes passion and empowerment will make it difficult for apathy to grow. It will make it easier to identify apathy because it will stand out in clear contrast to the dedicated people around it. The culture that is a fertile environment for passionate and committed people can quickly identify apathy and remove it. We also have a big advantage in that apathy is not fun and people are not naturally drawn to other people who just don't care and are not enjoying what they are doing every day.

> *When surrounded by hardworking, dedicated, optimistic, and passionate people, apathetic people will quickly stand out.*

We do have a great deal of control in that the right conditions for apathy should be avoided. In most cases we are focusing on the positive elements of a strong and new culture for IT, and by focusing on this positive challenge, we make it hard for apathy to find a place in our increasingly healthy culture of IT.

A zero-tolerance approach to apathy must come from leadership of course, but should be carried forward by every person in IT. This becomes a cultural identity. A culture of apathy makes every task difficult and greatness all but impossible, whereas a culture of passion and optimism will make anything possible.

A healthy and passionate culture will attract more people of like mind, and with each addition it becomes more difficult for apathy to find a foothold. Apathy can be contagious, so it's important that we make it difficult for apathy to get started. Prevention is a powerful cultural model and not just a powerful technical model. More good news—passion and commitment are more contagious than apathy, and this is another important aid for the future. Good trumps bad.

ENERGY

We close the discussion on Culture & People with a property that is not commonly discussed and not fully appreciated in IT today—energy. Energy is a vital resource for the IT organization of the future because it contains and reflects so much of what we need to make the rebirth of IT a success.

Energy gives us strength and vitality and brings us the resolve needed to carry through challenges we know will come as we make difficult changes; these challenges will not be few or easy to overcome. We learn a great deal about the character of a team and the character of a business when they are faced with hardship.

The level of energy present in an organization is a predictive measure: Energy is a reflection of the right behaviors, the right priorities, the right people, and the right leadership. Passion, discussed earlier in this chapter, is closely related to energy, but in this context we refer to energy as a collective whole, born of an organization and its culture. As such, energy will be something we can feel and something we can measure.

*To put some structure to this discussion,
consider the following equation that
helps to quantify the energy of the IT
organization:*

E=PxUxC

E is the collective energy of IT, P is the passion index, U is the unification index, and C is the customer connection index. To further break this down, we will assign a value for P on a scale of one to ten; we will also assign a similar value to the unification index that is from one to ten; and finally the C variable is the number of customers with which IT has created direct connections. This can be any value and is not limited to a given scale.

For each of the P and C scales, assume one is the lowest/ worst value and ten is the highest/best value. Of course, P and U are subjective measures, but in most cases we have a pretty good feel for where the organization is today.

In the case of passion (referenced earlier in this chapter), we look across the organization and assess how strongly and broadly passion is shown by our people and our teams. In the case of passion being clearly lacking, we would assign a value of one or two. In the case of passion being present but limited in scope and primarily present in a few key people or teams, we would assign a value of three or four. You get the idea.

*Similarly, we look at unification as an
evaluation of our journey to unify IT
(reference Chapter 7).*

In the case of traditional IT where the organization is primarily siloed and no real effort is under way to unify IT, we would assign a value of one or two. If an effort has begun to eliminate silos and create collaboration across IT, but this effort is in the early stages, we assign a value of three or four. If there is an active initiative in place to unify IT, a CIO driving this process, a number of silos have been eliminated, and a number of new cross-functional teams have been formed to work across IT and drive trans-IT business processes (reference Chapter 13), we assign a value of five or six. And, in the case of those organizations that are well on their way to unifying IT—including the successful elimination of most silos and a full number of cross-functional teams operating today as well as most business processes now in place and operating to drive the majority of work done in IT—we would assign a value of seven to nine. This, of course, assumes that very, very few IT organizations today could take a value of nine or ten.

The final metric is customers (reference Chapter 13), which captures the number of direct connections in place today, alive and well, if you will, and operating where an IT individual or team has a direct relationship with a customer and is leveraging that relationship to communicate on a regular basis. This would enable the customer to be actively providing input and feedback on the performance of existing solutions and/or the development and delivery of future solutions. This reference to a solution could include any product or service that is delivered by our business and enabled by the IT organization. The C then becomes a count of these connections and could range from zero to potentially hundreds or even thousands. It is important to be accurate to the best of our ability; this number has a significant impact on our total energy value.

The variations from company to company can be significant, but as a general guideline, we can consider the following numbers:

1. E<100: Very much a traditional IT model, much work to do.
2. 100<E<500 : An IT organization in the early to intermediate stages of transformation.
3. 500<E<1000 : IT organization in the intermediate to early advanced stages of transformation.
4. 1000<E: Likely an advanced IT organization into the later advanced stages of transformation with a growing track record of success and value.

It is true that the customer count can highly influence these numbers, so we have assumed that in the cases of #3 and #4 above, both P and U are likely greater than a score of four to five.

Each of these measures is very much an indication of the journey we have undertaken to remake IT and will be an indication of an organization that is in transition. Not precisely scientific, these measures are intended to help us stop and think for a minute about where we are today and how far we have come.

We could debate the numbers, but this equation is intended to capture the spirit of energy and reflects how important energy is to our future. It reminds us that where energy may have been lacking across IT in the past, it is now vital to the new IT.

KEY TAKEAWAYS: CULTURE AND PEOPLE

1. In many ways the transformation of IT is not just partly related to people—our people are at the very heart of the matter. This transformation and the ensuing rebirth of IT require many things at many levels, but a manifold truth is it all begins and ends with people and the cultural shift that is inseparable from our people.

2. Passion is a wonderful thing and should never be underestimated. In this chapter we introduce hope as a necessary companion to passion. Passion and hope make each other complete and multiply the goodness they can create together. Find and nurture passion among the staff we have today and when hiring opportunities come, passion should be on our short list for the must-have qualities for the IT staff of the future.

3. A critical thread of focus and thinking that will run through our new culture is a focus on the customer; hand in hand with our affection for the customer is taking a business approach to how we run IT every day. These two things become fundamental and are closely related, making the other focus both possible and successful.

4. New skills, new career paths, and more aggressive compensation arm IT with a motivated and talented workforce with which to face the challenges of the future. This is an exciting development for IT and quite practical—we can transform IT with the same strategy, thinking, people, and skills. We must get better—and get better at everything. This then creates a cycle of growth, recognition, and reward that will propel us into our exciting future.

CHAPTER 13

TRANS-IT BUSINESS PROCESS

The design and execution of businesses processes across all of IT is a critical but widely neglected strategy. This chapter will introduce and outline this strategy and explain why it is so important to the future of IT.

As we have touched on a few times, the creation and growth of IT over the past thirty years have centered on a model of localized domain expertise, localized software applications, a silo-based organizational model, and therefore a localized silo-based business process model. This model has been natural and convenient but imposes significant limitations and challenges that are born of the localized model itself.

The reality of the conventional IT organization is that we have teams of dedicated people working very hard on one piece of the IT business. At the same time, there are many other teams doing something very similar and with an equally local focus. Visibility across these numerous teams is nonexistent, as are communication and coordination. At our very best, we manage to get by with very hard work and some creative problem solving to meet our deadlines and to complete our deliverables.

> *But look closely—we are not getting better, we are not innovating, we are not thinking strategically. We are essentially living IT-hand to IT-mouth.*

There is, of course, a level of visibility at the office of the CIO and some VPs within IT, but as such this understanding of the broader IT operation is only present in a few roles and people.

Today, we now have the opportunity to change how we live and to create leverage in order to replace what has been a brute force model. The people in IT are smart and dedicated and will find a way to overcome. But this model won't scale, so we need to identify ways to get better, faster, more agile, and ready to scale.

The good news is that automation tools and the tools we have to support business process execution have improved dramatically over the past ten years and are now fit for purpose and able to help us in rebuilding the business process model across IT.

Broadening existing single-function or localized business process work to work fully across the scope of IT effectively brings together multiple existing workflows or business processes into a single integrated, efficient, and optimized team effort.

> *This model is powerful and brings us exponential improvements that create real leverage, visibility, and speed. This model changes how we live and elevates IT to a new standard of performance.*

VISIBILITY

Visibility is a wonderful thing and a powerful enabler to IT, although it has been often lacking in the past. This is a good place to start our deeper exploration of working together across IT. As we begin to contemplate designing, building, and operating trans-IT business processes, we immediately gain the benefit of improved visibility at the beginning of this process.

> **The first step in making these business processes a reality is bringing teams together for a cross-functional brainstorming and design process.**

These sessions can be informal discussions and whiteboard sessions, and visibility improves immediately. Every person in the room will learn something, and most people in the room will learn a lot. Visibility is not expensive or difficult. It is just a matter of taking a step back and looking at what has been there for a long time in most cases, albeit we are now seeing this with a different objective in mind, which immediately changes our perspective.

This improved visibility will happen for every person participating in the process. It changes how we see IT, how we think about the work we do every day, how we can do better, how we can save precious time, and so much more. We immediately have all our people thinking about IT as a whole versus the limited scope we focused on before.

> *But it all starts with visibility. We can't*
> *improve what we know nothing about.*

This is a reminder of the powerful enabler that visibility represents for us and how quickly it can improve, in a matter of hours; we then have created a remarkable and self-sustaining momentum that upsets the inertia of IT and sets us on a different course.

We now have momentum across all of IT where it did not exist before. Yes, it is possible there existed some momentum in the individual silos of IT, but these forces are insignificant when compared to the IT-wide strength we can create when our teams begin working together toward a common goal. We can't overstate this strength—it goes far beyond the work that is being performed at the moment. Yes, this is important, but we need to appreciate the remarkable power of having our teams across IT working toward common goals, thinking about solving common problems, and looking for smarter ways to work in the future.

IT is hard, and it is harder when our teams are not working together. Visibility is the start to creating a new model of cooperation across IT.

BRUTE FORCE & LEVERAGE

While there is something simple and raw about brute force, we can't continue to rely on this model for the future. Brute force can be habit forming; it can become the lifestyle of IT and how we get things done. But brute force does not scale, brute force is not strategic, brute force is never optimal, and brute force never creates leverage. With brute force, the return we get on effort is always exactly equal to the effort expended. In some cases it can be even less.

Leverage is a different thing entirely.

> *Leverage is a force multiplier. Leverage allows us to think differently. Leverage enables us to go faster with equal or less effort. Leverage scales where there was no hope of scaling previously.*

But we never achieve leverage by working locally within the existing silos of IT.

Leverage can only be created by looking beyond our existing

silos, to a more holistic set of synergies that allow us to save resources, to save time, and to work toward a common purpose. This common purpose is often the customer, or in some cases a business objective that can best be supported by all of IT coming together to work toward this common purpose. This unifying purpose brings us leverage where there is none when we are focused on local priorities and local objectives.

> *Leverage is a transformational and*
> *unifying call that fundamentally changes*
> *IT.*

It changes our mindset and changes how we work every day. All the staff of IT will rally around the search for leverage and look at everything we do every day differently. Leverage becomes the standard in everything we do, and all of us in IT will search for ways to create leverage in everything we do.

This is a remarkable shift. It creates a strategic mindset where there was only a tactical mindset previously. We begin to understand what leverage looks like and what it can do for us, and therefore, it becomes the standard for all we do. We then have everybody in IT casting a critical eye to the day-to-day operations for IT and applying the new standard of leverage and how we create it. Nothing else will do. This is a wonderful and healthy new standard that changes our perspective across IT. Every small step makes a big difference when it is born of leverage.

With brute force, improvement is difficult to come by and never accelerates. This is a trap that many organizations accept as a never-changing reality.

With brute force a small step is only a small step forever. With leverage, a small step can create disproportionately big results.

SYNERGIES

Synergies exist all across IT, waiting to be unlocked.

But by working in silos, by working locally to local objectives, we are never able to tap into these synergies, and they lie dormant. They are by definition inaccessible and disabled by the traditional model of IT.

As we begin to work across IT and build our broader workflows and automation models, synergies begin to emerge—born of the common goals and shared vision of the teams we form to design and operate these expanding business processes.

This new process is a powerful thing that provides goals that our teams can rally around. Synergies might begin small, but they will build quickly and ever expand in scope. Once begun, this process becomes natural. We won't return to the old silo models and localized workflow models of the past.

It is a simple and powerful axiom—the broader and more cross-functional we can build a repeatable business process, the greater the value and the greater the benefits.

Greater speed, agility, opportunity to innovate, cost savings, and reduced risk are a few of the benefits. Our goal is to build complete business processes that can then be automated across as many elements of IT as necessary to reduce or to eliminate entirely integrations and handoffs. Each of these gaps represents an opportunity for error and delay, and by eliminating them we fundamentally change the machine of IT into something superior.

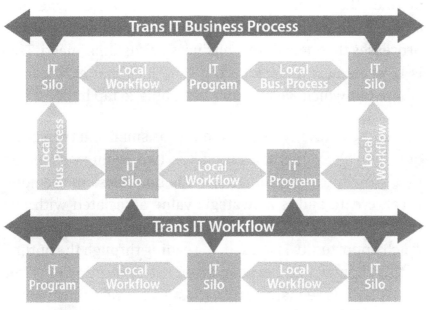

Figure 13.1 Local Versus Trans-IT Workflow

Figure 13.1 captures the contrast between a local business process, which is generally limited to just a couple of silos or programs, versus a trans-IT business process that reaches more broadly across IT and can include four, five, six, or even more silos and programs. There is no real limit to this number; in some cases the number of silos and programs we touch with a mature trans-IT process could be equal to the full sum of all IT silos and programs. This then creates a healthy cleansing of IT and will cause these silos to dissolve as they are less and less necessary. The speed and simplicity we get in return following the creation of these broad business processes are so immediately powerful, we quickly accelerate whatever works remain to bring IT together.

Think of this scrubbing process as eliminating any artificial boundaries or edges created by organizational models or roles that limit how our people or IT works. Synergies emerge when we focus on complete, end-to-end business processes that deliver to a business or customer need. This is IT at its best, unlocking the synergies that exist everywhere but which we have not been able to tap into.

Sometimes these synergies emerge as small and then grow quickly. This cooperation model of two or more elements that grow into a combined good is boundless in the good it can create and is a strategic value associated with our trans-IT business process work. Without this focus, so much opportunity is missed. In reading through the outline of this chapter, and the chapter on the unification of IT, for example, we see many similarities. This is no coincidence.

Broad and unifying strategies are at the heart of the new IT and represent not an incremental improvement but a completely new way of thinking and working.

Many of these elements and strategies are, in fact, inseparable, and as such, you might note a familiar outline or narrative to several of these chapters. This is as it should be and further highlights the common themes that run through the IT of the future. It is simple but should not be confused with *easy*.

MANAGING RISK

As we move faster, focus on the customer, and push ourselves to innovate and unify IT around common strategies, we can't be reckless. The need to manage risk does not go away. If anything, the need for IT to manage risk for the sake of IT and the business grows. Moving faster does not excuse us from the responsibility of managing risk, which in many cases is more complex and more important than ever.

All the change we are navigating in IT must be done for the common good while at the same time managing and then reducing organizational and business risk. This requires some attention and can't be taken for granted.

Many of our vertical markets today are shaped by governance, compliance, and audit-related requirements. The Imperative calls us to focus on strategic performance versus the tactical and localized IT objectives of the past, but we do so in a more global and complex business environment. If anything, the requirements associated with governance, compliance, and audit are growing and increasing in complexity. Threats are more sophisticated and come at us more often.

Managing risk in the context of trans-IT business processes involves recognizing a few key things:

1. We can manage risk more effectively when we do this holistically, across all of IT.
2. We must manage risk proactively, and not simply respond when risk escalates.
3. Key IT functions, including ITSM, ITAM, and Security, have common risks.
4. With common risks, we can more effectively use our resources across all of IT.
5. Automation is a great ally in managing risk.
6. IT will partner with the CEO, CFO, and CIO in addressing a full set of corporate risks.
7. Risk is visible at the Board of Directors level, and IT must now step up.
8. Assign key people in IT to focus on risk. Don't let it be a part-time thing.

All of IT should understand the risk management strategy, and with this alignment we can be successful on behalf of the business. If IT has a proactive risk management strategy, the risk of the business is greatly reduced. If IT has no risk management strategy, the risk of the business rises to unacceptable levels. In this, IT becomes a valuable partner to the business.

As stewards of our corporate assets, endpoints, and data, who is better able to protect the business? IT is ready to answer this important call.

Once again, this brings us back to the unique knowledge and skills of IT. Note the connections between a number of these initiatives. Trans-IT business processes are inextricably linked to automation, which enables us to more consistently and effectively manage risk. Speed is closely related to automation, which in turn enables us to be proactive in managing the changing landscape of risks to the business. Agility can be born in IT and is synergistic with speed and automation. And there are countless other connections in this web of value across the new IT.

ACCOUNTABILITY

An important matter, accountability. We certainly need more of it all across our business and more of it in IT as well. The challenge has not been the desire.

The challenge has been our ability to administer and enforce accountability fairly. The good people of IT will not shy away from this. In most cases they will welcome accountability, as it is likely to come with increased responsibility and empowerment. IT leadership will understand this and make it happen.

The design and operations of trans-IT business processes bring more clarity and remove much of the noise and distraction that exist in IT today. Beyond accountability that is highly enhanced, we will see improvements in communication, which then pays back to our ability to increase accountability.

**High-performing organizations are great
at creating accountability.**

Accountability becomes woven into the corporate culture; it is important to recognize that the company gives much to individuals and teams in order to create accountability, and the teams and individuals then give a lot back to the business.

The design of trans-IT business processes will call to attention the overlaps and redundancies that exist today across the multiple silos and functions of IT. This duplicity then creates some confusion about how work gets done, responsibilities, delays, redundant effort, communications, and much more. As we design our broader scope for business processes, we bring together functions including IT Service Management, Security, IT Asset Management, and Program Management. And as part of this process, we are able to identify a lot of the waste and overlaps that fight against the goals we have created for the IT organization of the future.

So, we get the benefits of the broader business processes themselves, and we are able to eliminate waste, move faster, save time, and improve communications all at the same time. We discussed the concept of leverage earlier—this is a great example of leverage at work. This leverage is about making a change to the traditional model of IT; we subsequently see a cascade of benefits, and these benefits keep coming over time, in ways we can't anticipate. Leverage gives us a great benefit/effort ratio. A ratio typical of brute force is around 1:1. A leverage ratio is more like 3:1, 4:1, or 5:1. Exceptional leverage can be even more. This is something to keep in mind as we rebuild IT and as we begin to enjoy small wins, then larger wins. The momentum builds and we continue to seek and find these points of leverage.

This brings us back to accountability and the many benefits it can create.

> *Accountability also brings us a number of intangible benefits that are more difficult to measure but no less important.*

One example would be the role modeling that occurs and how it shapes the culture of IT. Everybody takes notice when a strong performer accepts accountability along with responsibility, then delivers value to the business. Recognition then comes, and others want to be part of this healthy cycle—and so the culture changes. As more success occurs born of accountability, more change happens, and this role model influence grows and grows. This is real and lasting change for the good.

COMMUNICATION

Good communications make all surrounding people and processes better. Communication is not a natural competency of traditional IT, but it becomes a priority and a skill to be nurtured in the rebirth.

We will need to focus on the development of communications skills with our existing staff; when we hire new staff, communication skills move up our list of priorities and arrive in the top tier of skill needs. Good communications support our work with customers, our coordination across all IT teams, and our work with business owners to name a few.

The process of designing and operating trans-IT business processes is greatly enhanced with good communications. It brings us a better result and it gets us there faster.

This is our path to identify and brainstorm solutions that fulfill our need to create broader workflows and business process automation. Sometimes we will operate a business process manually for a period of time before we begin to automate the steps that make up the process. This manual operation for a time helps to validate our ground rules, decision criteria, timing, and dependencies, laying the groundwork for a successful business process and then for successful automation.

Throughout this work that sets the stage for a trans-IT success, communications are vital—and it is important to be inclusive. Best to include all the teams, individuals, process experts, and any others who help us design and operate a strong process. Communication helps us to move faster, drives us to the right results, and helps to prevent misunderstandings and wasted time. As we have begun to understand, time is precious, and we can't waste a second.

> *There is no cure-all for the challenges of IT, but we can identify a few things that come close. Good communication is one of those powerful agents of change that can improve so much of what we do.*

Communications are important from the very beginning of making trans-IT business processes a reality. For the sake of the discussion, let's assume we have identified candidate processes that work across the service desk, security, endpoints, and server teams in IT. The first step in making a broader business process a reality would be to bring members of these teams together for an introduction, overview, objectives summary, and brainstorming session. It is possible these teams have not been in a working session together before, so communications and coordination are the first step. With these basics in place, we will see some great ideas and real progress.

> *After a good start, communications play a vital role in keeping the teams coordinated and informed as we work toward making our trans-IT business processes a reality. Communications are a great preventer of problems as we travel this journey-within-the-journey.*

In the beginning it might be a single process that is designed and operated, which is okay; it serves to validate our model, what works and what does not work, and we can then be more productive in subsequent steps and projects. For some organizations, we might be able to create just a few trans-IT processes, and that is acceptable as each one will represent value and savings that pay back to us over time. In other large and more complex organizations, we might create many of our trans-IT processes. This is even more value and more savings.

Finally, communications play another important role in this context. When we do have success as trans-IT processes begin to come online, we need to shout these successes out to the organization. Make some noise. This is a key milestone for IT and for the business. We need to <u>celebrate success</u> and be proud of this creation of strong value.

This will bring well-deserved recognition to the trans-IT teams and individuals, and others will want to be part of it going forward. All good stuff, and made possible by communicating.

BUSINESS ACCELERATION

Acceleration is the brother of speed, and both are vital to the rebirth of IT—not just a part of what we are doing, but truly vital.

Acceleration is all about improving on the speed we have today. Finding the will and then the way to gain precious speed. Taking the necessary steps to move from slow to average, from average to above average, from above average to fast, from fast to very fast, and from very fast to world class.

Every step holds challenges, but every step holds tremendous value.

> *We should both recognize and embrace that we can always go faster. This mindset and soulful commitment will make everything possible.*

Improvements can be small, and improvements can be big. Both are important, and both add value. In some cases, a small and seemingly disconnected improvement in speed can clear the way for a much larger improvement later. The small issue can block our vision or obstruct our way in finding the next big leap forward. As such, every opportunity to accelerate should be embraced, be it seconds or days. When we look hard enough, we will find something.

A primary value of a trans-IT business process is in unlocking opportunities to accelerate the business. This speed has likely been trapped within existing, local, silo-born and -bred business processes that are inefficient, overly complex, fragile, disjointed, and ultimately slow.

In many ways these traditional processes are designed to be slow because our focus and priorities were elsewhere when they were originally designed and created.

Speed was simply not a priority, and speed does not happen by accident.

We can find lots of leverage here. And along the way we get to bring our teams together in new ways to work toward common goals. This is a very powerful thing and beautiful to behold when it unfolds. The more holistic the process, the more teams and mini-processes involved, the bigger the opportunity. If we take a typical IT organization model of something like eight to ten organizations and silos, the more we can involve, and the more we can encompass the new business process, the better.

> *We, therefore, can find more speed, more*
> *synergy, and eliminate more waste. More*
> *of everything good, and less of everything*
> *bad.*

Today, speed is strategic, and acceleration is a priority for all the work we do across IT. Our trans-IT business processes represent a great opportunity for us to create this acceleration while at the same time creating many of the other benefits we have highlighted throughout the chapter. These multi-function processes begin to reshape much of what we do in IT every day and ultimately improve how we service our existing customers and win new customers.

It does not get any better than that.

ALIGNMENT

There is a wonderful synchronization that happens between our teams and across IT when our people are aligned. Our efforts are complementary, we communicate better, waste is reduced, and we avoid redundant efforts. The challenge lies in how we achieve this alignment. It is not an easy thing and we don't get there by accident or by being lucky. Well, luck might come our way sometimes, but we can't count on luck alone as nice as that would be.

Yes, getting to alignment is not easy. It is always best when we have a natural business initiative to rally around, which brings with it alignment as an extension of our work on this initiative.

> *Trans-IT business process is one initiative that can bring us alignment and can be a great rallying cry; our scope is broad, and we are engaging the right teams across IT.*

In addition to this, we have process experts engaged in helping with the workflow and process design as well as the full attention of the CIO and IT leadership. In looking at these elements and characteristics, it begins to emerge as a great fit for helping us achieve the needed alignment within IT and between IT and the business.

This alignment is necessary in the design of our business processes that will span IT so that we are getting the benefits of alignment for our trans-IT business process work and for our potentially greater good of aligning our teams beyond IT—with the full organization. This is powerful, but in many ways just the beginning. The ceiling for potential in alignment is very high indeed, almost unlimited and fully worthy of our focus and attention.

We need to double-down when we find a project that brings us benefits on multiple levels, with this being one.

We get big value from the trans-IT business processes itself, plus the additional benefits of:

1. Speed
2. Agility
3. Improved communications
4. Elimination of waste and redundant effort
5. Simplification of the work required to achieve an outcome
6. Ability to scale with the growth of the business
7. Improved ability to support 24X7 operations
8. Supports the unification of IT
9. Brings IT closer to the strategy of the business
10. Better supports customer-facing engagement

And there are many other benefits we can call out. You will note the continued reminders of the remarkable synergies and linkages between the themes and strategies central to the Imperative.

There is a rich thread that runs through all the work we are doing and a reminder that we are not just getting better—we are taking a quantum leap forward to change IT and change the business.

ELIMINATION OF WASTE

This is a big topic, with lots of history and lots of depth.

IT is a mature organization, and it is only natural that waste has accumulated over time. The rebirth of IT is the perfect opportunity to take a fresh look at everything we do; we are sure to find waste, and we should be committed to immediately removing any form of it, be it small or large, and move on.

This cleansing is, in fact, a very good thing because any removal of waste brings us closer to our goals.

> *Waste slows us down, saps our organizational energy, costs money, and blocks us from strategic work.*

The removal of elements of waste also gives us a big emotional boost. We all like to get rid of waste—we know it is the right thing, it allows us to focus on the best part of our work, and we collectively feel like we have accomplished something important.

So, what does this have to do with trans-IT business processes?

As it turns out, they are closely related. The cross-functional work of designing and building our new trans-IT business processes creates a natural investigative evaluation of everything we do in our existing business processes, and this brings us the opportunity to question everything.

In fact, it is vital that we question everything in order to achieve the right result with our new business processes. In doing this, we are likely to find most if not all of the waste that exists in IT. Think of this as a ruthless audit and housecleaning exercise. As a quick reminder on what makes this work, *question everything* means question everything. We will discover work that is done, approvals that are accepted as necessary, activities, documentation, reviews, and more that just don't make sense or add value. Maybe they did at one time, but not now.

This scrubbing-through of everything we do is accomplishing something very important. Yes, it enables us to design and operate our new trans-IT business processes, and yes, we are eliminating waste, which is an enemy of the speed and agility that are so important to the rebirth of IT.

> *But we are doing something potentially even more important. We are changing the culture of IT and sending a message to everybody—this is how we work, this is what we stand for, and this is what the future looks like.*

We hold ourselves to the highest standard—and there is no place for waste. Everything we do is about value, building customer loyalty, and creating innovative competitive advantage. Waste is the natural enemy of these primary goals.

As a reference to other discussions throughout the book, apathy is another natural enemy of our primary goals. And these two are closely related. Apathy is the brother of waste, and the most fertile ground for waste is the work of people who simply don't care.

This is not us, and that will be clear as we build the new IT.

SCALABILITY

As we are rebuilding IT for the future, all the work we take on is important. But let's be clear, we can't really call all this work strategic. Some very important work is, in fact, tactical in nature and important to the improved day-to-day work we do across IT and the operational models that support this daily work. We need to pay attention to the fundamentals and take care to get those right. This is the foundation on which we build the future.

Scalability anticipates success. Scalability anticipates opportunity.

Scalability in our systems and infrastructure directly enhances the business; scalability allows us to seize new market opportunities; scalability encourages innovation and creativity; and as such, scalability is a strategic initiative that can be driven and delivered by IT. This is in recognition that in today's market, so much of scalability is related to technology and our systems.

Scalability comes in many different shapes. Sometimes

we can realize tremendous scalability improvements with small adjustments to our systems in IT. Other times, scalability requires a large and lengthy project in order to be successful. We will embrace all these opportunities in recognition that every incremental scalability improvement is valuable to the business today, and far into the future.

A few examples of the scalability IT can deliver:

1. The ability to support rapid growth in the number of employees
2. The ability to quickly open, operate, and close new facilities
3. A process for establishing operations in a new country
4. The ability to support rapid growth in the customer base
5. The capacity to support the rapid growth of IT assets
6. Support for the growth of service requests across IT
7. Support for the 24X7 operations of the business
8. The bandwidth to deliver reliable and fast Internet access
9. Security measures that anticipate the growing number and sophistication of threats in the market
10. A competence around the upgrades of systems and applications with zero downtime
11. The ability to enable the launch of new business products or services
12. A competency for onboarding people and systems acquired through mergers and acquisitions

13. A model for supporting multiple currency sales quotes and billing
14. A competency for making changes and enhancements quickly to existing systems
15. A healthy and current baseline of IT best practices
16. A high level of automation
17. Business processes that have been reviewed, modified, and validated
18. A plan for the unification of IT operations

It is simply a good exercise to ask ourselves many "what-if" questions. Better to ask ourselves these questions versus waiting for the business to come to IT in search of answers to questions we have not considered ourselves. What if we doubled the number of employees in the next twenty-four months? What if we opened a new office in Japan?

No doubt you can think of many other examples. It is a healthy planning exercise to look at a number of growth scenarios and engage some of our key people to look at these scenarios and create a framework plan. Even though they may not be implemented immediately, we have a rough plan ready to get a fast start should a planning scenario become reality.

One more good question to ask—what is the single growth scenario that scares us the most?

Then we look at why it concerns us. If it becomes reality,

what would we do? I highly recommend this exercise, which is very much in the spirit of *proactive* and *aggressive*.

Neither is easy and neither is comfortable, but that is a good thing in the end.

COMPETITIVE ADVANTAGE

An equally wonderful and worthy place for us to finish our discussion on trans-IT business processes is with a look at creating competitive advantage. A primary goal of the new IT, and part of what makes the rebirth of IT possible, is a focus on the business versus IT. This means a focus on external relationships, customers, revenue, and winning new customers.

This is not a casual, passing interest. This is a lasting focus that changes how we think and how we work in IT.

IT can now work with the business to drive competitive advantage, which directly supports these goals. When we show clear differentiation over the companies we compete with every day, we are building customer loyalty while at the same time winning new customers. This is our future and the lifeblood of the business, regardless of what business we are in.

Increasingly, in a global and highly competitive marketplace, we understand the importance of retaining customers. Once a client has selected to consume our products or services, we must build a strong relationship that will benefit both parties and last far into the future. I expect the replacement cycles in most markets to grow, meaning it becomes more important than ever to cultivate happy customers.

> *It is simple—we can best achieve this goal*
> *when the organization and IT are side by*
> *side through every step.*

IT can enable real innovation that, in turn, delivers value to our customers. IT can enable speed so we can deliver more quickly. IT can help to create agility so the business can better serve new customer needs, and IT can and should now support our competitive differentiation.

This brings us full circle back to our trans-IT business processes and the power they provide for these multiple objectives.

If we are running a bunch of silo-based, traditional business processes, we simply won't be able to answer the call for speed, agility, and everything else that is vital to our customers and prospects.

> *I can't overstate the importance of not*
> *just implementing these holistic processes*
> *across IT and moving beyond the silos that*
> *limit so much of what we do today—but*
> *doing this now and not waiting.*

We can't wait for a crisis in the business. We can't wait for the board of directors or the CEO or the COO to point a finger at IT and demand we make these changes. At that moment, it is too late.

So we start now to implement this and the other principles of the Imperative so IT is ready when the organization most needs us, and not a moment later.

And, my friends, that moment will come sooner than you might want to believe.

KEY TAKEAWAYS: TRANS-IT BUSINESS PROCESS

1. There is remarkable speed and leverage available to us by broadening the scope of our business processes in IT. Look for the natural model; this will capture how people naturally want to work and will span multiple silos. Welcome this as a natural unifier across IT and watch much of the waste we have today fall away.

2. Beyond the process improvements we naturally get with these broader business processes, we get a number of equally important team-related benefits: improved communication, visibility, and decision making, to name a few. It is an empowering process our people will experience as the teams work together to design the broader business process models.

3. Workflow models that span IT will naturally break down silos and eliminate waste. This removes noise and distractions that although individually are not strategic improvements, they do clear the way for time and thinking, spawning strategic ideas and innovations that can fundamentally change the business. The fragmentation of the silo model blocks

our ability to elevate the IT organization to a more strategic level. A few simple and tactical challenges must be addressed first.

4. As this work allows us to get our IT house "in order," it enables IT to work in a fundamentally different manner with the business. When IT brings speed, collaboration, and communication to the partnership with the business, we can in many cases lead the business to do the same. This creates a very powerful synergy with the business owners who are looking for every possible competitive advantage in the marketplace.

CHAPTER 14

LEVERAGING KNOWLEDGE

Knowledge holds an important place in the future of IT and is a strategic asset to the organization. This concept should not be confused with the Knowledge Management function of the service desk.

Traditionally, knowledge was viewed as a secondary or tertiary process and, as such, often placed amongst the many elements of IT that were considered to be tactical in nature. This is a serious misjudgment.

When properly cultivated, knowledge is so much more—a true strategic force multiplier for IT.

A remarkable characteristic of knowledge that should be recognized is its ability to be organically generated by our people as the organization evolves and changes.

This sets knowledge apart as a natural resource of sorts that is all our own.

However, while this wonderful resource stands in front of us every day, without planning and focus we are not able to leverage knowledge effectively. A few basic questions will allow us to get on the right track: Where does knowledge exist? How do we capture it effectively? How do we nurture the growth of knowledge in the future? How do we get this knowledge to the people who can best use it every day?

Figure 14.1 The Synergies of Knowledge

Figure 14.1 shows the interesting relationships that yield this powerful asset. We should begin with a knowledge strategy that provides context and guidance for how knowledge will be developed, nurtured, captured, and leveraged. Each of these actions contains much depth and drives the ultimate success of organic knowledge. With our strategy in place, we can effectively manage the knowledge that lives in our employees, in our customers, across the IT staff, and in our partners in addition to other constituents.

> *Note that our sources of knowledge can also be our users of knowledge—an important and sustainable cycle of reaping and sowing.*

Information underlies knowledge in a raw form, and when context is applied to data, we create a foundation that can be built and cultivated into knowledge. We can have data that does not yield knowledge, but if we have knowledge, it will always have a relationship with data and information. In other words, having lots of data and information does not guarantee that we will yield knowledge. It must be cultivated and safeguarded.

As we will explore in these pages, I like to recommend a process owner or mentor to drive key activities and change. Knowledge is a good example of where this can make sense. This is not limited to knowledge for ITSM or the service desk, but knowledge for all of IT.

THE CULTURE OF KNOWLEDGE

The future of IT will include a culture that values knowledge in recognition that knowledge is strategic and very much a corporate asset. This recognition runs wide and deep and begins with senior leadership; with this commitment comes the investment that is necessary to cultivate the growth of knowledge and the leveraging of existing knowledge.

As with many desirable cultural changes, the cultivation of knowledge is contagious.

When supported by executive and senior leadership, the appreciation of knowledge spreads quickly and naturally. This, in turn, recognizes our experts, which then enables and encourages us to focus on capturing and sharing the knowledge of our experts—which makes all our people better. We are paid back through a broader circle as less experienced staff recognize the value placed on knowledge and the associated experts, and this creates organic motivation on the part of our more junior staff, who develop a desire to grow into our experts of the future.

The cycle continues as our established experts mentor and nurture junior staff, who develop and grow into our experts of the future.

Then, remembering the mentoring they received in the earlier years, these domain experts will be more committed and generous with their time and will coach and mentor a new generation of staff who will then grow into our experts of the future. This creates the next generation of our people who will contribute to a growing treasure of corporate knowledge and expertise.

This is a cultural momentum of the very best kind. It is a characteristic of the rebirth of IT and a wonderful tapestry of giving and sharing.

Culture is very much at the heart of the new IT, and we see this theme running through many of our discussions, including cadence (Chapter 1), The Customer Connection (Chapter 2), and culture (Chapter 12) itself. Culture can be left to evolve naturally as a byproduct of business initiatives or it can be an explicit focus of the organization.

Traditionally culture has not been on our short list of priorities for IT; this is yet another shift that will come with the Imperative. Our transformation in IT over the next ten years simply can't be successful without a new focus on culture—a theme that runs through many of our seventeen elements, and is certainly the case with knowledge.

KNOWLEDGE STRATEGY

The organizational leveraging of knowledge does not happen by accident. It is born of a strategy that both recognizes the value of knowledge and then creates the investment and commitment necessary to harvest this value.

This takes time and careful planning. It is not necessary to create self-pressure to get this strategy exactly right from the very beginning, which is all but impossible.

> **What works best is a simple and clear strategy to enable us to get started, and to then plan for the evolution of this strategy over time.**

Even more so, embrace this evolution, knowing it is both necessary and the most productive model to arrive at a mature strategy in the least amount of time.

There are a few things the knowledge strategy must include:

1. The goal of knowledge in the organization

2. Key metrics and milestones to track progress
3. Key roles and responsibilities, including the knowledge owner
4. Technology investments necessary to support the strategy
5. Policies and procedures to cultivate the growth of knowledge
6. Capital investments required to support the strategy
7. A simple communication plan to support the knowledge strategy

Ownership is always important, and this is no exception. Owners might change over time and priorities might change as well, but establishing ownership will drive a number of desirable behaviors and outcomes.

Each of our strategic domains must have an owner who carries the responsibility to keep the right level of attention, resource, and investment to help ensure the success of the initiative. Knowledge is no exception. The knowledge strategy will set the direction for our development of the leverage we can create with knowledge and the role our experts will play every day.

The development of knowledge is closely linked with our culture and people. It is important that IT leadership communicate the importance of expertise and knowledge to the broader organization—this reinforces the right priorities and the right behaviors.

EXPERTS

Subject matter and business experts exist in every organization, and they are a treasure. These experts are the very sap of organizational capability and know-how.

The knowledge possessed by these experts is accumulated over many years and can greatly accelerate the learning of others in the organization when leveraged properly. Experts are often unselfish and make all the people around them better and smarter.

Beyond the face value of the knowledge held by these experts, there are a number of positive side effects that occur when we invest in the cultivation and leveraging of these experts:

1. Experts can help ensure key decisions are made correctly.
2. Experts greatly enhance and accelerate the training of other staff.
3. Experts are the foundation we must use for the automation of tasks and business processes. Automation is of no value if the answers are wrong.

4. Experts are great role models.
5. Experts help us to move faster in everything we do by eliminating indecision and confusion.
6. Experts create organizational competence and confidence. These qualities exist in every successful organization and are lacking in organizations that struggle and ultimately fail.
7. Experts are a natural source of motivation for junior staff members.
8. Experts are often key "witnesses" for management and leadership when faced with critical business decisions.
9. Experts can be utilized to support our strategic push to find better and smarter ways to work. This is often done by way of a task force.
10. Experts mentor a new generation of future experts.
11. Our experts are vital to the creation of automation and business process models.
12. Domain experts are often a source of innovative ideas.
13. Experts are critical to client escalations and problem solving.
14. Domain experts provide content that fuels our market-facing activities across sales and marketing organizations.

I described the importance of process owners across the business previously, and the experts we reference here are often one and the same.

Note that for many of the elements in the book, including automation and agility, experts are fundamental to making these elements successful.

THE KNOWLEDGE BASE

The knowledge base is an asset that will already exist in IT and in many cases as an element of a CMS or CMDB in concert with the service desk or IT Service Management solution. So, I am not suggesting something new here. The purpose of calling this out as a topic of discussion is to bring attention to the importance of keeping our knowledge base current and to ensure it is healthy.

We simply need up to date and clean here. No magic is required.

With the focus on knowledge will come a corresponding reliance on the knowledge base, and we don't want to be surprised by an unhealthy asset—one that stands in the way of the broader success of knowledge.

It is too often the case that the knowledge base languishes and receives little attention or upkeep. This is not a difficult problem to solve. A little bit of attention on a regular basis makes a big difference.

Throughout our discussion of the Imperative and the re-shaping of IT, I emphasize the importance of ownership. Ownership creates accountability, and accountability spawns many desirable behaviors and outcomes.

The knowledge base is no exception. I recommend a corporate knowledge owner to drive the elements highlighted in this chapter as an investment in the valuable asset of knowledge.

> ### *This a senior position in IT and one befitting the value of our knowledge assets.*

A key part of the activities driven by the knowledge owner will be the knowledge archive itself, which will support the many activities focused on leveraging knowledge across the organization.

The knowledge owner can establish guidelines for the updating and care of the knowledge base. This then helps to ensure the information is usable and available when needed by our teams. Increasingly, this activity includes client and employee access to knowledge and is not limited to analyst access as was sometimes the case in the past. This is a further recognition of the broader value of knowledge and how it can be helpful to all.

In fact, this is a good question to ask of any IT asset: Will it benefit our employees or our clients?

SHARING

The use of the term *sharing* here might bring a smile to your face, or it might cause you to scratch your head and wonder. Well, it is a great concept and one that is very much in line with the rebirth.

The essence of sharing is selflessness and transparency. It is about making others better.

These are great goals to have across the many activities of the new IT. Remember, we are trying to change perceptions and behaviors, recognizing we are living with the long legacy of IT. In some cases, IT was considered to be closed, parochial, and not great at communicating.

The Imperative calls us to turn this model on its head.

> *We nurture knowledge, not for the sole benefit of IT, but for the benefit of the broader organization.*

This elevates knowledge to be strategic. This elevates knowledge from a simple database to a corporate asset.

This elevates knowledge to drive competitive differentiation and happy clients. Sharing accelerates these desirable results and should be embraced as a goal from the very beginning of our commitment to the Imperative.

The people of IT, and especially the knowledge owner, should be proactive in contacting and communicating with all our teams across IT and beyond IT as well. This is an important outreach and reflects the right mindset. It is valuable role modeling and IT leading the people of IT and the organization.

Sharing is simple and very powerful.

Sharing is unselfish and enabling of others. Sharing creates a cultural energy and sense of optimism.

> *Assume the broader organization can benefit from the assets of IT and take proactive steps to liaison with business owners to identify how the right level of visibility and enablement can occur.*

IT must lead, encourage, and facilitate this behavior. This creates another source of leadership and value sprung from within IT.

EMPOWERMENT

Continuing to extend this concept of harnessing and leveraging the power of knowledge, we can't accomplish our goals here without the right level of empowerment. Empowerment has a remarkable effect on our people, the culture, and the organization.

> ***When we both empower our people and equip them to be successful, well, that is really something.***

The role of knowledge here is to serve as a primary element of equipping our teams with the right information to perform at a high level every day. It is a beautiful thing to behold when we have talented and passionate people working together as teammates to a common vision and the right level of empowerment to be successful.

The fuel that makes this possible is passion. The substance of knowledge complements the passion that we bring to bear and ultimately create a success. Passion in the absence of knowledge will not get us there. Knowledge in the absence of passion is equally lacking in the end. But when we combine the elements of **passion, knowledge, and empowerment,** we are likely to succeed—and the momentum ripples across the organization.

> ### *Note the synergies of these elements are important, none of which can stand alone and bring IT into the future.*

Often, we see passion and empowerment go hand in hand.

We all do our best work when we are working for leadership and with teammates who believe in us.

This is a fundamental benefit of empowerment. With empowerment, we also create the best kind of accountability, meaning that our individuals and teams are welcoming of the accountability, as it comes with the tools and resources to be successful. This is a very powerful force that creates further change to our culture. It is common to want accountability, but with no empowerment, lasting accountability is not possible. This is something for IT leadership to think about. Don't wait, lead with empowerment, and accountability will naturally follow.

RECOGNITION

When success begins to come, and when we see the right behaviors that precede and ultimately spawn success, it is important to recognize what we have sought and what we want to repeat itself in the future.

> *It is a remarkable machine, what recognition can bring. It is another case of small cost and big return.*

Recognition can take many forms and can be as simple as a kind word.

Small expressions of recognition can be very powerful and should not be underestimated. When possible, these expressions of recognition should be done publicly, as it brings great satisfaction to the individual or team, but also reinforces the right behavior and right results for all those present.

Recognition is another link in the cycle that rejuvenates our culture and transforms IT from within. Although we dedicate a chapter to culture later in the book, this theme runs throughout many of our discussions. Why? Because the Imperative only becomes reality with cultural change. It is possible to have the right processes and the right technology, but this alone does not allow us to create the new IT of the future.

Culture is the catalyst for change.

Knowledge cannot grow to its full potential without recognition. It is vital that the organization understands that knowledge is valuable, knowledge will be cultivated, and knowledge and the experts who hold and share this knowledge will be recognized and rewarded.

This encourages the further growth of knowledge. In the absence of this recognition, knowledge will be suppressed. The growth of knowledge with a lack of recognition might occur from time to time but it will be far from our full potential and far from becoming the strategic asset it can be for the organization.

As recognition is often directed at our current or future experts, we get the added benefit of motivating the very people who give us the most leverage.

RECRUITING AND RETENTION OF STAFF

All great organizations develop the ability to attract and retain talented people who are the key to our future. This does not come easily and needs to be an organizational priority. And the sooner we start, the more successful we will be. Make this a priority from the very beginning and note that our knowledge and our knowledge experts are in the middle of this.

Traditionally, this has not been a focus of IT, and as such IT was left to make the best of the efforts of the broader organization. The shift that we will create with the rebirth of IT is to make IT a leader in the recruitment of talented staff. A simple idea, but a big shift from the normal model of IT—not a common focus of the past.

It is another reminder that the Imperative is much more about people than it is about processes or technology. Yes, we love our technology in IT, and it will always have a place in the world of IT, but technology will not allow us to drive the transformation of IT.

This is very much about people and culture.

> *Technology does not give us leverage—*
> *leverage comes from people, knowledge,*
> *and a well-understood strategy.*

This concept of leverage is an important one and will appear over and over in our discussions throughout the book. If not a believer today, you will develop an appreciation for what leverage can do for the future of IT.

We should always be looking for ways to create leverage.

> *In the absence of leverage, we rely on the*
> *application of simple force, and this is a*
> *fool's errand.*

Force does not scale, and force is not strategic. Force can be a short-term solution, but only when we keep searching for true leverage.

This is the only way we can get better. Leverage scales, leverage is strategic, and leverage changes our life. We simply can't make the Imperative a reality without leverage. We have come back to leverage again because the recruitment and retention of talented people is thoroughly about leverage.

KEY TAKEAWAYS: LEVERAGING KNOWLEDGE

1. The beginning of our journey within a journey to leverage knowledge is a strong message that knowledge is to be valued and nurtured in every form. Too often we think of the data and information aspects of knowledge only and do not elevate knowledge itself in every form to occupy a strategic place in the business.

2. Focus on the people part of knowledge. The experts and mentors in IT can offer so much, and as we reinforce this value, we are sending a message to all our people and our teams that they are appreciated and recognized. This is a cultural catalyst that will more quickly grow the next generation of experts and mentors. Knowledge does not just appear and is not just found; it grows in our people.

3. Retention of staff is so important to the future of IT. Yes, we need to bring new skills to IT, but this is not enough. We need to nurture and develop the staff we have as a complement to any new skills that join the organization and then we must retain these teams and leverage tenure. This then allows the knowledge that is so precious to grow and to then be captured

and leveraged. This cycle will create value and accelerate the changing culture of IT, with knowledge being a key denominator. IT can't be scalable and good at change without leveraging knowledge.

CHAPTER 15

BUILT FOR CHANGE

It is not that change in our world is new—we know this is certainly not the case. What we face today is more a case of a new rate of change, and the degree of change that comes with it.

> *Meaning that change now comes at us*
> *much faster and with bigger consequences.*
> *Change now packs a global punch.*

This creates both great risk and, for some organizations, great opportunity.

What does that mean? What we will come to understand—although for many that insight will arrive too late—is that those organizations that plan for, design for, and embrace change will experience tremendous success in this dynamic global economy.

Those that deny, hesitate, or, worse yet, combat change

will suffer the consequences and are likely to ultimately lose customers; barring a dramatic turnaround, these organizations will in the end fail and be pushed aside or disappear from the market completely. This is not an exaggeration.

> *We need to make change a competency,*
> *make change something we know we are*
> *great at.*

Ambitious, yes, but not as hard as one might think. The key is to build change into everything we do from the very beginning. It will require the redesign or possibly the scrapping of some current systems, but that is perfectly okay and should be expected.

If anything, we should be alarmed if we are trying to move forward into the future with all our current systems in place. This just won't work—the technologies and systems of today are simply not up to meeting the demands of the Imperative and the next twenty-five years of the evolution of IT.

How could they be? Everything is changing.

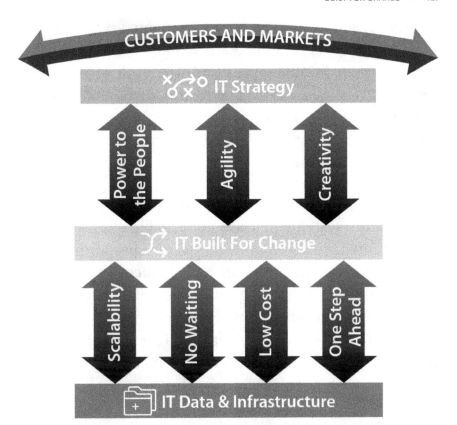

Figure 15.1 Making IT Ready for Change

Figure 15.1 calls out some of the elements that should be considered when developing a plan that makes IT equipped for change—big change and small change. As with anything that is important, this does not happen by accident, but it is within our reach. Change will be driven from outside, by customers and their markets, so as such we won't have a warning before change impacts us, nor will we know what the change will be. This is a reminder of how important flexibility will be—we can't know what change will come next, so we need to be ready for anything. This takes some thoughtful preparation and needs to be part of our IT strategy.

This is not simply a tactic. A few key characteristics include scalability, a path to immediate action, creativity, and the empowerment of employees and users. All of these elements will leverage the data and infrastructure of IT, recognizing there is more and more value and insight that lives within our data. Data is increasingly strategic, and so much opportunity lives there.

By both aligning existing systems to embrace change, and by replacing systems that are not capable of operating in this new high-change paradigm, we are preparing IT for this undeniable tide of change and, as such, preparing the full organization for making change a competency and then a competitive advantage. Change is not comfortable, but we are called to forge ahead. Our talented people will surprise us in how quickly they adapt. We only need a small nudge to make incredible things happen here.

AGILITY

Much has been made of the concept of agility for software development and for project management among other disciplines. This is a bit different.

In order for IT to be great with change, and comfortable with change, we must design in agility for every system and every process we both manage and build.

To use a sports analogy—it has been said that the difference between an average player and a great player is the thought that runs through their mind at the end of a close game. The average player says to himself, "Please, don't give me the ball," whereas the great player says to himself, "Please, give me the ball" and both players mean it and believe it 100 percent. This is only possible when we know deep down we are capable and ready.

The difference between an average IT organization and a great organization is that the great organization is ready for, almost to the point of eager anticipation, big changes so they can launch into action and leverage the design for agility that anticipates these big changes.

This is only possible with careful planning and design that removes every possible dimension and component that can block us or slow us down in IT when change comes.

Too many IT organizations *hope* change does not come, and this is futile. Yes, change might come slowly and these same organizations are lucky for a while, but change will always come. It is only a matter of when.

Agility in this context goes beyond the ability to change. It takes this idea further and requires that we can make these same changes quickly, and at a low cost. All of this together begins to capture what agility must be for IT.

You might note this is clearly NOT what many IT organizations are today. But in fairness, this capacity for change and agility was not demanded of IT in the past and so it was easy to keep many things as they were.

But today is the beginning of a new standard with the Imperative, and this is a key element of what we must be for the future: in many ways, the antithesis of the traditional IT model. The wonderful concept of agility says so much about what IT will become for the future, and I would offer that an agile IT organization says so much about our people and our leadership.

Knowing what it takes to arrive at agility, it will never be a mistake and can only be achieved with strategic planning, commitment, forward-looking design, and a disciplined implementation of the agility improvements.

A truly remarkable thing to see.

SCALABILITY

Plan for success. Plan for the growth that comes with success. Enjoy the fun that only comes with the combination of growth and success.

Plan for extreme growth, the growth we all dream about in business and are fortunate to be part of once or perhaps twice in our careers. This is a good mark to set and, better yet, it is fun. What could be more fun than planning for and anticipating success and then enjoying all the benefits that come along with winning, a prosperous business, and growing and keeping loyal customers?

IT is uniquely positioned to plan for this success and growth as IT knows our technologies and systems best. And few things will stop success faster than systems that can't scale.

It is a fundamental law of technology that designs taken early are the most cost-effective. Conversely, efforts to fix a faulty or limiting design later in the lifecycle of a system or a technology are far more expensive if even possible. Scalability follows this model. If anything, rebuilding systems to scale after they have been deployed and operating for a while is a very, very difficult and expensive undertaking. It is worth our time to thoughtfully build scalability into everything we do.

A few good questions to ask ourselves when evaluating an existing system or a planned new system:

1. What does it mean if our current volume of transactions doubles?
2. What does it mean if the number of users doubles? Increases by 10X? Increases by 50X?
3. What will happen to response time and performance at each volume level?
4. How does the system perform at these levels?
5. Does the system have a volume-related breaking point?
6. Are there any existing limits on the database(s) that support the system?
7. What are our license costs for any applications related to the system?
8. Does growth at these levels require new servers or any other asset investments?

With only a bit of planning, we can be far more confident in our ability to scale—these questions are just the beginning, of course, but exploring these answers can influence all the decisions we make going forward. Then, if the growth comes, we are prepared and confident in the ability of IT to enhance versus work against the business. If the growth does not come, then we have other issues that need attention. And so the cycle of business goes. With this proactive approach, IT moves into and stays in the category of enabler.

POWER TO THE PEOPLE

The rebirth of IT calls for us to create happy and empowered users of our IT systems.

This is leverage and helps us move away from the brute force model mentioned in other discussions throughout the book. This is a key principle. Why? Because a user who has more control is a user who can move more quickly, is engaged, happy, and less expensive to support.

An empowered user becomes a partner to the business and creates part of the momentum that ultimately creates the proactive model for IT that is so important. Taking this a step further, an empowered user with a sense of control begins to adopt a business mindset and thinks more like an entrepreneur than like a frustrated and powerless employee.

This is good for everybody and is an engine for both innovation and energy across the organization. It is a beautiful thing to behold. IT occupies a unique position in the organization in being able to create this model.

The paradigm of systems requiring special skills in order to make common changes is one that is slow, expensive, and frustrating to the users of these systems.

These checkpoints violate several of our Imperative principles. Anything that is slow can't be tolerated. We should all be ruthless in systematically eliminating anything in the business that slows us down. When we have an element of the business, in any shape or form, that is both slow and expensive, well, that is a big problem and the worst of all worlds.

Add to this a frustrated and unhappy internal or external customer, and what we have is a perfect storm of bad.

Systems must be designed to allow users to make most common changes themselves. Specialized tasks might require a different skill, but these tasks are increasingly unusual.

> *We can't allow administration of these systems to slow us down and take power away from our teams that are accountable for delivering completed projects and hitting the milestones that make the business run.*

It is a good exercise to ask ourselves, "How can we put the user in control of what they do every day?" If we start with this mindset, lots of progress will be made and over time the user can do everything.

The traditional IT paradigm had a level of fear in this

regard, but we now need to put this bias behind us. This paradigm was driven by some level of fear the user would create damage to our systems or create some number of other problems for these same systems. But the benefits of giving power to the users of these systems, the users who are driving the business, far outweigh whatever risks might remain.

It is important to note that the sophistication of our applications and systems have come too far and improved so dramatically, many of the risks that formed these concerns have been eliminated.

LOW COST

Building for successful change is not a single-track under-taking. It requires thoughtful design on a number of dif-ferent fronts. When embracing the mindset of the new IT, being great is not enough.

We have to be great and do it in a way that is optimal in terms of cost and people. We must embrace a strategy that is multidimensional and operate in a way that honors mul-tiple priorities. No, this is not easy, but IT will rise to the challenge.

Back to people and money—both are precious resources, and we need to treat them as such. Solving problems by throwing people or money at the issue is of little benefit. Yes, there was a time when we could operate that way, and some might cling to the idea, but those days are long gone. If you do operate in a business today with unlimited bud-get, please send me a note. I would love to hear from you! My Twitter handle is at the end of the book.

*When we recall that the resources of
capital and people in particular are so
precious, and when we take a long-term
view of the business and the organization,
we see things differently.*

The principle of cost is an overlay across scalability, ease of use, and agility, to name a few. As we design these important elements, we take on the additional responsibility of meeting these needs in a cost-effective way—not easy, but absolutely necessary and in line with managing multiple priorities. One key to managing our performance-related priorities while optimizing cost is to adopt this strategy across all teams from the beginning of each initiative or project.

*When we start any journey with this
mindset, we can be successful. However,
when we try to inject a cost-optimal
mindset into a project that is in flight, it
becomes very difficult and, ironically, more
expensive.*

The people of IT are very talented and will rise to any challenge when given the opportunity. Building the IT organization and the systems of IT for change is such an opportunity.

IT leadership won't have, and won't need to have, all the answers as we take on the elements of the initiative, including building our future for change. But that is okay. Leadership simply needs to provide the goals, some of the key assumptions, and let our good people run with the charter. This is healthy and empowering, and we will be amazed at what our talented people can accomplish.

People appreciate honest and authentic leadership and they appreciate being trusted and empowered. We can accomplish all these things within this initiative of *built for change* and the sub-initiative of *low cost*. Pick a small team of some of our best people and give them the charter to identify how we improve our existing IT systems to be more capable of making changes in the future, and to bring back to IT a new framework for how future systems will be designed for and operate successfully with a high level of change.

> *This strategy and work will be occurring in virtually every IT organization over the next five years. This is not an option. Being great at change becomes a core competency of IT, and we must lead the way for the full organization.*

NO WAITING

As we build IT for change, changes—when necessary—should be executed immediately.

> *Immediacy can't be left to chance; it should be designed for from the very beginning.*

The ability to make changes immediately is vital to the chain of actions that support our principles of *fast, low cost,* and much more. This chain of action can't be broken by delays in the ability to make changes to our systems. We will not normally know when change will occur, so our ability to respond immediately—or in some cases take proactive action that anticipates change—brings tremendous value to IT and the full organization.

No waiting for change can be accomplished in a number of different ways.

> *A preferred strategy is to design our systems to be flexible and agile, and at the same time to have the skills necessary*

to make these changes kept in-house. We want to have complete control.

It is difficult to rely on the specialized skills that we likely need to contract for when these skills are not with our people on staff. This was common in the past for IT but should be avoided with great vigor for the future. It creates a dependency that moves control of our timeline outside our organization, which goes against the Imperative that calls for us to focus on speed. This is a good strategy to carry forward with all that we do in IT.

If something is important, we want to have complete control over that element with no dependencies that can put us at risk. It's a great example of some thoughtful planning bringing back to us tremendous value in the future.

Because when we need this control, we really need it. And it can translate to competitive advantage for the business. For example, the business makes the decision to start doing business in a new country. This requires, among other things, the ability to create sales quotes and to do invoicing in a new language and a new currency. If IT does not have the ability to make these system changes independently, this can create both a significant cost and a significant delay. The delay associated with hiring consultants or submitting a change request to a software vendor and having these changes completed can be weeks or months.

A further risk associated with this path is simply not knowing how long it will take and not being confident in providing a timeline for this change back to leadership and the business.

A position of risk and poor control is one we need to avoid; if we find ourselves in this position, it weakens the confidence the organization has in IT.

However, if we have designed in the ability to make changes with in-house skills, we can expect this work to be completed in days, which is a significant time savings on the clock of business in the future, and another example of IT planning and acting strategically versus reacting to tactical needs. A possible exception here would be a capable service provider. The key being *capable*. Capable in terms of fast, capable in terms of skilled, and capable in terms of having the right level of capacity. This type of service provider can be a valuable extension of the IT organization and a strategic resource. This does however set a high bar for any service provider that can help us achieve the goals outlined throughout the book.

Absolute control gives us leverage, and leverage brings us value.

CREATIVITY

Creativity, long missing from many IT organizations, has a place in the strategic management of change and as such in the rebirth of IT. The element of creativity, as we will see here, is vital to managing change, but also plays an important cultural role.

> ***It is possible for creativity and technical expertise to coexist, and for each to enhance the other.***

This is not only possible, it should be encouraged and nurtured in IT. Some problems can't be solved with technical knowledge, nor by brute force, but require a new and creative solution that requires a different way of thinking and a different approach.

Sometimes the combination of these analytical skills and creative skills exist in the same person. This is not common, but some talented people have these skills, and these are people who have always been valuable contributors but become even more so in the future of IT. They must be recognized, managed for growth, and assigned to strategic projects where their unique skills can make a big contribution, while they at the same time find these assignments exciting.

Not all challenges that come with a high rate of change can be solved with technology.

When technology alone can be a solution, we take that quick win and move on. But in other cases we must look to creative solutions, doing what has not been done before, or taking a new vector from an existing solution. This is exciting for the organization and for our people.

> *We need to embrace this creative element and know that some of the best solutions delivered from IT in the next ten years will come from something completely new, a "crazy" idea, if you will.*

We can't expect IT leadership to have these answers—what we need from leadership is to recognize the value of an innovative solution and form a small team of our talented people, giving them the time and opportunity to brainstorm and bring new ideas back to IT.

> *Brainstorming is a healthy exercise and important to resetting the culture of IT and increasing our focus on innovating and the creative element.*

These are high-value solutions that have a high impact on the organization, but if people are not given the opportunity to think and explore new ideas, these solutions never see the light of day.

ONE STEP AHEAD

Being proactive is a desired lifestyle for IT, and a powerful lifestyle it is when it becomes reality. Long a pursuit of IT, the ability to stay one step ahead of the business is now within our reach.

An evolution of change in the business is anticipating change versus waiting for change to arrive and then taking action. This anticipation is part of the transformation cycle of proactive IT. When we anticipate change, our teams are enabled and empowered, and change does not knock us back. It's a much better way to operate every day, and further, it is all under our control.

A good model to anticipate change and stay one step ahead is to actively run "what-if" scenarios. War games, if you will. This is a healthy exercise.

We take a small team in IT and evaluate multiple scenarios around what can happen in the business, and what that change would mean to IT, our tools, our systems, and our technologies. Performing this exercise every day is not practical, but we need to make time for this planning on a regular schedule. Half a day on a quarterly basis is a good place to start.

As part of this exercise, good questions to ask ourselves are: What change would impact IT the most? What would we do? What can we do now to be better prepared?

Then, create a strawman plan for how we take this change head-on. This could include minor changes to systems or processes today that could save us significant time later.

> *Another question to ask is: What is the one change in the business that scares us the most? I use the word "scare" here by design, but there is a big difference between what concerns us and what scares us. A big difference.*

Then—what would we do if that time came? Is there anything we can do now? This is not an easy exercise, but a very healthy one. Even a short period of thought and planning makes a big difference versus a change arriving suddenly with no prior thought on our part.

Our goal should be to push our own planning process to ensure no change can arrive in the business that we have not considered. Of course, it is unlikely we can anticipate every permutation of every possible scenario, but this should be the goal. The pursuit of this goal causes us to be creative and think beyond the simple and obvious paths the business can take.

Then from time to time, a change will hit the business and one that has been discussed in our quarterly planning process.

> *When that does happen, we should do a debrief on reality as it unfolded versus our strawman plan and make any changes in our quarterly planning process that can make it better and more useful when a crazy idea becomes reality—because it will happen again.*

This gives us a cycle of improvement and lets us get just a little better each time. Over the course of months, quarters, and years, it makes a big difference in how we think and how we act in IT. Looking ahead creates a cultural change and shapes how all managers and front-line IT people view both IT and the broader organization.

KEY TAKEAWAYS: BUILT FOR CHANGE

1. Our world, the markets we serve, and the needs of our clients are changing faster than ever. This leaves us with a fundamental choice—do we suffer through each change hoping the next one will not come soon, or do we embrace change and make it a competency? Anticipate change and design for change in everything we do and expect to be great at executing changes at every level.

2. Planning for success and for the growth that accompanies success is both a healthy and a powerful mindset. A focus on success will often help to ensure that success does, in fact, come. And with growth comes change, so we can't allow a lack of scalability to stand in the way of success. Life is better in IT and across the business when we are successful; IT must build this scalability from the inside out, and with that will come a readiness that we must have in every organization when we are asked the question "What if..." On that day we will be able to answer that IT is ready. Don't wait on us.

3. The call of *built for change* extends from the largest and most complex corporate system to the single user needing to make a change in a simple application. Both are important and both must be

considered and anticipated in our broader change strategy. Every change that can be accommodated quickly and easily brings a great energy back to the organization. This creates an empowered, motivated, and engaged workforce supported by systems that can keep pace with the new speed of IT and business. If we are not built for change, we are built to fail in the rebirth of IT.

CHAPTER 16

BEST PRACTICES & METHODOLOGIES

We are fortunate today in the wonderful world of IT to have access to a historical high of best practices, models, standards, and methodologies to enhance the operations of the IT organization. This treasure is ultimately a very good thing, but it is important we keep these items in the proper perspective and leverage the right element at the right time and in the right role.

> *With any framework, methodology, or best practice that has experienced some success and an enthusiastic following, there is a tendency to take these elements above and beyond where they were intended to go.*

Any overreaching can create some risk that might diminish the effectiveness and value to the organization and, in the worst cases, cause the methodology to fail completely when it could have ultimately added value if kept in the proper context.

We will take a closer look at four of the more popular IT best practices and methodologies today: ITIL, SIAM, Dev Ops, and Agile. This is not intended to be a complete list or a complete technical description of each but rather an orientation to help us understand how these example items should be managed and what their place in IT is likely to be.

This approach could then be applied to any new methodologies that will appear in the future throughout the rebirth of IT over the next ten years, and we can be sure new ones will appear.

This evolutionary process will never stop.

Each of our examples is different yet with some striking similarities. Of course, new models and methodologies are emerging today, but the following discussion can likely apply to anything new that finds a place in IT over the next decade. And we should expect that some new methods will simply come and then fade away quickly, unable to prove their value or make IT perform better with regard to the elements laid out in this book.

With each of these elements, it is important to understand what the model was intended to do, and what it should not be expected to provide.

> *In each case, these elements are not the strategy; they must support the strategy of IT in a specific role and in a specific manner. They are role players.*

We need to ask a simple question—does the model directly support the strategy of IT, and does it make us better in delivering directly to this strategy? This is not to imply these roles are not important, because they certainly are, but make no mistake—each of these elements has a defined role. We will explore these roles more closely in the sections that follow.

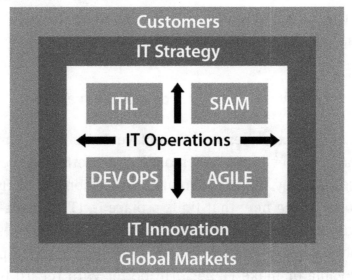

Figure 16.1 The Context of Best Practices & Frameworks

Figure 16.1 depicts a context for ITIL, SIAM, DevOps, and Agile as well as any others emerging today and in the future. Although our attention is often on this group today, there will be others and likely a few that will eclipse what we focus on today.

Regardless of the stature we might want to give these

models, it is important to remember to keep these best practices in the right place—supporting the strategy of IT. Each of these models can enhance innovation and enrich strategy, make no mistake, but the full strategy of IT is much broader and much richer than any single best practice or framework can provide. Of course, this full model is all about providing more value to our customers and the markets we serve.

As we prepare to invest in and implement any of these four, or any future best practice set, we should ask ourselves a few additional questions beyond the earlier one we posed:

1. How will this investment drive value to our customers?
2. Does the investment improve our competitive position in the market?
3. How will the investment improve the satisfaction of current customers?
4. Can the investment directly enable the business to win new customers?
5. What risks are we taking on with this investment and deployment?
6. What is the investment required to implement this initiative?
7. Do we have any experience with the methodology or best practice?
8. Have we defined a clear role for the framework in question?
9. How does this initiative directly support the strategy of IT?

10. Have we carefully set expectations across the organization?
11. What are the measurable benefits we expect to receive from the investment?
12. What is the definition of success?
13. Have we identified the people resources that will be assigned to and own this initiative?

This list will get you started; you will no doubt have many other good questions to add.

It is best to take these questions head-on and not have any surprises or mismatches of expectations later. For example, ITIL has suffered at times from unreasonable expectations and overly aggressive timelines. This has happened with the other three as well but perhaps not to the degree of ITIL.

These questions are intended to provide a pragmatic checkpoint recognizing how easy it is to quickly embrace something new and exciting because it is new and exciting. But our time and resources are precious, and neither of these should be invested before properly vetting any existing or new models or methods and asking some tough questions.

We should begin with the realization that if we allow any one or more of these elements to rise to be the strategy of IT, then we are diluting the overall effectiveness of IT. And as such, we divide our efforts when we should have all our resources working toward what must be a single and unifying strategy—one that is connected to the business and our customers.

ITIL

The IT Infrastructure Library has gained a well-deserved reputation as a versatile and robust framework for the Service Management practice within IT and in some cases now extending beyond IT in the form of Enterprise Service Management (ESM).

Although ITIL did not directly drive the growth of ESM over the past ten years, the terminology, process models, and structures it provides has helped fuel the maturity and refinement of ITSM across IT. And as such, it helped to make the appeal of ITSM stronger to the remainder of the business, thus encouraging the growth of ESM. But let's get back to ITIL within IT.

The ITIL framework has grown over the past fifteen years to now include approximately twenty-seven processes and functions.

While this expansion of the ITIL scope over the past fifteen years has provided a broader and more diverse framework

> *supported by more robust models for IT to leverage, it has brought with it some challenges.*

Some organizations with a high level of ITSM experience and a deeper pool of resources are able to take on a broader set of the ITIL framework and leverage the framework across IT successfully. These organizations have come to appreciate that the ultimate success of ITIL is very much a journey, often taken in carefully planned steps and phases, and supported by IT leadership with a degree of patience.

ITIL can't be pushed hard and fast. This is a formula for failure. When looking closely at an organization that has been successful with ITIL, the story of success will always include a patient and supportive management team along with a talented team of practitioners who have had some training and in most cases previous implementation experience with ITIL.

However, organizations with more limited ITSM experience or limited resources must make careful and smart choices around the processes of ITIL to focus on and determine which are the best fit for a particular organization with a particular set of challenges. This is a set of priorities and decisions that have proven to be complex and potentially overwhelming for some organizations.

To underscore a point made in the opening of this chapter, ITIL is at its best when supporting the broader strategy of IT, and should not be seen as providing us a strategy that is missing for the whole of IT. For example, the strategy of IT could include a new focus on customer engagement. And to make this strategy a success, we can leverage the service request, self-service, and service catalog elements of ITIL to help IT operate in a manner that creates happy and loyal customers.

This allows ITIL to assist the improved operations of IT and to thrive in the right role.

> *We could implement these self-serve models without ITIL, of course, but when used properly ITIL will likely get us there faster and with a more robust and scalable result.*

What we have in the end is IT operations working in line with the IT strategy and in line with the strategy of the business. This is exactly what our goal must be for the rebirth of IT and another example of how this powerful synergy exists in so many places across IT from top to bottom and left to right. Virtually boundless.

DEVOPS

DevOps has had a dramatic impact on IT, technology, and development organizations over the past ten years. Remarkably, we can trace the beginning of DevOps to 2007/2008, although it feels like it has been with us for much longer. This is a testament to the rapid and widespread adoption during this time and taking on a sometimes larger-than-life persona across IT.

It is easier to understand the success of DevOps when we take a closer look at exactly what DevOps represents. To a large degree, DevOps is not easy to define in simple terms as it is a combination of process, technology, philosophy, and culture. In many ways, this multidimensionality is exactly why DevOps has proven to be so useful to so many organizations.

We could use the following simple terms to describe DevOps:

1. Collaboration
2. Communication
3. Continuous integration
4. Lean

5. Adaptable
6. Organizational alignment
7. High quality and reliable

This is, of course, not a comprehensive list, but it captures some of the key points in DevOps for the purposes of this discussion. There is something significant in this profile that is begging to be addressed.

> *The nature of DevOps is very much a reflection of the future of IT and the forces that are driving our rebirth and the Imperative.*

It is certainly true that DevOps has created a focus on IT operations and development, but this is a micro model for what we must achieve across all of IT and then extend into every element and every corner of the business. The extension and expansion are unstoppable because these forces are so natural and powerful at the same time.

Taking this a step further, there is a powerful set of synergies that exists between the four highlighted elements in this chapter—SIAM, ITIL, DevOps, and Agile. Each shares some qualities with the others, and yet they are very different at the same time.

> *Some have suggested in recent years there exists some conflict or competition between different elements of these four. I could not disagree more.*

When implemented correctly, these four are highly synergistic and contribute value in different and necessary ways. We need each of these wonderful frameworks, philosophies, best practices, and operating models in order to first directly support the new strategy of IT and to help us operate IT better every day to make our strategy a reality. This distinction is important—we must start with strategy and how the model enables that strategy before digging into the details of how we operate.

The role of operations will become clear only in the light of strategy, which allows us to design, select, and deploy tools, technology, and techniques in order to bring strategy to life.

SIAM

The rapid evolution and growing complexity of IT today has created a strategic and tactical need for a scalable model for service integration and management (SIAM). Like other models reviewed here, the principles of SIAM will continue to adapt to the changing needs of our global IT markets, but the core principles have proven both valuable and essential to the IT organization of the future.

> ***In many ways, the practices of SIAM are a reflection of the transforming IT organization as a whole.***

In fact, the needs of a multi-sourced IT organization call to our attention the fundamentals of managing and integrating IT services internally, as well as from a dynamic network of service providers.

The principles that drive sound IT performance must apply to a small or a large network of service providers, integrators, and partners. This mix may change and likely will, but the objectives of how we work and what we deliver will remain consistent.

Today, the rapid growth of Cloud and the "As-A-Service" model as a readily available and proven, cost-effective, flexible, and scalable alternative for IT has further accelerated the evolution of SIAM. Another example of the layers of synergy that exist across SIAM is the adoption of Cloud solutions in IT today—at its heart, Cloud is very much complementary to SIAM as another readily available source of service providers and can be mobilized quickly and effectively to service the strategy of IT.

At the center of SIAM is the management of multiple service providers to a common set of goals carried forward by the IT organization. In particular, larger IT organizations must leverage a diverse network of service providers in a dynamic mix of services that meet the constantly changing needs of the market today. This provides flexibility and scalability that is very difficult to achieve with an "internal services only" model. As a further advantage of the multiple service providers model, IT is able to leverage specific vertical market, geographic, or domain expertise that is available through services specialists—expertise that can't be matched internally by IT.

To help understand the structural scope of SIAM, some of the building blocks leveraged include:

1. Service Desk
2. Service Catalog
3. Service Portfolios
4. Knowledge Management
5. Supplier Management and Coordination
6. Service Continuity

7. Service Testing
8. IT Information Security

To effectively leverage these building blocks and to create a flexible integration model, SIAM leverages what is effectively a matrix, where the integrator spans the network of providers and services and the relationship to customers. Managing this relationship can be done in a highly transparent manner, where the customer fully understands the network of providers, or in a much less transparent manner, where the customer does not have visibility of the combination of service providers and services, and the integrator manages the communications and expectations of the customer. This is a sensible model that provides the necessary flexibility in recognizing the very different needs of customer organizations and cultures today.

The widespread adoption of SIAM has only been possible as driven by a core set of benefits for IT today, including:

1. IT operating as a single virtual team leveraging the resources of the internal organization in synergy with an extensive network of experienced and skilled service providers
2. Ease and efficiency of onboarding new IT services and solutions
3. Optimal resource utilization at a reduced cost
4. High level of flexibility in addressing new solution requirements
5. Extended network of expertise and skills to drive innovation and proactive IT service

6. Improved controls and metrics across IT and all service providers

7. Ease of access to proven models, content, and methods that complement the business and markets served

8. Reduced implementation costs through reuse of proven models and methodologies—effectively a high-quality, out-of-the-box solution set

9. More consistent quality for IT service delivery

10. Improved scalability through proven service providers able to mobilize quickly while drawing on a large and dynamic resource pool

Note that like ITIL, DevOps, and Agile, SIAM relies on a core set of principles that emphasize flexibility, scalability, and adaptability without sacrificing quality and the integrity of the solution that is ultimately provided by IT.

This is a great model that can be leveraged by the evolving IT organization and a fundamental driver for both the value and the staying power of SIAM.

AGILE

Agile methodology has a place in this chapter given its current widespread use in project management and software development—but it goes far beyond this. Agile as a methodology has proven to be remarkably adaptable and resilient. We have and will continue to see new and creative applications of the fundamental agile strategy and principles.

As with the other three elements of this chapter, *agile* offers strong value in its own model, but reflects many of the principles driving the rebirth of IT and the framework of our Imperative.

A few key points to capture the agile approach:
1. Work performed is incremental and highly iterative
2. Teams retain a high level of authority and decision making
3. It focuses on high-value work elements
4. Every work process must include a high level of customer interaction

5. A commitment to collaboration with all stakeholders is vital
6. It's designed for frequent deliveries of the product
7. Testing occurs constantly
8. Assume requirements will change frequently

Of course, there is a great deal of meaning and detail behind each of these points, but this profile captures the essence of agile.

In a rapidly changing global market, and with increasing customer expectations and competitive forces, we can see the natural fit for agile in driving our success in IT and across the full business.

Although not stated as a specific point, speed and flexibility are implied. This takes us back to the heart of what we must be in the future of IT and what the business must become in order to be successful in the decade ahead.

Agile did not suddenly appear on the scene as a new and completely unique framework of all-original ideas.

In fact, agile borrowed and adapted ideas and models from existing methodologies, including:

1. SCRUM
2. DSDM
3. Crystal
4. Extreme Programming
5. Theory of Constraints
6. Pragmatic Programming

7. Adaptive Development

As agile continues to develop and we look at the history of agile and the adaptations that are natural given this is one of the core principles of agile itself, we are reminded of the contrast between traditional approaches and agile. Here are a few examples:

Old Way:	Agile Way:
1. Limited customer involvement	1. Constant customer engagement
2. Long development cycles	2. Short iterations
3. Poor readiness for changes	3. Be great at adapting to change
4. High focus on process	4. Results rule over process
5. Decisions take time	5. Fast decision making is paramount

Agile continues to remind us of how useful it can be both in the daily operations of and in supporting the future strategy of IT.

There is a clear intersection between the core principles of agile and the Imperative driving the rebirth of IT, including:

A. Customer satisfaction takes priority over all else.
B. We must be flexible and great at change.
C. All delivery timelines must be fast.
D. Business people and technology people must form a virtual team.

E. We must create constant communications.

F. Build a highly skilled and highly empowered culture.

> *With these striking synergies, agile can be leveraged as an important resource to help accomplish our short-term and longer-term objectives in the transformation of IT.*

We should also watch the continued evolution of agile in order to further leverage new advancements and innovations that will likely spring from agile over the next ten years.

Like DevOps, SIAM, and ITIL, there is a community of very dedicated and talented people driving agile forward, and these people all want the same thing—to make a meaningful contribution to the future of technology, IT, and the business. With this commitment, they are likely to be successful. We can all benefit from the amazing value these four methodologies will continue to bring us far into the future.

KEY TAKEAWAYS:
BEST PRACTICES & METHODOLOGIES

1. Although there are many best practices, frameworks, and methodologies available to IT today, I have selected four of the best known and impactful as examples for this discussion—ITIL, DevOps, Agile, and SIAM. As an IT professional, it is likely you have had some experience with one or more from this group. A key point to remember is to be clear on what each of these is, and what they are not. Each has had a big impact and has gained a loyal following, but this should not be confused with the strategy and mission of IT. In a supporting role, any combination of this group can be valuable and enhance IT performance, but we must be as clear about their limitations as we are about the upside.

2. Whether it be ITIL, DevOps, SIAM, or Agile, set the right expectations from day one. Each of these elements carries a big reputation and we need to guard against irrational exuberance and runaway expectations that can't be met. One part of these expectations to watch is the timeline of implementation. A meaningful investment of time and resource will be required to get the most from any of these four, and this should be understood and quantified. Be very

clear on this point. A proven approach includes multiple phases with phase debriefs, so have a model in mind for these iterations.

3. Know what success looks like before embarking on the journey with any combination of these four methodologies. This is not something to figure out later, and our view of success should include specific measurements that can be quantified as well as feedback from key stakeholders. Then, when success does come we will have the support of business owners, happy stakeholders, and a message that is ready to be delivered to the organization in support of the investment that was made.

CHAPTER 17

THE STRATEGIC CIO

The world of the CIO today is very different than that of just a few years ago, and the forces of change are growing rapidly, driven by a dynamic and global set of market forces that won't be denied and won't subside.

While the fundamentals of IT remain constant—managing and securing the assets of the organization while ensuring the delivery of quality services—a rapidly changing world-wide marketplace has created a great deal of new complexity for the CIO and for IT.

A few examples of this new complexity include:
1. Governance and compliance
2. Sophisticated security threats
3. Increased global competition
4. An increasingly mobile workforce
5. Aggressive technology audits
6. Rapid proliferation of endpoints
7. Adoption of the Cloud

8. Evolving audit and regulatory standards
9. An always-on business model
10. Navigating the rapid transformation of IT
11. Increased business dependency on technology
12. The need to safeguard and leverage an enormous volume of corporate data

Of course this is just the beginning. The strategic CIO understands the timeline of change is unpredictable and will never stop. This can be an opportunity for IT and the full business, and this begins with the CIO and IT.

The CIO sets the tone for all that happens across the IT organization. If the CIO is seen to embrace a strategic focus that governs all we do in the day-to-day operations of IT, this style is quickly adopted by the VPs, directors, managers, and every staff member in IT. The CIO sets the new cultural tone for everything we do.

This is a fundamental part of the transformation of IT. It begins with the transformation of our tactical CIO of the past, moving to the strategic CIO, who is so essential to making the new IT a reality.

This shift brings with it a new strategic agenda for IT that overlays the many day-to-day operational responsibilities that won't disappear altogether.

CUSTOMER FOCUS

The strategic CIO faces many challenges as we highlighted in the introduction on the previous pages, and these are but a few examples. At the top of these growing priorities might very well be bringing a customer focus to the IT organization.

This focus best comes from leadership and must include a cultural change in addition to many other elements that will make this change complete. Every member of the IT organization, be it small or one that supports a global 50 enterprise, must understand and feel the passion for customers. And this must be reinforced every day by the CIO and the senior leadership of IT.

> *If the CIO models this passion every day,*
> *it will be contagious throughout IT. Good*
> *people are easy to convince the customer*
> *has ascended to the top of our priorities.*

This focus takes many forms and must include the direct connection we described in The Customer Connection (Chapter 2), and it should also be reflected in the investments made by IT. This is an important clarification—if we say the customer is important but when faced with tough choices related to our budgets and investments, we consistently cut customer-related programs in favor of internal-focused programs, then we are sabotaging the customer passion we are working so hard to create.

Figure 17.1 The Essence of the Strategic CIO

While the strategic CIO must balance many things, Figure 17.1 shows a few of the key things close to the heart of the CIO, and this begins with the customer. The CIO should set the tone across IT, and a passion for everything customer related will begin here.

Also note that the CIO will understand how important it is to be a master recruiter and talent developer, one who seeks strong partnerships, many of which are external to IT and to the business, and a true innovator. It is, of course, not easy to balance these things, but the strategic CIO will understand what is at stake, will be a strong leader, and will be up to the task.

Because we want to keep this chapter at a strategic level, we will keep our focus on the broader mission of the CIO. This begins with the conviction of the CIO and the cultural change it will create.

This is a simple but very powerful concept—make it clear every day that nothing takes priority over the customer throughout IT, and there will be no stronger influence over the transformation of IT.

> *This makes decisions clear, gives our people something to rally around, reinforces where we should spend our time, and brings a shape to the purpose of our technology, systems, and data.*

And, of course, the examples go on from there.
If the strategic CIO can do but one thing to effect real and lasting change in IT, this authentic and consistent focus on the customer would likely be that thing.

With this, we simply can't get far off course, and everything becomes more clear.

A VISION & ROAD MAP FOR IT

The strategic CIO will have a living vision for IT which must be understood by the IT leadership team, the IT front-line management team, and all the operations and execution teams.

The vision of the CIO has always been important, but today it is more vital than ever. In many cases, this vision will serve as the catalyst for the rebirth of IT and for both challenging and changing much of what we do today.

It is not a stretch to say the IT organization needs the vision of the CIO more than ever. The need and hunger do not stop there—the business needs the vision of the CIO because it is capable of unlocking the synergies and innovative forces that are so vital to future success in the local and global marketplaces.

The road map supports the vision. It is our compass for the operations and execution of the IT organizations and helps us to navigate each and every day.

This vision can and should be a simple statement, but also taking the form of key actions, deliverables, and milestones that can be captured in the form of a road map. The road map is a valuable tool in communicating the direction of IT across the organization and across the business, helping all our people to understand the vision, buy in to what lies ahead, and stay synchronized in the work we do every day.

There is no right or wrong way to build a road map, but a few things should be included:

1. A high-level vision statement that is easy to understand and provides context
2. A three- to five-year road map horizon—not too short, not too long
3. A core set of actionable goals that support the vision statement
4. Key milestones and deliverables that are a must for success (this is not a detailed project plan, so only a few milestones per year is about right)
5. An expectation from the beginning that the road map is a living thing and will be updated as needed
6. A process for communicating the road map and future new versions to the organization
7. Key principles that enable IT to make the tough decisions we know will come
8. A few success criteria so IT understands what success looks like

This is not a long document; in fact, short and simple is better. It is not enough for the CIO and the CIO staff to understand the road map. We need everybody in IT to have a basic understanding of what the road map contains.

> *This is a vehicle to help us create the*
> *cultural understanding and alignment that*
> *is so important to the rebirth of IT.*

The road map will also offer very practical uses. The IT road map will serve as a valuable reference when setting priorities, assigning resources, and allocating budgets for the work we do every day. All of these decisions and work efforts should be aligned with the road map and bring us closer to making the vision a reality.

In some cases and depending on many factors, it can be a daunting task to create the first version of the road map. That is understandable.

> *However, creating a road map is vital, so*
> *an option to help us get started is to pull*
> *back to a smaller scope for the road map.*
> *A good place to start is with our mission*
> *critical systems.*

Mission critical systems are systems the business relies on every day to keep the business running. If we lose one of these systems, there is an immediate impact on customers or revenue. By creating a draft of the IT road map for these mission critical systems, we streamline the work necessary to get the first version done, and at the same time address the strategy and plan for the core systems that are most vital to the business.

The mission critical systems IT road map can then be shared and discussed, and any necessary updates can be made. This basic plan now in place brings a great deal of value to IT and to the extended business. As a next step, we can expand the scope of this first version to include critical projects for the coming year or some other set of investments that are timely and should be addressed.

With the cycle now established, it gets easier to keep the road map fresh and, as such, provide a valuable reference to IT.

A BUSINESS MINDSET

IT has a rich history of technology expertise. This has been our core competence from the beginning and, as such, our top priority.

Today, what the business needs from us is changing, a bigger change than we have seen in the past thirty years. The need for technology and data expertise has not gone away. But we in IT are now called to possess business skills and aptitude in addition to our technology charter.

> **Where before we worked on the single level, or single plane of thought if you will, of technology, we must now think and act on two levels—how can we best leverage technology and data for the greater good of the business?**

More than this really, how can we innovate and leverage the technology we have at hand to better serve our customers and create a competitive advantage in the market? This changes everything.

And it is simply a fact that IT is best qualified to deliver this to the organization. It is natural for IT. If forced to find another solution, the business will no doubt find one. But it will take more time and be costly. The fastest and optimal solution to the challenge of innovating and how we best use technology to create happy customers is a solution that is delivered by IT.

The business mindset begins with an understanding of the business and a desire to create positive business outcomes, and how IT can contribute directly to this outcome. This will require improved communications and new partnerships across the organization. We will need a direct and open dialogue with sales, marketing, technical support, R&D, and services, to name a few.

This section name referenced "mindset" because this is where the business focus begins—the business is on our mind all day, every day, and it begins to shape our every action. This consistency of thought makes everything else possible.

With our mindset focused on the business and driving the right outcomes, we will need to evolve the skills and people of IT. Most of our people will quickly adapt to this new focus on the business, and we are likely to find a natural attraction throughout IT for anything customer related.

A few people might not be able to make this shift, but they will be the exceptions. As we hire in the future, business skills and communications skills will climb our list of priorities in new candidates.

> *As so, over time we will bring some of*
> *these new people with new skills into IT,*
> *and this will form a great complement to*
> *the existing good people of IT, making a*
> *stronger team for the future. This mix is*
> *healthy, and this mix makes us strong.*

This further supports our focus on the business, but also brings better communications, better customer engagement, improved innovation, and a more proactive IT. All these desirable characteristics and behaviors are related and build upon one another. We simply need to set the course and give our people the encouragement and empowerment they need.

Then, watch amazing things happen across IT every day.

VENDOR CONSOLIDATION

The IT portfolio of technology, software, hardware, mobile devices, integrations, services, and more has exploded over the past decade. This must stop and is very much on the mind of the CIO today.

In particular, software applications and the related integrations and configurations are increasingly problematic.

The complexity of this portfolio creates risk, makes accountability difficult, slows down IT, and makes agility and managing change all but impossible.

The strategic CIO recognizes we must consolidate the portfolio of software vendors in order to achieve the following:

1. A smaller group of core software vendors that are partners with IT
2. Greatly increased sense of accountability
3. Stronger communications and transparency
4. Improved ability to perform system upgrades
5. Significantly reduced operating costs

6. A reduced number of systems integrations and associated risks
7. A high level of agility
8. An enhanced ability to manage changes to the business
9. Reduced risk to IT and the business
10. Stronger contracts and better business terms

This creates a new opportunity for IT and for the software application vendors. The strong separate themselves from the others and emerge as a strategic partner with IT. This is good for the IT organization and good for the vendors able to display strong value and a vision that matches that of the strategic CIO.

A few key characteristics the strategic CIO will seek in vendors best qualified to consolidate the IT application portfolio:

1. Shares a vision of partnership
2. An established vendor with a strong client list
3. A vendor that invests aggressively in R&D, committed to innovation
4. A vendor with a broad and balanced view of the global market
5. Willing to offer favorable contract and pricing terms
6. A vendor with a broad and deep product portfolio
7. A solution set with a favorable and proven total cost of ownership
8. A business with a strong financial profile, built for the future

The right partner will welcome this scrutiny and understand

the long-term opportunity is valuable to both parties. This is an important decision and investment for IT. The closer the CIO looks, the better the right partner will look.

It is also important to take notice of how the vendor conducts themselves during this evaluation—we are looking for honesty, transparency, and good communications. The same qualities that are important to the go-forward partnership. Through this process of consolidation, the exceptional vendors will rise and stand clear of the other vendors.

This is exactly as it should be.

FAIL AND LEARN

This is a simple yet very powerful model.

And another important cultural shift that must come from leadership is the simple axiom that it is okay to make mistakes. Mistakes of commission are, in fact, a healthy thing for the organization, and when we have people working hard and taking action, some mistakes will occur. But with this behavior we will be much further ahead in advancing the new IT agenda than if we acted with great caution, and therefore slowly, in fear of mistakes.

When we fail, it is in order to learn, and the sooner we learn, the sooner we make progress.

> *This is a vital cycle in an organization that is alive and moving forward. The CIO must make it clear this is how we work, and this is the culture we create together.*

Of course, we don't set out to make mistakes. We simply know that with action, and with moving fast, some mistakes will occur and are born of good actions. With this model established by the leadership team of IT, it quickly becomes a cultural style and a natural part of how we work. The momentum builds quickly. Working fast, being more aggressive, thinking more creatively, and not looking over our shoulder is a great way to work.

You may very well be nodding your head in agreement while reading this, but it is striking in that this is not normal for IT today.

> *And so this becomes another important part of the transformation of IT that cascades from what are somewhat small changes when taken individually but together become something remarkably powerful.*

This fail-and-learn culture must come from the CIO so that all know this is now how we work and that the consequences of not moving fast, not being aggressive, and not being proactive are far greater than waiting, not taking action, working reactively, or moving slowly.

As a final point, it is important that when we do make those mistakes and outcomes are not what we expect, we immediately reinforce that this is okay. It is going to happen, and we immediately shift our focus to learning—what happened, why did we not get the result we expected, what adjustments should be made next time, and then we move on.

Our teams will notice exactly what happens in these cases;

the example that is set must be clear and will be widely understood immediately. With this, our speed increases and our willingness to take reasonable chances and act proactively increases along with it. This is a powerful way to work every day and a product of the strategic CIO.

AGILE IT

Much has been made of agility across the business, but it has a specific and strategic meaning to the IT organization and to the strategic CIO. In many ways, agility can have its most important mission in IT as this will govern our ability to manage both technology and information for the greater good of IT and, as a result, for the complete business.

This then creates an agile organization, which in turn translates into a competitive advantage.

Our emphasis on agility will require us to review both our business processes and our systems. Automation can be an asset here (again) but only if the automation elements are designed to be changed and adapted quickly, because the rate of change in the market and thus in the business is accelerating, not slowing.

But lasting agility begins with a mindset, and this is best coming from IT leadership. The CIO can set a valuable tone with this message. We must be agile, we must anticipate change, and we must be great at this—not just for IT but for the business.

The agile IT organization is the single best enabler of an agile business, and an agile business is a force to be reckoned with in the marketplace.

The systems that run our business every day are often the very elements that stand in the way of agility, which brings us back to the importance of making IT agile. This is often the source of innovation, and increases in the speed of our performance are just bonuses. It is not simply a matter of agility for the sake of agility; there are real and hard benefits associated with this, and they line up remarkably well with our Imperative.

I mentioned two real benefits of agility earlier —speed and innovation. That is just the beginning, as we also get the benefits of providing more personalized service to our customers, being able to change quickly when market conditions change, providing a more consumer-like IT experience, and the list goes on. The strategic CIO will be committed to agility and recognize the cascade of benefits that follow. Did I mention it is just more fun to work in an agile organization? We are constantly greeted with new challenges and refuse to accept conventional thinking. This then attracts more talented and creative people to IT, which allows us to better innovate, to move faster, and to be a better enabler to the business.

And so the new cycle of IT repeats and enriches itself.

CULTIVATE TALENT

With the rebirth of IT, we take a fresh look at our people—a talented and dedicated group who will play an important role in the sweeping change and acceleration that comes with rebirth.

But we simply can't meet the challenges of the future with the traditional skills of IT. Our eyes have been opened to the broader needs of the organization and in an increasingly global marketplace that changes more quickly than ever while we are trying to please a demanding and impatient customer.

It is surely not the case that the traditional CIO has not been keen to attract and develop talent. They have.

But the strategic CIO is now faced with the need to integrate new skills into the organization while at the same time leveraging the current subject matter and technology experts of IT in a new and more optimal way.

These new skills will be addressed throughout the book; new skills are tightly coupled with the new strategies and operating models reshaping the future of IT and making our rebirth a reality. These new skills will include business analytics skills, customer-facing skills, communications skills, innovation focused staff, customer use case skills, and much more.

Of course, the cultivation of talent takes on a much bigger meaning and is not just about hiring new skills.

> *We must also develop the skills of our current team and, in some cases, assign talented up-and-coming staff to new roles.*

This is an encouraged practice and healthy for the organization. It also means it is more important than ever to retain our key people over time. The best organization will retain the talented and high-impact staff and find ways to keep them motivated, challenged, and fairly compensated.

This requires a strong partnership with human resources, for example, including an IT-focused personnel development and retention plan. If this does not exist today for IT specifically, now is the time. None of this comes as a shock to an experienced executive.

What might be new is the focus this now requires from the CIO, and the emphasis required by IT as an organization. Traditionally, organizations including development, sales, and marketing received much of the hiring and personnel development focus from HR and from the broader organization.

With the rebirth of IT and the value that IT now brings to the business, IT is elevated to an equal investment along with these other organizations, and in some cases IT becomes priority #1.

When we look at the impact the new IT organization can bring to the top line, the value IT can deliver to customers, and the innovation that can spring from IT, this is a shrewd investment and one the CEO and CFO will support.

DESIGN FOR RAPID CHANGE

Hand in hand with agility is our ability to anticipate—and then to embrace—changes in the business. *Embrace* might be a bit of a stretch, but you get the idea. We know change is going to happen and we know it is not easy. But by designing our processes and systems for change, we can minimize the impact, minimize the disruption, execute change quickly, and create a competitive advantage.

This concept is not a natural one in IT today, so it should come from the CIO. In some cases, this idea can be part of the vision to be created and shared by the strategic CIO of the future.

It's a case where a little bit of thoughtful planning makes a big difference and saves us a great deal of pain.

Often, the systems managed by IT can slow us down or cause delays in the business when change happens. For newer systems this might not be as much risk as with older systems.

Given our increased focus across IT and a push to align with the business, IT should conduct a proactive review of all systems in order to evaluate our state of readiness to make changes when change becomes necessary.

And change will come; it is only a matter of time. This is clearly a "when" question and not an "if" question. As such, we should not wait—when the time does come, it is too late.

We never want IT to be on the critical path for making a strategic or tactical change to the business or our business model. For example, what is the impact to IT if sales adds new product SKUs to the price list? If we start doing business in a new country and must provide price quotes in a new currency? I'm sure you can think of many other examples. Picking a few that are most relevant to your organization, what is your timeline to make these changes to your systems? Can this be done quickly, or will it take weeks, months, or even longer in some cases to complete?

The point is that we need to push ourselves in IT sooner and faster than the business would to make these changes. This is a cultural change, a new lifestyle for IT.

When we take this proactive approach, we save valuable time and missed opportunities versus waiting for the business to demand these changes. This is integral to IT aligning with the business, shifting to proactive action, innovating to create value, and ultimately to IT leading the business forward. All these elements are related.

Extending this value chain a bit further, it is important to appreciate this is not about rapid change for the sake of being rapid alone. Rapid change extends all the way to the customer, and the business that gives the customer what they want and when they want it wins. It's that simple.

A STRONG IT INFRASTRUCTURE

It has been said that when our IT infrastructure is secure and highly available, life is good for all.

Well, this might be oversimplifying things a bit, but there is a lot of truth here. We simply can't be successful in IT if we don't do the basics well. The basics include ensuring our assets, hardware, data, software, applications, and systems are healthy and ready to service the organization. This is a foundation on which the strategic CIO can build the future of IT and drive the future of the business.

> *The relationship between the fundamentals of IT and the new strategic dimensions of IT is something the strategic CIO understands well and embraces.*

We must forever do the fundamentals of IT well, but this is no longer enough given the world we conduct business in today.

It is true in today's world that this is not enough for IT to be successful. However, at the same time we should recognize that IT can't be successful without a few fundamental building blocks in place, and a healthy and available IT infrastructure is one of these foundational elements. The implementation of strategic programs in IT won't matter much if we don't have a highly available and robust IT infrastructure.

This is an important issue with regard to the key issue of "balance" the strategic CIO must appreciate. Do the basics well, and this will pave the way for a more strategic IT. Without the basics in place, there can be no strategic IT.

A strong IT infrastructure must be many things, including:

1. Highly available
2. Resilient
3. Adaptable
4. Scalable
5. Highly secure
6. Operates 24X7
7. Cost effective
8. Highly automated
9. User friendly
10. Based on a high level of customer engagement
11. Innovative
12. Based on governing standards
13. Able to accommodate integrations
14. Designed for change

This is a mix that allows IT to operate effectively today and puts us on a path to support successful business performance over the next ten years. We should anticipate both small impacts as well as large and plan for both. The strategic CIO understands this balance and is ready for the challenge.

Don't be confused—a strong IT infrastructure is not tactical. Far from it.

A high-performing IT infrastructure that is scalable, adaptable, and resilient is so much more. This infrastructure gives us leverage and creates competitive advantage—another great example of IT leading the business from within. When the business can leverage technology, systems, and data to perform better and to create happy customers, IT is ready and has planned for this moment.

SELF-SERVICE FIRST

Ah, self-service returns to our discussion, which should not be a surprise. Self-service can do so much for us, it is easy to love. The strategic CIO does not see self-service as simply helpful, but a model that can play a key role in the transformation of IT.

Self-service gives us leverage, and by now we know how important leverage is.

The leverage of self-service is a combination of the following:

1. Supports our 24X7 operation of IT
2. Makes customers happy
3. Offloads the staff of IT, enabling more time for strategic activities
4. Saves money
5. Increases the speed of IT
6. Assists IT in scaling effectively
7. Creates a significantly higher level of agility
8. Is a productive use of automation
9. Supports self-education of users

10. Effective for both internal use and external customer support

Note these elements cut across much of what is shaping the future of IT. The model of self-service is a very effective asset in delivering on the agenda of the strategic CIO and is top of mind in pushing IT through the barriers that stand between us today and the IT organization of the future.

There is a big difference between evaluating self-service <u>as one option</u> among many to be utilized when implementing the operational models that will shape the future of IT, versus leading with self-service as <u>the favored option</u> in order to maximize how we leverage the compelling attributes of the self-service model.

Only a few of these were highlighted in the list of ten above.

Where we find leverage, real leverage, we double down.

We don't have many of these proven performers in the organization, and self-service is certainly one. Remarkably, self-service is relatively young and has already had a significant impact; the good news is that self-service will get better in virtually every respect over the next ten years. It will get smarter, faster, easier to deploy, easier to use, and as a result save us even more money.

INNOVATION

Innovation has always been important to the organization, but not often considered to be in the charter of IT. This is now changing and changing quickly. With the natural technology aptitude we have in IT and with IT moving closer to the business, suddenly IT has the opportunity to lead.

I'm convinced that one day we will look back on this and see it as an obvious thing, but that has certainly not been the case. Far from it.

> *IT has too often been seen as something of a laggard—the antithesis of innovative, if you will. IT simply implemented, purchased, or configured what we innovated elsewhere.*

This is an exciting development, and the creative energy that has been dormant within IT can now rise to the aid of the organization. This opportunity will be recognized by the strategic CIO, who will be in a unique position to both encourage and then enable this innovation to take a path forward. It starts with a business need or the need of a customer. These needs are everywhere and are not difficult to identify. We only need to be looking and to be open to the opportunity.

An initial level of innovation would be taking action to solve an existing problem. This is a great place for IT to start, as it brings an immediate impact to the business.

The strategic CIO can encourage or in some cases lead the investigation and set the tone with IT—we are mobilizing our talented people to be proactive and more aggressive in solving business challenges that can be addressed with technology, information, and process.

This is a valuable evolution of our IT culture.

The next level of innovation would be to develop solutions for future challenges—not as easy as the first level, but potentially more valuable and impactful. This does require a higher level of vision—as these problems are not in front of us today—and a higher level of patience, as the delivery timeline can be more extended. But IT is up to the challenge, and the skills and problem-solving abilities are here among us. It is a wonderful quality of leadership to see an opportunity, match it to a capability, make the connection, and then take action. This is the cycle of innovation and a calling of the strategic CIO.

A PARTNERSHIP MODEL

The potential of IT as a partner to the business has long been part of our dialogue. But how often has this become a reality? It is likely we can all agree it is not as often as we would like, and there are many good reasons behind this. One benefit of this dialogue is the increased awareness of an IT desire and capability to become this partner.

These forces have been building for the past decade, and we have now reached a critical mass of need on the business side, and aptitude coupled with motivation on the IT side.

Now, we can come together and make the business stronger.

The strategic CIO can once again be the catalyst and carry the vision that makes this partnership a reality.

He/she will see partnership opportunities everywhere—across the business, with vendors, with partners, and with customers.

And the wonderful thing about partnerships is they are to the benefit of both parties. A healthy partnership makes everybody better.

The partnership model begins with both a recognition of the value created through partnerships and the willingness to dedicate resources to bring these partnerships to life. This does not require a lot of time but does require *some* time. We have previously discussed the new skills that will flourish in IT, and this is another example. IT need not dedicate resources to partnerships exclusively, and it could be combined with the client-facing skills or business analyst skills. This commitment of resources and bandwidth then accelerates the growth of the partnership ecosystem throughout IT and the organization.

Many would quickly think IT is an unlikely origin for these partnerships, but the Imperative holds some surprises for us, this being but one. When we take a moment to consider the unique knowledge, aptitude, and resources of IT, the possibilities come more into focus. What we are lacking in many cases is the vision to see a connection between the growing needs of the business and these riches that lie in IT, largely untapped.

This then becomes a void that can be uniquely filled by the strategic CIO.

EXTERNAL RELATIONSHIPS

The circle of relationships for the CIO is growing.

Predominantly driven by internal relationships in the past, the strategic CIO now becomes far more focused on growing external relationships. This brings a more balanced and broader perspective to IT and is very much in line with our customer focus and our focus on partnerships. It also plants the seeds of a business focus and is a healthy source of communications and contacts that can enrich the operations of IT and the broader business.

The shift of the CIO agenda is one that will bring much-needed sources of information that enrich the expertise and skills we possess in IT.

The strategic CIO understands the need for external influences and the value these relationships can bring, including:

1. Emerging business best practices we can leverage in IT
2. A network of CIO relationships that can bring lessons learned and other valuable information to IT

3. New training and ongoing education opportunities for staff development

4. A natural extension of our growing customer focus

5. New strategic partnerships with technology and service specialists to complement the skills we have in IT

6. Increased CIO and executive profile at industry and community events; the CIO becomes an adjunct member of the spokespeople team working with corporate public relations

7. Brainstorming on innovative solutions with peer organizations

8. A larger network and referral network for hiring new skills and new people into IT

External relationships are another element of our strategy that can bolster our focus on the business and on customers and stimulate our process of innovation with additional streams of influence.

> *The pursuit of meaningful innovation with an exclusively internal focus is folly.*

We simply can't bring a sound strategy and strong execution to the IT organization of the future without the clarity of a market- and customer-oriented view. Looking at the market, networking with peer organizations and leadership, and working directly with customers brings knowledge and insights that are simply not possible when our focus is internal. Yes, an internal focus is easier and more convenient. These touchpoints and sources of information are within our own walls.

But this internal focus is ultimately a comfortable trap.

The market and our customers hold many surprises, insights, and changes that are invisible to the internal focus. Navigating through these surprises and changes is not easy, and it takes time and commitment, but ultimately it is the only complete view of today and the only foundation on which to base our planning for the future.

The strategic CIO understands this and will drive the easy and the hard changes across IT that bring us these external relationships and the market-based and customer-based inputs that will reshape our IT strategy and tactics for the future.

KEY TAKEAWAYS: THE STRATEGIC CIO

1. As captain of the IT ship, the CIO carries a great deal of responsibility on their broad shoulders, now more than ever. This chapter outlines a number of those key areas, but where we begin should be simple—making a cultural shift that is all about our focus on the customer. This must include a direct connection with the customer and a cultural spirit that we will do whatever it takes to create successful customers. Think of this as starting with the customer and working our way back into the business and IT.

2. The strategic CIO will understand they must develop the skills and careers of the current people of IT and attract new talent to build our team for the future. Both are equally important. This is closely related to the cultural evolution that is so central to the remaking of IT. The CIO must be a master recruiter and understand the importance of talented and passionate people, extending to career path development and compensation. Many people in IT will step up, but the rebirth of IT will not be for everybody; some people will need to be transitioned out of IT, making room for the new skills and mindset we need.

3. The rebirth of IT will include a shift from the

traditional focus on internal relationships to a focus on external relationships. The CIO will lead this shift as well as being the primary advocate for these external relationships—of course, beginning with the customer but extending further to partners, analysts, market influencers, specialized consultants, service providers, and much more. This enhances the connection IT will cultivate with the markets we serve and be an engine for innovation and bring a new balance to the mindset of our people in IT. It is a big world.

CHAPTER 18

FINAL THOUGHTS

We are all truly fortunate to be working in IT today as we embark upon this exciting rebirth and the remarkable transformation that will occur in the next ten years.

I'm confident the best days of IT are ahead of us, and ultimately how we shape this exciting future is up to us. We are the stewards of this future.

I hope the previous chapters have provided a useful outline for the Why, What, and How of this rebirth and that you will take away a few good ideas that can be put into action for your organization.

Even if you have found only one useful idea in these pages, I'm thrilled to have helped.

With these powerful forces swirling faster than ever, I'm increasingly convinced that IT can become a capable if somewhat unlikely leader for the overall business in the years ahead. Let's take this a step further—the business needs the leadership of IT more than ever, and the talented people of IT will rise to the challenge. This might surprise many people, but if we look closely, there are many signs it will happen. Sometimes great leadership comes from places that surprises those people who believe they know the most about the future. Just when we begin to think IT is traveling a given course, we are gently reminded that this journey is anything but predictable.

Make no mistake, this exciting journey will not be easy. Our world is changing, and on that point most of us can agree.

But we should recognize this pace of change won't slow down—if anything it is likely to accelerate in the years ahead. We are faced with new and sophisticated threats, global competitors that want to take our customers, and impatient and demanding clients. These big challenges offer an opportunity for a new success for the organization that can only be achieved through the leadership and innovation that comes through the rebirth of IT, driven by the elements outlined in the preceding pages.

It bears saying again that as much as we love our technology, this is all about people and culture. This theme of our wonderful people and the culture they form was present throughout the book, and it becomes clear this is central to the rebirth of IT.

A remarkable and dynamic mix is formed uniquely with humanity and technology.

Looking ahead, the evolution of technology will never stop, and we will continue to be surprised by the launch of new products that can make our lives and our work better.

An IT organization of passionate and empowered people—propelled by the right strategy and supported by a new generation of IT leadership—is an awesome and unstoppable force. More than this, a dynamic new IT organization is the key to the future success of every business.

Enjoy the journey, my friends, take time to celebrate your hard-earned success, and I look forward to hearing your stories when our paths cross.

Kevin

@kevinjsmith4IT

REFERENCES

Prove It! Stacey Barr. Wiley, 2017.

The Practical Guide to World-Class IT Service Management. Kevin J. Smith. The Anima Group, 2017.

Agile Project Management. Marcus Ries, Diana Summers. 2016.

SIAM Principles and Practices for Service Integration and Management. Dave Armes, Niklas Engelhart, Peter McKenzie, Peter Wiggers. Van Haren Publishing, 2015.

World Class IT. Peter A. High. John Wiley & Sons, 2009.

DevOps. Christopher Weller. Christopher Weller, 2017.

NOTES

_____

_____

_____

_____

_____

_____

_____

_____

_____

_____

_____

_____

_____

_____

_____

_____

_____

_____

_____

_____

_____

NOTES

NOTES

NOTES

NOTES

_____

_____

_____

_____

_____

_____

_____

_____

_____

_____

_____

_____

_____

_____

_____

_____

_____

NOTES

NOTES

NOTES

NOTES

NOTES

NOTES

NOTES

NOTES

NOTES

NOTES

NOTES

NOTES

NOTES

NOTES

NOTES

NOTES

NOTES

NOTES

_____
_____
_____
_____
_____
_____
_____
_____
_____
_____
_____
_____
_____
_____
_____
_____
_____
_____

NOTES

NOTES

NOTES

NOTES

NOTES

NOTES

NOTES

NOTES

NOTES

NOTES

NOTES

NOTES

NOTES

NOTES

NOTES

NOTES

NOTES

NOTES

NOTES

_____

_____

_____

_____

_____

_____

_____

_____

_____

_____

_____

_____

_____

_____

_____

_____

_____

NOTES

NOTES

NOTES

NOTES

NOTES

NOTES

NOTES

_____

_____

_____

_____

_____

_____

_____

_____

_____

_____

_____

_____

_____

_____

_____

_____

_____

_____

_____

NOTES

www.ingramcontent.com/pod-product-compliance
Lightning Source LLC
Chambersburg PA
CBHW071354050326
40689CB00010B/1636